A Paddler's Guide To
Northern Georgia

A Canoeing and Kayaking Guide to the
Streams of the Cumberland Plateau,
Blue Ridge Mountains and Eastern Piedmont.

A Paddler's Guide To
Northern Georgia

A Canoeing and Kayaking Guide to the
Streams of the Cumberland Plateau,
Blue Ridge Mountains and Eastern Piedmont.

By Bob Sehlinger
and Don Otey

Menasha Ridge Press
Birmingham, AL

Cover Photo: William Clay running Sock'em Dog Rapid,
    owned by William Clay.
Cover Design: Icon Graphics, Birmingham, Alabama

Library of Congress Cataloging-in-Publication Data
Sehlinger, Bob, 1945-
    Northern Georgia Canoeing: A canoeing and
kayaking guide to the streams of the Cumberland Plateau, Blue Ridge Mountains, and Eastern Piedmont.
Bibliography: p. Includes index.

    1. Canoes and canoeing—Northern Georgia—Guide-
books. 2. Northern Georgia—Description and travel—
Guidebooks. I. Otey, Don, 1950- joint author II. Title.

84-115766
ISBN 0-89732-134-0

Menasha Ridge Press
3169 Cahaba Heights Road
Birmingham, AL 35243
(800) 247-9437

This book is dedicated to three special friends,

Helen & Wilbur Otey, Jr.,

who also happen to be very good parents, and

Cyril Sehlinger,

who has never parented anyone (as far as is known) but has managed nonetheless to live surrounded by lovely ladies and to have this book dedicated to him.

Acknowledgments

Though many individuals and organizations contributed toward the writing of this guide, there were a special few whose enthusiasm and dedicated efforts actually made the work possible. We wish to thank, therefore, Marty Otey for her tireless assistance and support; Harold Golden, Associate District Chief of the Water Resources Division of the Georgia District, U.S. Geological Survey, who granted us access to the U.S.G.S. data base and allowed us to camp in his office for a week while we were computing technical data; Gary DeBacher, who assisted with the research of several streams and served as general adviser to the entire project; Bill Conger, friend, outdoorsman, and mathematician, who supervised the computation of technical data; Jerry Penland, whose river research assistance was invaluable; Jim and Jeanette Greiner and their wonderful staff at Wildwater, Ltd., on the Chattooga, who provided Bob Sehlinger with a base of operations during his field research; *Brown's Guide to Georgia*, which unselfishly provided dozens of professional quality photographs for inclusion in the guide; and Russ Rymer, who, like Gary DeBacher, lead us to some beautiful little streams we had overlooked and supplied the data necessary to include them in the guide.

The following is a partial list of yet more wonderful folks who contributed significantly to the finished product:

River Research

John Lott	Terry Bramlett
Toby Thomas	Ben Parker
Gerald Marshall	Liz Cornish
Bob Brooksher	Preston Justice
Eddie Jones	

Technical & Editorial Assistance

Mary Joscelyn	Tara Cope
Kathy Jackson	Ann George
Donna Brown	Rita Mirus
Marilyn Marshall	

Data Collation

U.S. Geological Survey	Phillip Allen
Mary Bergner	Rod Smith

Photography

Fred Brown
Robert Harrison
Dick Murless
Wilderness Southeast
Georgia Department of Industry and Trade
Okefenokee National Wildlife Refuge

Special Assistance & Advice

Ron Odom, Georgia Senior Biologist for
    Endangered Species
Oscar Dewberry, Regional Game Supervisor
BMC Stephen Taylor, U.S. Coast Guard
BMC C. D. Harmon, U.S. Coast Guard
U.S. Forest Service
Lloyd Culp, Okefenokee National Wildlife Refuge
Max Walker, Georgia Department of Natural
    Resources
Rob Holland, U.S. Army Corps of Engineers
Juanita Guinn
Buckhorn Mountain Shop
SAGE Outfitters
High Country Outfitters
Georgia Department of Transporation

Contents

Introduction

For years we've been coming to the Chattooga, myself and my friends and practically every aspiring whitewater paddler from Chicago to Boston. And with each trip we were filled with the peace and euphoria that come as surely as the pulse-quickening, foam-flecked rapids. To us the Chattooga *was* paddling in northern Georgia, or southern Georgia, or anywhere in the Southeast, for that matter. But even so, we could not help wondering, "Are there other streams in Georgia that compare with the Chattooga?"

Don Otey knew the answer, but nobody was paying attention, . . . at least not at first. An expert boater, Don elected to forgo distant treks to Canada, the Colorado, and the Allagash, instead concentrating his paddling time on the rivers of Georgia's Blue Ridge Mountains, Cumberland Plateau, and eastern Piedmont. Don discovered water treasures throughout northern Georgia and carried a map on which, circled in red, were dozens more streams waiting to be uncovered. "Why drive a thousand miles," he said, "when it's all right here."

Don was right, and, if anything, his case was understated. Rolling out of northern Georgia is more beauty and diversity of nature, more majesty, more serenity, and more pristine paddling enjoyment than a person could appreciate in a lifetime. Don generously shared the streams of northern Georgia with me, and collectively we have prepared this guide to share those waterways with you. So paddle northern Georgia with us when you can, and, in between, feel free to dream along.

Bob Sehlinger

How to Use Stream Information

For each stream in this guide you will find a general description and at least one stream data list and map. By definition, a stream is flowing water and may be a river, creek, or a branch or fork of a river; therefore lakes are not included here. The streams are grouped roughly by geological region, that is, Cumberland Plateau, Blue Ridge Mountains, and eastern Piedmont. Only the northern portions of the lengthy Chattahoochee, Savannah, and Oconee rivers are found in this book. For a description of the southern portions of these rivers, see the companion book, *Southern Georgia Canoeing: A Canoeing and Kayaking Guide to the Streams of the Western Piedmont Coastal Plain, Georgia Coast and Okefenokee Swamp.*

Stream Descriptions

The descriptions that accompany the maps and data lists are intended to give you a feel for the stream and its surroundings and are presented in general, nontechnical terms.

Stream Data

Each stream data list provides the necessary technical and quantitative information for each of the streams listed, as well as some additional descriptive data. Occasionally certain facts will be covered in both the general description and in the data list for added emphasis. Listed below are fuller explanations of many of the categories found on the data lists.

Each list begins with the specific stream **section** to which the data apply and the **counties** in which the stream is located.

Suitable For. While most streams described in this book are best suited to *day cruising*, some provide the opportunity for *canoe camping*. A few, because of their convenient access and configuration, are designated as being good for *training* runs.

Appropriate For. This item was included strictly for convenience. For a better idea of whether or not a listed stream is for you, evaluate yourself according to the paddler self-evaluation format on pages 4–5 and match your numerical score with the numerical point rating of the river. For definitional purposes, *families* connotes adults of various skill levels who want to take nonswimming adults or children in the canoe with them. We always assume that personal flotation devices (PFD's), e.g., life jackets, will be worn by all parties on moving water. We also assume that no passengers will be carried in whitewater.

Beginners are paddlers with a knowledge of strokes and self-rescue who can maneuver their boat more or less intuitively on still water (lakes and ponds). True *intermediates* meet all beginner qualifications, have a working knowledge of river dynamics, have some ability in rescuing others, and (for our purposes) are competent and at home on Class II whitewater. *Advanced paddlers* (not experts) are paddlers who possess all the foregoing qualifications in addition to specialized rescue skills, and who are competent and at home on Class III and IV whitewater. *Experts* are paddlers who easily exceed all the above qualifications. Needless to say, these definitions could be refined or elaborated ad infinitum. They are not intended to be all-inclusive but rather to give you a reasonable idea of how to classify yourself and how experienced practitioners of the sport may tend to classify you.

Months Runnable. The months given are based on the average rainfall for a year. Different sections of rivers may be runnable at different times. Some rivers are not necessarily runnable at a given time of year but are only runnable after a heavy rainfall or when a dam or powerhouse is releasing enough water.

Section: Goshen Rd. (Afton) to Etowah River

Counties: Dawson

Suitable For: Cruising, camping, training[1]

Appropriate For: Beginners, intermediates, advanced above GA 53; intermediate and advanced paddlers from GA 53 to the Etowah River
Months Runnable: March through July

Interest Highlights: Scenery, wildlife, whitewater

Scenery: Exceptionally beautiful to spectacular

Difficulty: International Scale I-IV (V)
Numerical Points 5-29

Average Width: 30-40 ft.
Velocity: Fast
Gradient: 5-80 ft./mi.

Runnable Water Level: Minimum 0.8 ft. above GA 53;
0.6 ft. below GA 53
Maximum 2.5 ft., open; 3.5 ft., decked

Hazards: Strainers, deadfalls, undercut rocks, difficult rapids
Scouting: At major rapids below GA 53

Portages: As required by water level

Rescue Index: Accessible to extremely remote

Mean Water Temperature (°F)

| Jan 42 | Feb 44 | Mar 49 | Apr 56 | May 62 | Jun 68 |
| Jul 72 | Aug 70 | Sep 64 | Oct 55 | Nov 50 | Dec 44 |

Source of Additional Information: Buckhorn Mountain Shop (404) 536-0081

Access Point	Access Code	Access Key
A	2357	1 Paved Road
B	2357	2 Unpaved Road
C	2357	3 Short Carry
D	1367	4 Long Carry
K[2]	2357	5 Easy Grade
		6 Steep Incline
		7 Clear Trail
		8 Brush and Trees
		9 Launching Fee Charged
		10 Private Property, Need Permission
		11 No Access, Reference Only

[1] Above GA 53
[2] On the Etowah River

Interest Highlights. This category includes special *scenery, wildlife, whitewater, local culture and industry, historical locations,* and unusual *geology.*

Scenery. Taste is relative, and in the absolute sense ours is no better or worse than anyone else's. Our preference is that you form your own conclusions about the comparative beauty of the streams listed in this guide. Knowing, however, that it takes a long time to run all of the state's major drainages, we were presumptuous enough to include a comparative scenery rating based strictly on our own perceptions. The ratings run from *unattractive,* to *uninspiring,* through gradations of *pretty* and *beautiful,* to *spectacular.* To indicate how capricious taste is, some popular canoeing streams in surrounding states are rated:

Tuckasegee River .... Pretty in spots
(North Carolina)   to pretty
Nantahala River .... Pretty to beautiful
(North Carolina)   in spots
Hiwassee River .... Beautiful in spots
(Tennessee)   to beautiful
Suwannee River .... Beautiful
(Georgia)
Conasauga River ...... Exceptionally beautiful
(Tennessee)
Chattooga River, Section IV .... Spectacular
(Georgia)

Difficulty. The level of difficulty of a stream is given according to the International Scale of River Difficulty and according to the river evaluation table on page 3. Both ratings are relative and pertain to the stream described under more or less ideal water levels and weather conditions. For streams with two International Scale ratings, the first represents the average level of difficulty of the entire run and the second (expressed parenthetically) represents the level of difficulty of the most difficult section or rapids on the run. Paddlers are cautioned that changes in water levels or weather conditions can alter the stated average difficulty rating appreciably.

Average Width. Rivers tend to start small and enlarge as they flow toward their confluence with another river. Pools form in some places, and in other places the channel may constrict, accelerating the current. All of these factors affect the width and make the average width a very approximate measure.

Velocity. This represents the speed of the current, on the average, in nonflood conditions. Velocity can vary incredibly from section to section on a given stream depending on the stream's width, volume, and gradient at any point along its length. Velocity is a partial indicator of how much reaction time you might have on a certain river. Paddlers are known to describe a high velocity stream as "coming at them pretty fast," meaning that the speed of the current does not allow them much time for decision and action.

Rivers are described here as *slack, slow, moderate,* and *fast.* Slack rivers have current velocities of less than a half mile per hour; slow rivers have velocities over a half mile per hour but less than two miles per hour. Moderate velocities range between two and four miles per hour, and fast rivers are those that exceed four miles per hour.

Gradient. Gradient is expressed in feet per mile (ft/mi) and refers to the steepness of the stream bed over a certain distance. It is important to remember that gradient (or "drop" as paddlers refer to it) is an average figure and does not tell the paddler when or how the drop occurs. A stream that has a listed gradient of 25 feet per mile may drop gradually in one- or two-inch increments (like a long, rocky slide) for the course of a mile, or it may drop only slightly over the first nine-tenths of a mile and then suddenly drop 24 feet at one waterfall. As a general rule, gradient can be used as a rough indicator of level of difficulty for a given stream (i.e., the greater the gradient, the more difficult the stream). In practice, gradient is almost always considered in conjunction with other information.

Runnable Water Level: Minimum. This represents the lowest water level at which a given stream is navigable. For purposes of continuity and because of disagreement in many instances between depth markers on the same stream, most water levels are expressed in terms of volume as cubic feet per second (cfs). The use of cfs is doubly informative in that knowledge of volume at a gauge on one stream is often a prime indicator of the water levels of ungauged runnable streams in the same watershed or for other sections of the gauged stream, either up- or downstream.

Maximum. In this book, "runnable" does not mean the same thing as "possible." The maximum runnable water level refers to the highest water level at which the stream can be safely run (this may vary for open and decked boats). With few exceptions (which can only be run when flooded), this categorically excludes rivers in flood.

Hazards. Hazards are dangers to navigation. Because of the continuous action of the water, many of these hazards may change and new ones might appear. *Low-hanging trees*, which can be a nuisance, may become *deadfalls*, and *strainers*. Human intervention creates hazards such as *dams, low bridges, fences* (an especially dangerous "strainer"), and *powerboat traffic*. Some watersheds have soils that cannot retain much water and the streams in that watershed may have a *flash-flood* potential. Additionally, geologically young rivers, usually whitewater rivers, may have *undercut rocks, keeper hydraulics, difficult rapids,* and a *scarcity of eddies.*

Scouting. In this guidebook we attempt to list spots on specific rivers where scouting is required, i.e., recommended for the continuation of life and good health. Because many hazards may change in a short period of time, we also subscribe to the rule of thumb that you should scout any time you cannot see what is ahead (whitewater or flatwater and even on familiar rivers); that small, turning drop that you have run a thousand times may have a big log wedged across it today.

Portages. We adhere to the rule that dams should be portaged. Additionally, portages are recommended for certain rapids and other dangers. The fact, however, that a portage is not specified at a certain spot or rapid does not necessarily mean that you should not portage. It is the mark of a good paddler to be able to make safe and independent decisions about his or her own ability to run a given river or rapid.

Rescue. Many of the streams in this book run through wild areas. A sudden serious illness or injury could become an urgent problem if you can't get medical attention quickly. To give you an idea of how far you may be from help, a brief description is given of what might be expected. *Accessible* means that you might need up to an hour to secure assistance, but evacuation is not difficult. *Accessible but difficult* means that it might take up to three hours to get help and evacuation may be difficult. *Remote* indicates it might take three to six hours to get help; *and extremely remote* means that you could expect to be six hours from help and would need expert assistance to get the party out.

Water Temperature. This figure is the average temperature for each month of the year computed over a minimum ten-year period. Because it represents an average, actual water temperatures on a given day may vary considerably from the stated average. The statistic is included to help paddlers determine the need for special warm- or cold-

Table 1: Conversion Table
Degrees Celsius (°C) to degrees Fahrenheit (°F)*
(Temperature reported to nearest 0.5°C)

°C	°F	°C	°F	°C	°F	°C	°F	°C	°F
0.0	32	10.0	50	20^0	68	30.0	86	40.0	104
0.5	33	10.5	51	20.5	69	30.5	87	40.5	105
1.0	34	11.0	52	21.0	70	31.0	88	41.0	106
1.5	35	11.5	53	21.5	71	31.5	89	41.5	107
2.0	36	12.0	54	22.0	72	32.0	90	42.0	108
2.5	36	12.5	54	22.5	72	32.5	90	42.5	108
3.0	37	13.0	55	23.0	73	33.0	91	43.0	109
3.5	38	13.5	56	23.5	74	33.5	92	43.5	110
4.0	39	14.0	57	24.0	75	34.0	93	44.0	111
4.5	40	14.5	58	24.5	76	34.5	94	44.5	112
5.0	41	15.0	59	25.0	77	35.0	95	45.0	113
5.5	42	15.5	60	25.5	78	35.5	96	45.5	114
6.0	43	16.0	61	26.0	79	36.0	97	46.0	115
6.5	44	16.5	62	26.5	80	36.5	98	46.5	116
7.0	45	17.0	63	27.0	81	37.0	99	47.0	117
7.5	45	17.5	63	27.5	81	37.5	99	47.5	117
8.0	46	18.0	64	28.0	82	38.0	100	48.0	118
8.5	47	18.5	65	28.5	83	38.5	101	48.5	119
9.0	48	19.0	66	29.0	84	39.0	102	49.0	120
9.5	49	19.5	67	29.5	85	39.5	103	49.5	121

*°C = 5/9 (°F - 32) or °F = 9/5 (°C) + 32.

weather clothing or equipment. At water temperatures below 50°F a wet suit is recommended in case of an upset. Table 1 presents equivalent Celsius and Fahrenheit temperatures.

Sources of Additional Information. Various sources of additional information on water conditions are listed. Professional outfitters can provide both technical and descriptive information and relate the two to paddling. TVA and the various hydraulics branches of the respective district Corps of Engineers' offices can provide flow data in cfs but will not be able to interpret the data for you in terms of paddling. Other sources listed (forest rangers, fish and wildlife officers, police departments, etc.) will normally provide only descriptive information, e.g., "The creek's up pretty good today," or, "The river doesn't have enough water in it for boating."

Access Code. Access codes correspond to the letter-denoted access points on accompanying maps. The code is usually four digits, but it may be more or less. Each digit relates to a description of the actual access point on the river. For example, the access code 1357 indicates that (1) a paved road goes to the river; (3) it is a short carry from your vehicle to the water's edge; (5) you don't have to carry down a steep hill or embankment; and (7) there is a clear trail, road, or path to the river. The number 9 means that the access is on private land and permission must be secured to put in or take out a boat. Absence

of the number 9 does not necessarily mean that the access is public, it could mean that the landowner has historically granted access and that it is not essential for each boater to secure permission individually. It could also mean that the landowner is nonresident or extremely difficult to locate. The rule of thumb is to respect property.

Maps

The maps in this book are not intended to replace topographic quadrangles for terrain features. Rather, they are intended to illustrate the general configuration of the stream, its access points, and the surrounding shuttle network of roads.

The scale of these maps, unless otherwise stated, is one inch (the approximate length of the end portion of your thumb) equals one mile, and north is at the top of the page. A legend explaining the map symbols is found inside the front cover. A general map of Georgia counties and the rivers described in this book is found inside the back cover.

Some of the maps are congested to the point that access letters may not represent exact location, but are only in the general vicinity. You may have to scout the area before launching. Approximate river miles and car shuttle miles from one access point to the next are provided with the maps.

Additionally, the names of the 7½-minute topographic quadrangles on which the streams appear are provided with the maps. To order these maps, see the address list in "Where to Buy Maps" in the Appendix.

A Paddler's Guide To
Northern Georgia

*A Canoeing and Kayaking Guide to the
Streams of the Cumberland Plateau,
Blue Ridge Mountains and Eastern Piedmont.*

Chapter 1

Paddler Information

Rating the River—Rating the Paddler

For several years concerned paddlers have sought to objectively rate rivers. Central among their tools has been the International Scale of River Difficulty. While certainly a useful tool, and by no means outdated, the International Scale lacks precision and invites subjective, judgmental error. A more objective yardstick is the recently developed difficulty rating chart that is based on a point system. While more cumbersome, it does succeed in describing a river more or less as it really is. Gone is the common confusion of a single rapid being described as Class II by the veteran while the novice perceives a roaring Class IV. Also eliminated is the double standard by which a river is rated Class III for open canoes but only Class II for decked boats. Instead, points are awarded as prescribed for conditions observed on the day the river is to be run. The total number of points describes the general level of difficulty.

Once the basic difficulty rating is calculated for a river, however, how is it to be matched against the skill level of a prospective paddler? The American Whitewater Affiliation relates the point system for rivers back to the International Scale and to traditional paddler classifications.

This helps, but only to the extent that the individual paddler understands the definitions of "Practiced Beginner," "Intermediate," "Experienced," and so on. If, paddlers finds these traditional titles ambiguous and hard to differentiate, they will probably classify themselves according to self-image. When this occurs, we're back to where we started.

Correctly observing the need for increased objectivity in rating paddlers as well as in rating rivers, several paddling clubs have developed self-evalua-

tion systems where paddlers are awarded points that correspond to the point scale of the river rating chart (Table 2). Thus an individual can determine a point total through self-evaluation and compare his or her skill, in quantified terms, to any river rated through use of the chart. The individual paddler, for instance, may compile 18 points through self-evaluation and note that this rating compares favorably with the difficulty rating of 17 points and unfavorably with a difficulty rating of 23 points. It should be reiterated here, however, that river ratings obtained from the river difficulty chart pertain to a river only on a given day and at a specific water level. Generalized ratings, when given, represent the difficulty of the river under ideal weather and water conditions.

The most widely publicized of the *paddler* self-evaluations was created by the Keel-Haulers Canoe Club of Ohio. This system brings the problem of matching paddlers with rivers into perspective but seems to overemphasize nonpaddling skills. A canoe clinic student who is athletically inclined but almost totally without paddling skill once achieved a rating of 15 points using the Keel-Haulers system. His rating, based almost exclusively on general fitness and strength, incorrectly implied that he was capable of handling many Class II and Class III rivers. A second problem evident in the system is the lack of depth in skill category descriptions. Finally, confusion exists in several rating areas as to whether the evaluation applies to open canoes, decked boats, or both.

To remedy these perceived shortcomings and to bring added objectivity to paddler self-evaluation, Bob Sehlinger has attempted to refine the paddler rating system. Admittedly the refined system is

Table 2: Rating the River

| Points | Secondary Factors — Factors Related Primarily to Success in Negotiating | | | Primary Factors — Factors Affecting Both Success and Safety | | | Secondary Factors — Factors Related Primarily to Safe Rescue | | | | |
	Obstacles, rocks and trees	Waves	Turbulence	Bends	Length (feet)	Gradient (ft/mile)	Resting or rescue spots	Water Velocity (mph)	Width and depth	Temp °(F)	Accessibility
0	None	Few inches high, avoidable	None	Few, very gradual	<100	<5, regular slope	Almost anywhere	<3	Narrow (<75 feet) and shallow (<3 feet)	<65	Road along river
1	Few, passage almost straight through	Low (up to 1 ft) regular, avoidable	Minor eddies	Many, gradual	100–700	5–15, regular slope		3–6	Wide (<75 feet) and shallow (<3 feet)	55–65	<1 hour travel by foot or water
2	Courses easily recognizable	Low to med. (up to 3 ft), regular, avoidable	Medium eddies	Few, sharp, blind; scouting necessary	700–5,000	15–40, ledges or steep drops		6–10	Narrow (<75 feet) and deep (<3 feet)	45–55	1 hour to 1 day travel by foot or water
3	Maneuvering course not easily recognizable	Med. to large (up to 5 ft), mostly regular, avoidable	Strong eddies and cross currents		>5000	>40, steep drops, small falls	A good one below every danger spot	>10 or flood	Wide (>75 feet) and deep (>3 feet)	<45	>1 day travel by foot or water
4	Intricate maneuvering; course hard to recognize	Large, irregular, avoidable; or med. to large, unavoidable	Very strong eddies, strong cross currents								
5	Course tortuous, frequent scouting	Large, irregular, unavoidable	Large scale eddies and crosscurrents, some up and down								
6	Very tortuous; always scout from shore	Very large (>5 ft), irregular, unavoidable, special equipment required					Almost none				

SOURCE: Prepared by Guidebook Committee—AWA (From "American White Water," Winter, 1957)

Table 3: Ratings Comparisons

International Rating	Approximate Difficulty	Total Points (from Table 2)	Approximate Skill Required
I	Easy	0–7	Practiced Beginner
II	Requires Care	8–14	Intermediate
III	Difficult	15–21	Experienced
IV	Very Difficult	22–28	Highly Skilled (Several years with organized group)
V	Exceedingly Difficult	29–35	Team of Experts
VI	Utmost Difficulty-Near Limit of Navigability		

more complex and exhaustive, but not more so than warranted by the situation. Heavy emphasis is placed on paddling skills, and description has been adopted from several different evaluation formats, including a non-numerical system proposed by Dick Schwind.*

*Schwind, Dick; "Rating System for Boating Difficulty," *American Whitewater Journal,* Volume 20, Number 3, May/June 1975.

Rating the Paddler

Instructions: All items, except the first, carry points that may be added to obtain an overall rating. All items except "Rolling Ability" apply to both open and decked boats. Rate open and decked boat skills separately.

1. Prerequisite Skills. Before paddling on moving current, the paddler should:
   a. Have some swimming ability.
   b. Be able to paddle instinctively on nonmoving water (lake). (This presumes knowledge of basic strokes.)
   c. Be able to guide and control the canoe from either side without changing paddling sides.
   d. Be able to guide and control the canoe (or kayak) while paddling backwards.
   e. Be able to move the canoe (or kayak) laterally.
   f. Understand the limitations of the boat.
   g. Be practiced in "wet exit" if in a decked boat.

2. Equipment. Award points on the suitability of your equipment to whitewater. Whether you own, borrow, or rent the equipment makes no difference. *Do not* award points for both *Open Canoe* and *Decked Boat.*

Open Canoe

0 Points	Any canoe less than 15 ft. for tandem; any canoe less than 14 ft. for solo.
1 Point	Canoe with moderate rocker, full depth, and recurved bow; should be 15 ft. or more in length for tandem and 14 ft. or more in length for solo and have bow and stern painters.
2 Points	Whitewater canoe. Strong rocker design, full bow with recurve, full depth amidships, no keel; meets or exceeds minimum length requirements as described under "1 Point"; made of hand-laid fiberglass, Kevlar®, Marlex®, or ABS *Royalex®*; has bow and stern painters. Canoe as described under "1 Point" but with extra flotation.
3 Points	Canoe as described under "2 Points" but with extra flotation.

Decked Boat (K-1, K-2, C-1, C-2)

0 Points	Any decked boat lacking full flotation, spray skirt, or foot braces.
1 Point	Any fully equipped, decked boat with a wooden frame.
2 Points	Decked boat with full flotation, spray skirt and foot braces; has grab loops; made of hand-laid fiberglass, Marlex®, or Kevlar®.
3 Points	Decked boat with foam wall reinforcement and split flotation; Neoprene spray skirt; boat has knee braces, foot braces, and grab loops; made of hand-laid fiberglass or Kevlar only.

3. Experience Compute the following to determine *preliminary points,* then convert the preliminary points to *final* points according to the conversion table.

Number of days spent each year paddling
   Class I rivers   × 1 = _____
   Class II rivers   × 2 = _____
   Class III rivers × 3 = _____
   Class IV rivers   × 4 = _____
   Class V rivers   × 5 = _____
   Preliminary Points Subtotal___
Number of years paddling
   experience_____ × subtotal =
       Total Preliminary Points   _____

Note: This is the only evaluation item where it is possible to accrue more than 3 points.

Table 4: Conversion Table

Preliminary Points	Final Points
0–20	0
21–60	1
61–100	2
101–200	3
201–300	4
301–up	5

4. Swimming

0 Points	Cannot swim
1 Point	Weak swimmer
2 Points	Average swimmer
3 Points	Strong swimmer (competition level or skin diver)

5. Stamina

0 Points	Cannot run mile in less than 10 minutes
1 Point	Can run a mile in 7 to 10 minutes
2 Points	Can run a mile in less than 7 minutes

6. Upper Body Strength

0 Points	Cannot do 15 push-ups
1 Point	Can do 16 to 25 push-ups
2 Points	Can do more than 25 push-ups

7. Boat Control
0 Points	Can keep boat fairly straight
1 Point	Can maneuver in moving water; can avoid big obstacles
2 Points	Can maneuver in heavy water; knows how to work with the current
3 Points	Finesse in boat placement in all types of water, uses current to maximum advantage

8. Aggressiveness
0 Points	Does not play or work river at all
1 Point	Timid; plays a little on familiar streams
2 Points	Plays a lot; works most rivers hard
3 Points	Plays in heavy water with grace and confidence

9. Eddy Turns
0 Points	Has difficulty making eddy turns from moderate current
1 Point	Can make eddy turns in either direction from moderate current; can enter moderate current from eddy
2 Points	Can catch medium eddies in either direction from heavy current; can enter very swift current from eddy
3 Points	Can catch small eddies in heavy current

10. Ferrying
0 Points	Cannot ferry
1 Point	Can ferry upstream and downstream in *moderate* current
2 Points	Can ferry upstream in *heavy* current; can ferry downstream in *moderate* current
3 Points	Can ferry upstream and downstream in *heavy* current

11. Water Reading
0 Points	Often in error
1 Point	Can plan route in short rapids with several well-spaced obstacles
2 Points	Can confidently run lead in continuous Class II, can predict the effect of waves and holes on boat
3 Points	Can confidently run lead in continuous Class III; has knowledge to predict and handle the effects of reversals, side currents, and turning drops

12. Judgment
0 Points	Often in error
1 Point	Has average ability to analyze difficulty of rapids
2 Points	Has good ability to analyze difficulty of rapids and make independent judgments as to which should not be run
3 Points	Has the ability to assist fellow paddlers in evaluating the difficulty of rapids; can explain subtleties to paddlers with less experience

13. Bracing
0 Points	Has difficulty bracing in Class II rivers
1 Point	Can correctly execute bracing strokes in Class II water
2 Points	Can correctly brace in intermittent whitewater with medium waves and vertical drops of 3 ft. or less
3 Points	Can brace effectively in continuous whitewater with large waves and vertical drops (4 ft. and up)

14. Rescue Ability
0 Points	Self-rescue in flatwater
1 Point	Self-rescue in mild whitewater
2 Points	Self-rescue in Class III; can assist others in mild whitewater
3 Points	Can assist others in heavy whitewater

15. Rolling Ability
0 Points	Can only roll in pool
1 Point	Can roll 3 out of 4 times in moving current
2 Points	Can roll 3 out of 4 times in Class II whitewater
3 Points	Can roll 4 out of 5 times in Class III and IV whitewater

Hazards And Safety

Hazardous situations likely to be encountered on the river must be identified and understood for safe paddling. The lure of high adventure has in part explained why there are so many more paddlers these days. Unfortunately, an alarming number were not prepared for what they encountered and lost their lives.* They didn't use good judgment or just didn't understand the potential dangers. In some cases the use of alcohol has been a factor in bad judgment, just as it is in driving and private flying. In swiftly moving water you need all your faculties to handle the rapid, critical decisions.

---

*Paddling Fatality Facts: (1) Over three-quarters of the operators in canoe/kayak accidents have not had any formal instruction; (2) 86 percent of fatalities occurred within 90 minutes of departure on an outing; (3) approximately 74 percent of the victims encountered water temperatures less than 70°F. (From a presentation by the U.S. Coast Guard at the 1976 American Canoe Association instructors' conference in Chicago.)

American Whitewater Affiliation Safety Code

The American Whitewater Affiliation's safety code is perhaps the most useful overall safety guideline available.

I. Personal Preparedness and Responsibility

1. **Be a competent swimmer** with the ability to handle yourself underwater.

2. **Wear a life jacket.**

3. **Keep your craft under control.** Control must be good enough at all times to stop or reach shore before you reach any danger. Do not enter a rapid unless you are reasonably sure you can safely navigate it or swim the entire rapid in the event of capsize.

4. **Be aware of river hazards and avoid them.** Following are the most frequent killers.
   a. **High Water.** The river's power and danger and the difficulty of rescue increase tremendously as the flow rate increases. It is often misleading to judge river level at the put-in. Look at a narrow, critical passage. Could a sudden rise in the water level from sun on a snow pack, rain, or a dam release occur on your trip?
   b. **Cold.** Cold quickly robs your strength, along with your will and ability to save yourself. Dress to protect yourself from cold water and weather extremes. When the water temperature is less than 50°F, a diver's wet suit is essential for safety in event of an upset. Next best is wool clothing under a windproof outer garment such as a splashproof nylon shell; in this case one should carry matches and a complete change of clothes in a waterproof package. If after prolonged exposure a person experiences uncontrollable shaking or has difficulty talking and moving, he or she must be warmed immediately by whatever means available.
   c. **Strainers.** Brush, fallen trees, bridge pilings, or anything else that allows river current to sweep through but pins boat and boater against the obstacle. The water pressure on anything trapped this way is overwhelming, and there may be little or no whitewater to warn of this danger.
   d. **Weirs, reversals, and souse holes.** Water drops over an obstacle, then curls back on itself in a stationary wave, as is often seen at weirs and dams. The surface water is actually going *upstream*, and this action will trap any floating object between the drop and the wave. Once trapped, a swimmer's only hope is to dive below the surface where current is flowing downstream or to try to swim out the end of the wave.

5. **Boating alone is not recommended.** The preferred minimum is three craft.

6. **Have a frank knowledge of your boating ability.** Don't attempt waters beyond this ability. Learn paddling skills and teamwork, if in a multi-person craft, to match the river you plan to boat.

7. **Be in good physical condition** consistent with the difficulties that may be expected.

8. **Be practiced in escape** from an overturned craft, in self-rescue, and in artificial respiration. Know first aid.

9. **The Eskimo roll should be mastered** by kayakers and canoeists planning to run large rivers or rivers with continuous rapids where a swimmer would have trouble reaching shore.

10. **Wear a crash helmet** where an upset is likely. This is essential in a kayak or covered canoe.

11. **Be suitably equipped.** Wear shoes that will protect your feet during a bad swim or a walk for help, yet will not interfere with swimming (tennis shoes recommended). Carry a knife and waterproof matches. If you need eyeglasses, tie them on and carry a spare pair. Do not wear bulky clothing that will interfere with your swimming when water-logged.

II. Boat and Equipment Preparedness

1. **Test new and unfamiliar equipment** before relying on it for difficult runs.

2. **Be sure the craft is in good repair** before starting a trip. Eliminate sharp projections that could cause injury during a swim.

3. **Inflatable craft should have multiple air chambers** and should be test inflated before starting a trip.

4. **Have strong, adequately sized paddles or oars** for controlling the craft and carry sufficient spares for the length of the trip.

5. **Install flotation devices** in non-inflatable craft. These devices should be securely fixed and designed to displace as much water from the craft as possible.

6. **Be certain there is absolutely nothing to cause entanglement** when coming free from an upset craft; e.g., a spray skirt that won't release or that tangles around the legs; life jacket buckles or clothing that might snag; canoe seats that lock on shoe heels; foot braces that fail or allow feet to jam under them; flexible decks that collapse on boater's legs when trapped by water pressure; baggage that dangles in an upset; loose rope in the craft or badly secured bow and stern lines.

7. **Provide ropes to allow you to hold on to your craft** in case of upset and so that it may be rescued. Following are the recommended methods:
   a. **Kayaks and covered canoes** should have 6-inch diameter grab loops of ¼-inch rope attached to bow and stern. A stern painter 7 or 8 feet long is optional and may be used if properly secured to prevent entanglement.
   b. **Open canoes** should have bow and stern lines (painters), securely attached, consisting of 8 to 10 feet of ¼- or ⅜-inch rope. These lines must be secured in such a way that they will not come loose accidentally and entangle the boaters during a swim, yet they must be ready for immediate use during an emergency. Attached balls, floats, and knots are not recommended.
   c. **Rafts and dories** should have taut perimeter grab lines threaded through the loops usually provided on the craft.

8. **Respect rules for craft capacity** and know how these capacities should be reduced for whitewater use. (Life raft ratings must generally be halved.)

9. **Carry appropriate repair materials:** tape (heating-duct tape) for short trips, a complete repair kit for wilderness trips.

10. **Car-top racks must be strong and positively attached** to the vehicle, and each boat must be tied to each rack. In addition, each end of each boat should be tied to the car bumpers. Suction-cup racks are inadequate. The entire arrangement should be able to withstand all but the most violent accident.

III. Leader's Preparedness and Responsibility

1. **River conditions.** Have a reasonable knowledge of the difficult parts of the run, or, if making an exploratory trip, examine maps to estimate the feasibility of the run. Be aware of possible rapid changes in river level and how these changes can affect the difficulty of the run. If important, determine approximate flow rate or level of the river. If the trip involves important tidal currents, secure tide information.

2. **Participants.** Inform participants of expected river conditions and determine whether the prospective boaters are qualified for the trip. All decisions should be based on group safety and comfort. Difficult decisions on the participation of marginal boaters must be based on group strength.

3. **Equipment.** Plan so that all necessary group equipment is present on the trip: 50- to 100-foot throwing rope, first aid kit with fresh and adequate supplies, extra paddles, repair materials, and survival equipment, if appropriate. Check equipment as necessary at the put-in, especially life jackets, boat flotation, and any items that could prevent complete escape from the boat in case of an upset.

4. **Organization.** Remind each member of individual responsibility in keeping the group compact and intact between the leader and the sweep (a capable rear boater). If the group is too large, divide into smaller groups, each of appropriate boating strength, and designate group leaders and sweeps.

5. **Float plan.** If your trip is into a wilderness area, or for an extended period, your plans should be filed with appropriate authorities or left with someone who will contact them after a certain time. Establishing of checkpoints along the way from which civilization could be contacted if necessary should be considered; knowing the location of possible help could speed rescue in any case.

IV. In Case of Upset

1. **Evacuate your boat immediately** if there is imminent danger of being trapped against logs, brush, or any other form of strainer.

2. **Recover with an Eskimo roll** if possible.

3. **If you swim, hold on to your craft.** It has much flotation and is easy for rescuers to spot. Get to the upstream side of the craft so it cannot crush you against obstacles.

4. **Release your craft if this improves your safety.** If rescue is not imminent and water is numbingly cold, or if worse rapids follow, then strike out for the nearest shore.

5. **When swimming rocky rapids,** use backstroke with legs downstream and feet near the surface. If your foot wedges on the bottom, fast water will push you under and hold you there. Get to slow or very shallow water before trying to stand or walk. Look ahead. Avoid possible entrapment situations: rock wedges, fissures, strainers, brush, logs, weirs, reversals, and souse holes. Watch for eddies and slackwater so that you can be ready to use these when you approach. Use every opportunity to work your way to shore.

6. **If others spill, go after the boaters. Rescue boats and equipment only if this can be done safely.**

V. International Scale of River Difficulty

(If rapids on a river generally fit into one of the following classifications, but the water temperature is below 50°F, or if the trip is an extended one in a wilderness area, the river should be considered one class more difficult than normal.)

Class I   Moving water with a few ripples and small waves; few or no obstructions.

Class II   Easy rapids with waves up to 3 feet, and wide, clear channels that are obvious without scouting; some maneuvering is required.

Class III   Rapids with high, irregular waves often capable of swamping an open canoe; narrow passages that often require complex maneuvering; may require scouting from shore.

Class IV   Long, difficult rapids with constricted passages that often require precise maneuvering in very turbulent waters. Scouting from shore is often necessary, and conditions make rescue difficult. Generally not possible for open canoes; boaters in covered canoes and kayaks should be able to Eskimo roll.

Class V   Extremely difficult, long, and very violent rapids with highly congested routes that nearly always must be scouted from shore. Rescue conditions are difficult and there is significant hazard to life in event of a mishap. The ability to Eskimo roll is essential for kayaks and canoes.

Class VI   Difficulties of Class V carried to the extreme of navigability; nearly impossible and very dangerous; for teams of experts only, after close study and with all precautions taken.

Injuries and Evacuations

Even allowing for careful preparation and attention to the rules of river safety, it remains a fact of life that people and boats are somewhat more fragile than rivers and rocks. Expressed differently, accidents do occur on paddling trips, and *all* boaters should understand that it can happen to them. Although virtually any disaster is possible on the river, there seem to be a small number of specific traumas and illnesses that occur more frequently than others. These include:

1. Hypothermia
2. Dislocated shoulder (especially common in decked boating)
3. Sprained or broken ankles (usually sustained while scouting or getting into or out of the boat)
4. Head injuries (sustained in falls on shore or during capsize)
5. Hypersensitivity to insect bite (anaphylactic shock)
6. Heat trauma (sunburn, heat stroke, heat prostration, dehydration, etc.)
7. Food poisoning (often resulting from sun spoilage of foods on a hot day)
8. Badly strained muscles (particularly of the lower back, upper arm, and the trapezius)
9. Hand and wrist injuries
10. Lacerations

What happens when one of the above injuries occurs on the river? Many paddlers are well prepared to handle the first aid requirements but are unfortunately ill prepared to handle the residual problems of continued care and evacuation. The following is an excerpt from *Wilderness Emergencies and Evacuations* by Ed Benjamin, Associate Program Director at SAGE, School of the Outdoors in Louisville, Kentucky, "When a paddler is injured during a river trip he can usually be floated out in a canoe. Unfortunately, however, circumstances do sometimes arise when the victim is non-ambulatory, or when lack of open canoes or the nature of the river preclude floating the injured party out. In such a situation the trip leader would have to choose between sending for help or performing an overland evacuation."

When sending for help, send at least two people. Dispatch with them a marked map or drawing showing your location as exactly as possible. (Yes, that means pencil and paper should be part of every first aid kit). Also send a note giving directions for finding you plus information on the nature of your emergency and the type of assistance you require. Have your messengers call the proper agencies, such as local police, a rescue squad, the U.S. Forest Service, the state police, plus any unofficial parties such as professional river outfitters who could lend special expertise to the rescue. This having been done, the messengers should be instructed to report the situation simply and factually to the families of the persons involved.

Many paddlers, unfortunately, do not know where they are except in relation to the river, and all too few carry topographical maps. Rescuers need to know exactly where you are in terms of the land, roads, etc. A helicopter pilot will not make much sense of the information that your victim is on the left bank below Lunchstop Rapid. Establish shelter for yourselves and your victim; any rescue is going to take a long time. In the time it takes your messengers to walk out, organize help, and return to you, many hours or perhaps days will pass. Psychologically prepare yourself for a long wait. To expedite the rescue attempt, build a smoky fire to help your rescuers locate you.

Many people believe that if they are ever hurt in the wilderness, a helicopter will come fly them out. This is not necessarily so. Only if you are near a military air base or a civilian air rescue service do you have a good chance of getting a helicopter. Even if one is available, there are several serious limitations to this type of rescue. A rescue helicopter will not fly in bad weather, over a certain altitude, or at night. A helicopter needs a clear area about 150 feet in diameter that is reasonably level on which to land. Moreover, the pilot will probably need some sort of wind indicator on the ground such as a wind sock or a smoky fire. All helicopters are not the same; most do not have a cable on which to raise a victim, and all have limitations on where they may hover. If a helicopter is successful in landing near you, do not approach the craft until the crew signals you to do so, and then only as the crew directs. In most situations the availability or usefulness of a helicopter is doubtful. More likely you will be rescued by a group of volunteers who will drive to the nearest roadhead, reach you on foot, and carry the victim out on a litter. Be advised that volunteer rescue teams are usually slow and sometimes lack adequate training (particularly for a river or climbing rescue). Occasionally you may encounter a top-notch mountain rescue team, but this is rare.

If help cannot be obtained, or if you have a large, well-equipped group, it may be possible to carry the victim out yourself. A litter can be improvised from trees, paddles, packs, etc. Any litter used should be sufficiently strong to protect your victim from further injury. If you do attempt to evacuate the victim yourself, be advised that overland evacuations (even with the best equipment) are extremely difficult and exhausting and are best not attempted unless there are eight or more people to assist. When carrying a litter, a complement of six bearers is ideal. Not only does this spread the load, but, if one bearer loses footing, it is unlikely that the litter will be dropped. Bearers should be distributed so that there are two by the victim's head, two by the feet, and one on each side in the middle. Those carrying at the head of the victim must pay careful attention to the victim. An unconscious victim requires constant checking of vital signs. A conscious victim will be uncomfortable and frightened and will need reassurance. Bear in mind also that a day warm enough to make a litter carrier perspire may be cool enough to induce hypothermia in an unmoving victim. Always have one bearer set the pace and choose the safest and easiest route. Go slow and easy and be careful. Always use a rope to belay the litter from above when ascending or descending a slope—a dropped litter can slide a long way. Paddlers should insist that their partners learn first aid. First aid gear (including pencil and paper), extra topographical maps, and rope should be carried in the sweep boat.

Hypothermia

Hypothermia, the lowering of the body's core temperature, and death from drowning or cardiac arrest after sudden immersion in cold water are two serious hazards to the winter, early spring, and late fall paddler. Cold water robs the victim of the ability and desire to save him- or himself. When the body's temperature drops appreciably below the normal 98.6°F, sluggishness sets in, breathing is difficult, coordination is lost to even the most athletic person, pupils dilate, speech becomes slurred, and *thinking irrational*. Finally unconsciouness sets in, and then, death. Hypothermia can occur in a matter of minutes in water just a few degrees above freezing, but even 50°F water is unbearably cold.

To make things worse, panic can set in when the paddler is faced with a long swim through rapids. Heat loss occurs much more quickly than beleived. A drop in body temperature to 96°F makes swimming and pulling yourself to safety almost impossible, and tragically, the harder you struggle, the more heat your body loses. Body temperatures below 90°F lead to unconsciousness, and a further drop to about 87°F usually results in death. (But this same lowering of the body temperature slows metabolism and delays brain death in cases of drowning, therefore heroic rescue efforts have a higher chance of success.)

Paddlers subjected to spray and wetting from waves splashing into an open boat are in almost as much danger of hypothermia as a paddler completely immersed after a spill. The combination of cold air and water drains the body of precious heat at an alarming rate although it is the wetness that causes the major losses since water conducts heat away from the body twenty times faster than air. Clothes lose their insulating properties quickly when immersed in water, and skin temperatures will rapidly drop to within a few degrees of the water temperature. The body, hard pressed to conserve heat, will then reduce blood circulation to the extremities. This reduction in blood flowing to arms and legs makes movement and heavy work next to impossible. Muscular activity increases heat loss because blood forced to the extremities is quickly cooled by the cold water. It's a vicious, deadly cycle.

The best safeguards against cold weather hazards are: recognizing the symptoms of hypothermia, preventing exposure to cold by wearing proper clothing (wool and waterproof outerwear or wet suits), understanding and respecting cold weather, knowing how the body gains, loses, and conserves body heat, and knowing how to treat hypothermia when it is detected. Actually, cold weather deaths may be attributed to a number of factors: physical exhaustion, *inadequate food intake, dehydration of the body,* and psychological elements such as fear, panic, and despair. Factors such as body fat, the metabolism rate of an individual, and skin thickness are variables in a particular person's reaction and endurance when immersed in cold water. Since the rate of metabolism is actually the rate at which the body produces heat from "burning" fats, carbohydrates, and proteins, one person may have a higher tolerance for cold weather than another. Stored fatty tissues also help the body resist a lowering of its core temperature. Shivering is "involuntary exercise"— the body is calling on its energy resources to produce heat. Proper food intake and sufficient water to prevent dehydration are important in any cold weather strenuous exercise, especially paddling.

The key to successfully bringing someone out of hypothermia is understanding that their body must receive heat from an *external source*. In a field situation, strip off all wet clothes and get the victim into a sleeping bag with another person. Skin-to-skin transfer of body heat is by far the best method of getting the body's temperature up. By all means don't let the victim go to sleep, and feed him or her warm liquids but not alcohol, which is a depressant. Build a campfire if possible. Mouth-to-mouth resuscitation or external cardiac massage may be necessary in extreme cases when breathing has stopped, but remember that a person in the grips of hypothermia has a significantly reduced metabolic rate, so the timing of artificial respiration should correspond to the victim's slowed breathing.

Legal Rights of Landowners

Landowners' rights to prohibit tresspassing on their land along streams, if they so desire, is guaranteed; therefore, access to rivers must be secured at highway rights-of-way or on publicly owned land if permission to cross privately owned land cannot be secured. In granting you access to a river, landowners are extending a privilege to you such as they extend to hunters who stop by their doors and seek permission to shoot doves in their cornfields. Don't betray landowners' trust if they give you permission to camp or launch canoes or kayaks from their riverbanks. Always pick up your litter, close any gates you open, and respect planted fields. Tenure of land, landholding, and the right to do with it what you want, is serious business to some landowners. Many farmers do not subscribe to the concept of "land stewardship." They do not feel any responsibility towards the paddling community, and in some cases might even resent people driving hundreds of miles for the pleasure of floating down a river.

On the other hand, it may be that the landowner you seek permission from is intrigued with paddling and will be quite friendly and approachable. Value this friendship and don't give cause for denying access at some time in the future. Remember also that your conduct and courtesy (or lack thereof) shape a landowner's opinion of paddlers in general. Discourteous behavior by a single individual can easily result in a landowner cutting off access to all. A positive approach is the best approach; take up the slack when you encounter evidence that others have been careless or irresponsible. Allow a few extra minutes to share the virtues of your sport with the landowner if it seems welcome. Pick up and carry out garbage and refuse you find along the stream or where paddlers park. Beware of sensitive issues such as changing clothes in view of others.

Paddlers are trespassing when they portage, camp, or even stop for a lunch break. If you are approached by a landowner when tresspassing, by all means be cordial and understanding and explain what you're doing (making a lunch stop or portage). Never knowingly camp on private land without permission. If you do encounter a perturbed landowner, don't panic. Keep cool and be respectful.

Ecological Considerations

Presenting a set of ecological guidelines for all paddlers sounds like preaching, but with the number of people using our creeks and rivers today, it is indeed a valid point. Many of the streams listed in this guide flow through national parks and forests, state-owned forests and wildlife management areas, and privately owned lands that in some cases are superior in quality and aesthetics to lands under public ownership. It is the paddling community's responsibility to uphold the integrity of these lands and their rivers by exercising ecologically sound guidelines. Litter, fire scars, pollution from human excrement, and the cutting of live trees is unsightly and affects the land in a way that threatens to ruin the outdoor experience for everyone.

Paddlers should pack out everything they packed in: all paper litter and such nonbiodegradable items as cartons, foil, plastic jugs, and cans. Help keep our waterways clean for those who follow. If you are canoe camping, leave your campsite in better shape than you found it. If you must build a fire, build it at an established site, and when you leave, dismantle rock fireplaces, thoroughly drown all flames and hot coals, and scatter the ashes. Never cut live trees for firewood (in addition to destroying a part of the environment, they don't burn well). Dump all dishwater in the woods away from watercourses, and emulate the cat, bury all excrement.

Chapter 2

Stream Dynamics

Understanding Hydrology

Understanding hydrology—how rivers are formed and how they affect man's activities—is at the very heart of paddling. To aid the paddler, here is a brief discussion of the effects on paddling of seasonal variations of rainfall, water temperatures, volume, velocity, gradient, and stream morphology.

The most basic concept about water that all paddlers must understand is the hydrologic (water) cycle, which moves water from the earth to the atmosphere and back again. Several things happen to water that falls to the earth: it becomes surface runoff that drains directly into rivers or their tributaries, or it is retained by the soil and used by plants, or it may be returned directly to the atmosphere through evaporation, or else it becomes ground water by filtering down through subsoil and layers of rock.

Local soil conditions have a great deal to do with streamflow as do plant life, terrain slope, ground cover, and air temperature. In summer, during the peak growing season, water is used more readily by plants, and higher air temperatures encourage increased evaporation. The fall and winter low-water periods are caused by decreased precipitation, although since the ground is frozen and plant use of water is for the most part halted, abnormally high amounts of rain, or water from melting snow, can cause flash floods because surface runoff is high—there's no place for the water to go but into creeks and rivers. Though surface runoff is first to reach the river, it is ground water that keeps many larger streams flowing during rainless periods. Drought can lower the water table drastically. Soil erosion is related to surface runoff—hilly land in intensive agricultural use is a prime target for loss of topsoil and flashflooding.

The Water Cycle

The water on and around the earth moves in a never-ending cycle from the atmosphere to the land and back to the atmosphere again. Atmospheric moisture flows constantly over Georgia, and the amount that falls on the state now is much the same as it was when only the Indians worried about dried-up springs and floods in their villages.

Beginning the cycle with the oceans, which cover some 75 percent of the earth's surface, the movement of the water follows these steps:

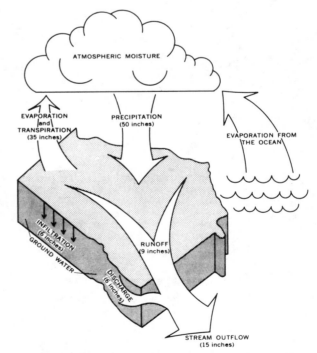

SOURCE: *Water Resources Investigations in Georgia, 1974.* U.S. Dept. of Interior Geological Survey.

Figure 1: Water Cycle in Georgia

1. Water from the surface of the oceans (and from the lands between) evaporates into the atmosphere as vapor. This water vapor rises and moves with the winds.

2. Eventually, either over the ocean or over the land, this moisture is condensed by various processes and falls back to the earth as precipitation. Some falls on the ocean; some falls on the land where it becomes of particular concern to man.

3. Of the rain, snow, sleet, or hail that falls on the land, some runs off over the land, some soaks down into the ground to replenish the great ground-water reservoir, some is taken up by the roots of plants and is transpired as water vapor, and some is again evaporated directly into the atmosphere.

4. The water that flows over the land or soaks down to become ground water feeds the streams that eventually flow back into the oceans, completing the cycle.

The key steps in this great circulation of the earth's moisture are evaporation, precipitation, transpiration, and streamflow. All occur constantly and simultaneously over the earth. Over Georgia and its river basins the quantities in any part of the cycle vary widely from day to day or from season to season. Precipitation may be excessive or may stop entirely for days or weeks. Evaporation and transpiration demands are lower in winter and higher in July and August. Streamflow depends on the interrelation of these processes.

Rainfall and Weather in Georgia

Rainfall in Georgia averages about 50 inches a year, but it is not uniformly distributed by season or location. The Augusta area annually receives about 43 inches while a small area in the mountains of northeastern Georgia receives nearly twice that amount. Most of Georgia's rainfall comes from warm, moist, air masses formed over the Gulf of Mexico. Lesser amounts of rainfall come from air masses that form over the Atlantic Ocean. The average annual rainfall decreases with distance from the Atlantic Ocean and the Gulf of Mexico up to the Fall Line. The Fall Line is the discernible geologic break between the hard rock strata of the Piedmont and the more easily eroded rock of the Coastal Plain. This line, which roughly parallels the eastern seaboard, is marked by steep cliffs, waterfalls, and rapids. North of the Fall Line average rainfall increases because the moist air is forced to rise thus precipitating moisture as it passes over the ridges and mountains.

In addition to the above, there are also seasonal variations in rainfall. More rain falls in winter,

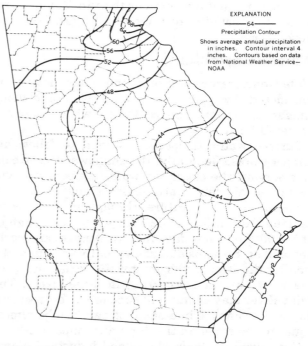

SOURCE: *Water Resources Investigations in Georgia, 1974.* U.S. Dept. of Interior Geological Survey.

Figure 2: Average Annual Precipitation, in Inches, 1936–65

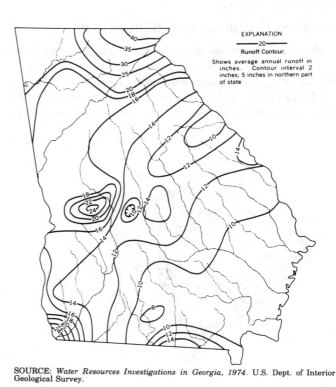

SOURCE: *Water Resources Investigations in Georgia, 1974.* U.S. Dept. of Interior Geological Survey.

Figure 3: Average Annual Runoff, in Inches, 1938–62

early spring, and midsummer than in May or June or in the usually dry months of October and November.

Water Temperature

Water temperature is another important factor to be considered by paddlers because of the obvious dangers of encountering cold water when you're not prepared for it.

Surface water temperatures tend to follow air temperatures. Generally, the shallower the stream or reservoir, the closer the water temperature will be to the air temperature. Streams show a wide variation in temperature throughout the years, ranging from a low of 32°F in winter to a high of about 90°F on some days in July, August, and early September. Streams also show a daily variation: the smaller the stream, the greater the variations, with the least variation occurring in large rivers. The Flint River may change only one or two degrees in a day while changes in a small stream can be almost equal to the range in the day's air temperature.

Coal-burning steam plants and industrial plants may influence the water temperature in some rivers through thermal discharges. Usually, the added heat is lost within twenty miles downstream from the entry point, but this heat loss depends on the amount of water used, the temperature of the waste water, the size of the stream, the air temperature, and other factors.

Stream Evolution and Morphology

Often, when teaching canoeing or paddling socially, someone will fix an inquisitive stare at a large boulder in midstream and ask, "How in the blazes did that thing get in the middle of the river?" The frequency of being asked this and similar questions

about the river has prompted us to include in this book a brief look at river dynamics.

Basically river dynamics represent the relationship between geology and hydraulics, or, expressed differently, what effect flowing water has on the land surface, and, conversely, how the land surface modifies the flow of water.

To begin at a rather obvious point, we all know that water flows downhill, moving from a higher elevation to a lower elevation and ultimately flowing into the sea. Contrary to what many people believe, however, the water on its downhill journey does not flow as smoothly as we sometimes imagine the water in our home plumbing flows. Instead, to varying degrees depending on the geology, it has to pound and fight every inch of the way. Squeezed around obstructions, ricocheted from rock to rock, and funneled from side to side, almost any river's course is tortuous at best. This is because the land was there first and is very reluctant to surrender its domain to the moving water, and therefore it does so very slowly and grudgingly. In other words, the water must literally carve out a place in the land through which to flow. It accomplishes this through erosion.

There are three main types of moving-water erosion; downward erosion, lateral erosion, and headward erosion. All three represent the wearing away of the land by the water. *Downward erosion* is at work continuously on all rivers and can be loosely defined as moving water wearing away the bottom of the river, eroding the geological strata that compose the river bottom, and descending deeper and deeper down into the ground. A graphic example of downward erosion in its purest form is a river that runs through a vertical-walled canyon or gorge. Here the density of the rock forming the

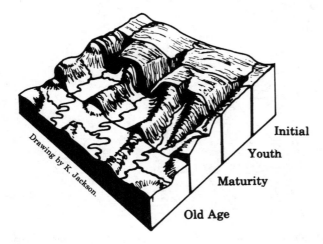

Figure 4: Stages of Erosion, Evolution of a Landscape

Drawing by K. Jackson.

Figure 5: Headward Erosion: Waterfalls

canyon walls has limited erosion to the side and left most of the work for downward erosion. Down and down the river cuts without proprotional expansion of its width. A gorge or canyon is formed this way. (see Figure 4.)

Most of the time, however, two and usually three kinds of erosion are working simultaneously. When the water, through downward erosion, for example, cuts into the bottom of the river, it encounters geological substrata of varying density and composition. A layer of clay might overlay a shelf of sandstone, under which may be granite or limestone. Since the water is moving downhill at an angle, the flowing water at the top of a mountain might be working against a completely different type of geological substratum than the water halfway down or at the foot of the mountain. Thus, to carve its channel, the water has to work harder in some spots than in others.

Where current crosses a seam marking the boundary between geological substrata of differing resistance to erosion, an interesting phenomenon occurs. Imagine that upstream of this seam the water has been flowing over sandstone, which is worn away by the erosive action of the current at a rather slow rate. As the current crosses the seam, it encounters limestone, which erodes much faster. Downward erosion wears through the limestone relatively quickly while the sandstone on top remains little changed over the same period of time. The result is a waterfall (see Figure 5). It may only be a foot high or it may be 100 feet high, depending on the thickness of the layer eaten away. The process is complete

when the less resistant substratum is eroded and the water again encounters sandstone or another equally resistant formation. The evolution of a waterfall by downward erosion is similar to covering your wooden porch stairs with snow and then smoothing the snow so that from top to bottom the stairs resemble a nice snowy hill in the park, with the normal shape of the stairs being hidden. Wood (the stairs) and snow can both be eaten away by water. Obviously though, the water will melt the snow much faster than it will rot the wood. Thus, if a tiny stream of water is launched downhill from the top of the stairs, it will melt through the snow quickly, not stopping until it reaches the more resistant wood on the next stair down. This is how erosion forms a waterfall in nature.

Once a waterfall has formed, regardless of its size, headward erosion comes into play. *Headward erosion* is the wearing away of the base of the waterfall. This action erodes the substrata in an upstream direction toward the headwaters or source of the stream, thus it is called headward erosion. Water falling over the edge of the waterfall lands below with substantial force. As it hits the surface of the water under the falls, it causes a depression in the surface that water from downstream rushes to fill in. This is a hydraulic, or what paddlers call a souse hole. Continuing through the surface water, the falling current hits the bottom of the stream. Some of the water is disbursed in an explosive manner, some deflected downstream, and some drawn back to the top where it is recirculated to refill the depression made by yet more falling current. A great deal

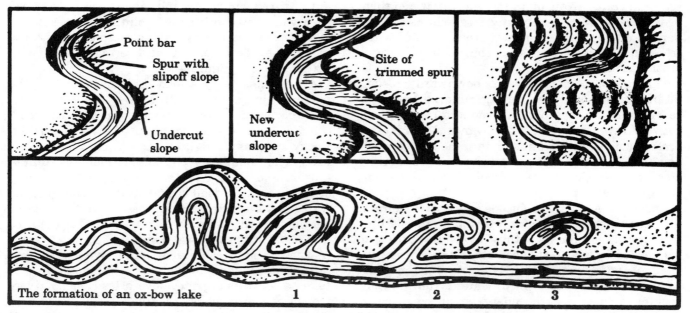

Drawing by K. Jackson.

Figure 6: Meanders and Oxbow Lakes

of energy is expended in this process and the ensuing cyclical turbulence, which combines with bits of rock to make an abrasive mixture, carves slowly away at the rock base of the falls. If the falls are small, the turbulence may simply serve to smooth out the drop, turning a vertical drop into a slanting drop. If the falls are large, the base of the falls may be eroded, leaving the top of the falls substantially intact but precariously unsupported. After a period of time the overhang thus created will surrender to gravity and fall into the river. And that is one way that huge boulders happen to arrive in the middle of the river. Naturally the process is ongoing, and the altered facade of the waterfall is immediately attacked by the currents.

Lateral erosion is the wearing away of the sides of the river by the moving current. While occurring continuously on most rivers to a limited degree, lateral erosion is much more a function of volume and velocity (collectively known as discharge and expressed in cubic feet per seconds, cfs) than either downward or headward erosion. In other words, as more water is added to a river (beyond that simply required to cover its bottom), the increase in the volume and the speed of the current cause significant additional lateral erosion while headward and downward erosion remain comparatively constant. Thus, as a river swells with spring rain, the amount of water in the river increases. Since water is noncompressible, the current rises on the banks and through lateral erosion tries to enlarge the river bed laterally to accommodate the extra volume. Effects of this activity can be observed every year following seasonal rains. Even small streams can widen their beds substantially by eroding large chunks of the banks and carrying them downstream. Boulders and trees in the river are often the result of lateral erosion undercutting the bank.

Through a combination of downward erosion, lateral erosion, and meandering, running water can carve broad valleys between mountains and deep canyons through solid rock. Downward and lateral erosion act on the terrain to determine the morphology (depth, width, shape, and course) of a river. Headward erosion serves to smooth out the rough spots that remain.

Curves in a river are formed much as waterfalls are formed; i.e., the water will follow the path of least resistance and its path will twist and turn as it is diverted by resistant substrata. Rivers constantly change and do not continue indefinitely in their courses once they are formed. Water is continuously seeking to decrease the energy required to move from the source to the mouth. This is the essence of all erosion.

As we have observed, headward erosion works upstream to smooth out the waterfalls and rapids. Lateral erosion works to make more room for increased volume, and downward erosion deepens the bed and levels obstructions and irregularities. When a river is young (in the geological sense), it cuts downward and is diverted into sharp turns by differing resistance from underlying rock layers. As a stream matures, it carves a valley, sinks even closer to sea level, and leaves behind, in many instances, a succession of terraces marking previous valley floors.

Moving water erodes the outside of river bends and deposits much of the eroded matter on the inside of the turn, thereby forming a sand or gravel bar. Jagged turns are changed to sweeping bends. The results in more mature streams is a meander, or the formation of a series of horseshoe-shaped and geometrically predictable loops in the river (see Figure 6). A series of such undulating loops markedly widens the valley floor. Often, as time passes, the current erodes the neck of a loop and creates an island in midstream and eliminates a curve in the river; this is called a meander by-pass or cut-off island.

In the theoretically mature stream, the bottom is smooth and undisturbed by obstructing boulders, rapids, or falls. Straight stretches in the river give way to serpentine meanders, and the water flows at a very moderate rate of descent from the source to the sea. Of course, there are no perfect examples of a mature stream, although rivers such as the Ohio and the Mississippi tend to approach the mature end of the spectrum. A stream exhibiting a high gradient and frequent rapids and sharp turns is described as a young stream in the evolutional sense of the word (stream maturity having more to do with the evolutional development of a stream than with actual age; see Figure 4).

All streams carry a load that consists of all the particles, large and small, that are a result of the multiple forms of erosion we discussed. The load, then, is solid matter transported by the current. Rocky streams at high altitudes carry the smallest loads. Their banks and bottoms are more resistant to erosion and their tributary drainages are usually small. Scarcity of load is evident in the clarity of the water. Rivers such as the Mississippi and Ohio carry enormous loads collected from numerous tributaries as well as from their own banks and bottoms. Water in these and in similarly large rivers is almost always dark and murky with sediment. Since it takes a lot of energy to move a load, many rivers transport conspicuous (readily visible) loads only during rainy periods when they are high, fast, and powerful. When the high waters abate, there is insufficient energy to continue to transport the large load that then, for the most part, settles as silt or alluvium on the bottom of the stream.

Understanding stream dynamics gives any boater an added advantage in working successfully with the river. Knowledge of stream evolution and morphology tells a paddler where to find the strongest current and deepest channel, where rapids and falls are most likely to occur, and what to expect from a given river if the discharge increases or decreases. But more, understanding the river's evolution and continuing development contributes immeasurably to the paddler's aesthetic experience and allows for a communion and harmony with the river that otherwise might be superficial.

Volume, Velocity and Gradient

Being able to recognize potential river hazards depends on a practical knowledge of river hydrology—why the water flows the way it does. Since river channels vary greatly in depth and width and the composition of stream beds and their gradients also enter into the river's character, these major components of streamflow bear explanation.

Discharge is the volume of water moving past a given point of the river at any one time. The river current, or velocity, is commonly expressed as the speed of water movement in feet per seconds (fps),

and stage is the river's height in feet based on an arbitrary measurement gauge. These terms are interrelated; increased water levels mean increased volume and velocity.

Another factor in assessing stream difficulty is gradient, which is expressed in feet per mile (ft/mi). As gradient increases, so does velocity. The streams profiled in this book have gradients that range from about one foot per mile to an astounding 200 feet per mile. The gradient in any stream or section of a stream changes with the landforms, the geology of the basin. If a river flows over rock or soil with varying resistance to erosion, ledges, waterfalls, and rapids sometimes form and dramatically affect gradient.

Velocity is also affected by the width and depth of the stream bed. Rapids form where streams are shallow and swift. Large obstructions in shallow streams of high velocity cause severe rapids. Within a given channel there are likely to be rapids with different levels of difficulty. The current on straight sections of river is usually fastest in the middle. The depth of water in river bends is determined by flow rates and soil types; water tends to cut away the land and form deep holes on the outside of bends where the current is the swiftest.

Chapter 3

Georgia's Land and Water

Physiographic Regions of Georgia

To understand and appreciate the varied and beautiful waterways of Georgia, it is necessary to understand something of the geology and topography of the state. Water shaped Georgia into its present physical form by attacking, eroding and dissolving the land for millions of years. Everytime it rains a little more of Georgia is carried away to the sea as grains of sand or dissolved salts. The rock shapes resulting from this continual action of water make possible the division of the state into five major physiographic provinces or regions. (See Figure 7.)

Distinguishing these provinces are differences in rock strata. Some rocks lie flat, one on top of the other like the pages in a book. Other rocks are folded, while still others are broken, cracked, and without apparent layering. Each of these rock types reacts differently to the action of water.

Georgia has been subjected to the unheavals of the earth time after time in recent millenia. Oceans sweeping across the state have eroded the land in one place and built it up in others. In northwestern Georgia, the Cumberland Plateau region and the Valley and Ridge region are characterized by parallel valleys and ridges that are underlain by Paleozoic sedimentary rocks, some of which lie nearly flat and some are much folded. The Blue Ridge region is a mountainous area underlain by very hard crystalline rocks. The Piedmont, adjacent to the south, is a hilly rolling area where the ridgetops have a uniform level and slope southward. It is underlain by the same crystalline rocks as the Blue Ridge region. The Coastal Plain, stretching south from the Piedmont to Florida and the sea, is nearly flat everywhere and is underlain by thick beds of sand and limestone that were deposited in an ocean whose shoreline was north of Macon. The streams of

the lower sections of the state are found in a companion book, *Southern Georgia Canoeing: A Canoeing and Kayaking Guide to the Streams of the Western Piedmont, Coastal Plain, Georgia Coast and the Okefenokee Swamp.*

Climatic conditions are similar in all parts of Georgia although northern Georgia is slightly cooler and wetter than southern Georgia. Geology, topography, and stream channel development, however, vary significantly from region to region.

Cumberland Plateau Region and the Valley and Ridge Region

The Cumberland Plateau region and the Valley and Ridge region grade one into the other; the rocks of the plateau lie almost flat, whereas those of the Valley and Ridge are folded. The latter province gets its name from the many long valleys and ridges that resulted from the erosion of the folded rocks that extend into Tennessee and Alabama.

Erosion is the process by which water, wind, and weather break down rocks. It works fastest on the limestone that underlies most of the valleys. Not only is the limestone broken up by other rocks carried by moving water, but it is also dissolved by the water itself. This erosive action has carved an extensive network of interconnected subterranean channels and caverns. Through these large openings, the water moves as freely as it would through a city main. Since the underground channels are connected under large areas, water that falls as rain in Tennessee may flow underground and emerge in Georgia, or water that falls in Georgia may surface in Alabama.

Both regions are drained by a network of streams that yield substantial river flow. Those in the northwestern part of the state drain north into the Tennessee basin; the remainder drain southwest into the Mobile basin. The streams generally flow in deep channels meandering in wide floodplains. Where they cut through the ridges in the water gaps, they are shallow and swift and have numerous rapids. Steep slopes give rise to rapid runoff and flashflooding is not uncommon.

Average annual runoff of streams averages from 18 to 24 inches (compared with a state average of 14 inches). In the Valley and Ridge region, many streams are sustained during dry weather by the numerous springs that are characteristic of the region. Streams of the Cumberland Plateau have lower flow during dry weather because they are not fed by so many springs.

Blue Ridge Mountain Region

The Appalachian Mountains of the eastern United States extend southwestward from the state of Maine to the Blue Ridge province of Georgia. This region is the coolest and wettest part of the state. Average annual rainfall in the region ranges from 55 to more than 80 inches per year, with the greatest amount falling in higher altitudes. The average annual temperature is about 58°F, ten degrees cooler than in southern Georgia.

The Blue Ridge Mountain region contains thousands of acres of forest, mountains, and rivers. The area is not farmed extensively nor is it densely populated. The steepness of the topography makes the land more suitable for forest than for farms.

The region is drained by the headwaters of four basins; the Tennessee, the Savannah, the Chattahoochee, and the Coosa. The rivers within the region are small and have small drainages, but they have the highest flow for their size in the state. Their channels are steep and rocky, and water flows swiftly over an abundance of rapids and falls.

The Blue Ridge Mountain region is underlain by rocks that the geologists refer to as "crystalline," which includes granite, slate, gneiss, and other dense, hard rocks. The mountains are high and steep and have nearly V-shaped valleys covered with luxurious forests and thick soil, which retard runoff.

Piedmont Region

The Piedmont region is the most densely populated part of the state. About 66 percent of Georgia's population inhabits this region, which contains 31 percent of the state's area. The Piedmont was primarily an agricultural region for two centuries. In the last half century, however, the textile industry has expanded, and in recent years a completely diversified industrial expansion has taken place.

The Piedmont is underlain by the same crystalline rocks as the Blue Ridge, but it lacks the high relief of the Blue Ridge Mountain region. Instead it is an area of rolling plain broken occasionally by narrow stream valleys and prominent hills. The soil cover in the Piedmont is not as thick or as capable of slowing runoff as that of the Blue Ridge.

The Piedmont region includes parts of several drainages. The Savannah, Ogeechee, Ocmulgee, and Oconee rivers drain into the Atlantic Ocean while the Flint and Chattahoochee drain into the Gulf of Mexico. Throughout most of the region the main streams flow southeastward, the direction of the general slope of the upland, and cross the underlying rock structure at right angles. In the northwestern section of the Piedmont, the Chattahoochee and some streams in the Mobile basin tend to parallel the direction of the rock strata. Rivers there generally have moderate slopes interrupted by occasional rapids and falls and flow in well-defined channels within comparatively narrow valleys.

The ridges between the major drainage systems of the Piedmont are broad and rather sinuous and have the region's primary cities, highways, railroads, and farmlands concentrated on top of them. Towns were established on the ridges along the old wagon trails and railroads because the ridges were well-drained routes that required a minimum number of bridges and were free of the danger of floods.

Rainfall along the northern Piedmont, the area of highest elevation, averages more than 50 inches annually. To the south and east the rainfall is less. The Augusta area receives less than any other part of the state, a little more than 42 inches annually.

Coastal Plain Region

Over sixty percent of Georgia lies in the Coastal Plain, with the population concentrated along the Fall Line (where the Piedmont descends to the Coastal Plain) in the cities of Augusta, Macon, and Columbus, and in the coastal city of Savannah.

Because of the great difference in the runoff characteristics of the Coastal Plains streams, hydrologists differentiate between the upper Coastal Plain and the lower Coastal Plain. Streams in the upper Coastal Plain have relatively uniform flows and high volume because of small storm runoff and large groundwater inflow. The very small streams commonly have very little runoff because the permeable soil absorbs rainwater rapidly and the channels are not entrenched deeply enough to intercept much groundwater flow. The average annual runoff of the larger streams ranges from 12 to 28 inches. The streams are generally sluggish and flow in deep meandering, low-banked, tree-choked channels bordered by wide, swampy, densely wooded valleys.

The lower Coastal Plain generally has the least runoff of any part of Georgia, averaging from 9 to 14 inches annually. The streams wander in wide, swampy, heavily wooded valleys separated by very wide and very low, flat ridges. Swamp vegetation consumes large quantities of water and evaporation loss is high.

Cretaceous sand aquifers, a blanket of sand and gravel, begin at the Fall Line and thicken to the south. Rainfall filters into this sand blanket and recharges the sand aquifer with water. When the stream levels are high, water moves from the streams into the sands. When the stream levels are low, water feeds back from the sands into the streams.

In the southwestern area of the upper Coastal Plain, near Albany, limestone–sand aquifers give rise to lime sinks, caves, underground rivers, and artesian wells. These features are formed by the solvent action of water on limestone. When the limestone is dissolved, caverns and interconnected channels are left below the surface. If the cavern roof collapses, sink holes are created.

Streams originating in the Coastal Plain generally carry very little sediment. Running over sand and sandy clay, their waters flow clear and sparkling, colored a reddish tea color by tannic acid derived from decaying vegetation. Streams crossing the Coastal Plain that originate in the Piedmont or in the Blue Ridge transport heavy loads of sediment.

The annual rainfall in the Coastal Plain averages from 45 to 52 inches, draining slowly over the flat terrain, with the part that does not sink into the ground quickly evaporated or consumed by vegetation.

Water and Rivers in Georgia

Georgia receives approximately 50 inches of rainfall each year, primarily in the winter and early spring. Due to the varied topography of the state, the mean annual precipitation varies from place to place and ranges from a maximum of 68 inches to a minimum of 40 inches.

Of the state's mean annual average rainfall of 50 inches, only 9 to 24 inches (depending on the part of the state) becomes a part of the surface or ground-water system. The remaining inches return to the atmosphere by evaporation or transpiration.

Since the greater part of the rainfall occurs during the winter when plant life is dormant, the soil must store moisture for plant use during the periods of minimum rainfall. However, the capacity of the soil to retain moisture varies considerably over the state. A soil of one type can receive more rainfall than another but can experience drought conditions quicker because of its inability to hold moisture.

Several of the chief surface-water systems in

Georgia are dam controlled. The smaller tributaries of these great systems are not regulated. Their flow varies greatly from year to year, from month to month, and from day to day. Average streamflow in a wet year may be five or ten times that in a dry year, but flow in a wet month may be several thousand times that in a dry month, and the flow during the instant of flood peak may be tens of hundreds of thousands times greater than the minimum daily flow. The low flow dependability of the streams of the state varies according to their geographic location.

Georgia Streamflow

The amount of water that finds its way into the stream channels of Georgia is on the average less than half of the rain that falls on the state. Streamflow is residual water that is left over after the heavy demands of evaporation and transpiration have been met.

Streamflow is made up basically of two runoff components. These are direct runoff, or the water that flows over the ground or just under the surface during and immediately after a rainstorm, and ground-water storage that comes out in seeps and springs for days and weeks after the rain. Direct runoff supplies most of the volume of streamflow in flood periods. Ground-water runoff feeds the streams in the periods between rains.

The proportion of total streamflow that comes from direct runoff or ground-water runoff varies among streams, depending on such watershed features as elevation of the land and the density and type of vegetation.

The Major Drainages of Georgia*

Georgia, the largest state east of the Mississippi River, encompasses nearly sixty thousand square miles and has ten major river basins. It is estimated that there are over 20,000 miles of streams in Georgia. All of Georgia's rivers flow south except tributaries of the Tennessee River. The Coosa River and its tributaries in northwest Georgia represent the eastern headwaters of the Alabama River system and cross out of the state into Alabama. All other large drainages flow within Georgia though the Savannah has numerous South Carolina tributaries and the Chattahoochee has many Alabama tributaries. Two of Georgia's largest rivers, the Flint and the Chattahoochee, meet at Lake Seminole near the southwestern corner of the state to form the Apalachicola River, which runs through Florida to the Gulf of Mexico. These rivers, therefore, are

*Much of the information in this section was derived from *Water Resources Development in Georgia*, South Altantic Division, U.S. Army Corps of Engineers.

Figure 7: Physiographic Regions of Georgia

SOURCE: *Water Quality Monitoring Data for Georgia Streams, 1977.* Georgia Department of Natural Resources, Environmental Protection Division. Drawing by K. Jackson.

considered part of the Apalachicola system.

Rivers of the Savannah, Altamaha, Apalachicola, and Ogeechee systems flow through two or more physiographic regions and their flow characteristics change to reflect regional differences in rainfall, runoff, topography, and rock structure.

The Satilla flows entirely within the Georgia Coastal Plain while the Ochlockonee and Suwannee systems originate in the Coastal Plain and cross into Florida. In the far southeastern corner of Georgia the St. Marys River forms the Florida–Georgia boundary.

Flow from the Savannah, Ogeechee, Altamaha, Satilla, and St. Marys systems empties into the Atlantic Ocean while the Apalachicola (Flint and Chattahoochee), Ochlockonee, Alabama (Coosa), and Suwannee drain into the Gulf of Mexico.

The Savannah, Altamaha, Ogeechee, Alabama, and Apalachicola systems carry large sediment loads and are therefore considered to be "alluvial rivers." Distinguished from these rivers are those drainages that originate on the Coastal Plain. The Coastal Plain drainages run over sandy beds and transport very little suspended sediment. Their water is characteristically colored red from the tannic acid released by tree roots and decaying vegetation. Because the red water appears glossy and black in direct sunlight, these streams are known as "blackwater rivers."

The Altamaha is the largest river lying wholly within Georgia's boundaries. Originating in the Piedmont, flowing across the Coastal Plain and entering the Atlantic near St. Simons Island, the Altamaha drains 14,200 square miles. The longest river in Georgia is the Chattahoochee, which runs 436 miles from source to mouth. The Chattahoochee's 8,770 square mile drainage area includes part of southeastern Alabama and lies in three physiographic regions, the Blue Ridge, the Piedmont, and the Coastal Plain.

Of the four major systems that cross the Piedmont into the Coastal Plain, only the Ogeechee remains free flowing. All of the others (Apalachicola, Savannah, Altamaha) are punctuated to varying degrees with dams, lakes, and other navigational and flood control projects.

Alabama–Coosa River Basin of Alabama and Georgia

The upper reaches of the Coosa and Tallapoosa rivers drain about 5,350 square miles in northwestern Georgia. This area is a part of the extensive Alabama–Coosa river basin, which extends about 320 miles from southeastern Tennessee and northwestern Georgia diagonally across Alabama to the southwestern corner of that state.

The Coosa River is formed by the junction of the Oostanaula and Etowah rivers at Rome. Their headwaters, which rise in the Blue Ridge Mountains, include the Conasauga, Coosawattee, Cartecay, and Ellijay rivers, all scenic mountain streams flowing through steep, narrow, forested valleys among high, rounded mountains. The Oostanaula River is 47 miles long and has a relatively flat slope. The Etowah River is 150 miles long. Rising in the Blue Ridge Mountains, the Etowah falls steeply for about 60 miles, then more moderately for the remaining distance to its junction with the Oostanaula. From its beginning at Rome, the Coosa River flows westward though a wide valley between high ridges for about 30 miles before reaching the Alabama line. This part of the Coosa River passes through the old Corps of Enginners' Mayos Bar Pool and the Alabama Power Company's Weiss Lake. The Coosa River and its headwaters drain about 4,630 square miles in Georgia.

The Tallapoosa River begins about 40 miles west of Atlanta and flows southwestward through hilly terrain for about 45 miles in Georgia before entering Alabama. It drains about 720 square miles in Georgia.

Rainfall is plentiful in the basin, and generalized storms periodically inundate bottom lands along the principal streams in Georgia. Streamflows, if controlled, would be adequate for foreseeable water supply needs along the larger streams. Unfortunately, pollution is a problem near large population centers.

Agriculture is a major factor in the economy of the area, but, as a result of rapid industrial development, manufacturing has become an integral part of the economy. Major industries produce textiles, machine parts, and wood and food products. Manufacturing is centered mainly in Rome, but it is also scattered in smaller urban areas throughout the region.

Apalachicola–Chattahoochee–Flint River Basin of Florida, Georgia and Alabama

The Apalachicola–Chattahoochee—Flint River system drains an area of 19,600 square miles, of which 8,770 square miles lies along the Chattahoochee River arm, 8,460 square miles lie along the Flint River arm, and the remaining 2,370 square miles lie along the Apalachicola River below the confluence of the Chattahoochee and Flint rivers. Beginning in northeastern Georgia, this basin extends for 385 miles to the Gulf of Mexico. It covers most of northern and western Georgia, an area of about 14,400 square miles, and extends into southeastern Alabama and northwestern Florida. The largest Georgia cities in the basin are Atlanta, Albany,

Drawing by K. Jackson.

Figure 8: Canoeing Divisions

Bainbridge, and Columbus.

The main stem of the system is the Apalachicola River, which flows southward across northwestern Florida from the vicinity of the Georgia line to the Gulf, a distance of about 108 miles. The Apalachicola is formed by the junction of the Chattahoochee and Flint rivers in the southwestern corner of Georgia.

The Chattahoochee River flows 120 miles southwestward from the Blue Ridge Mountains in northeastern Georgia near the western tip of South Carolina. It then flows southward for 200 miles, forming the boundary between Georgia and Alabama and between Georgia and a small portion of Florida.

The Flint River flows south in a wide eastward arc from the southeastern edge of Atlanta for 349 miles to its junction with the Chattahoochee River.

The topography of the Apalachicola–Chattahoochee–Flint river basin varies widely; elevations range from 4500 feet above mean sea level to sea level. In Georgia, the land is low, rolling, clay hills and sandy bottoms along the lower Chattahoochee River and broad, often swampy, flatlands along the lower Flint River that extend to the Fall Line, which is the transition zone between the Coastal Plain and the upland plateau of the central part of the state. Both rivers fall about 375 feet in this transition zone. Practically all the fall on the Chattahoochee River has been developed for power generation by a series of privately owned dams betwen West Point and Columbus. The upper reaches of the Flint River and about 200 miles of the Chattahoochee River above the Fall Line flow through a plateau characterized by red hills somewhat steeper than those of the Coastal Plain. The uppermost reaches of the Chattahoochee River watershed extend into the Blue Ridge Mountains, where rugged, densely wooded knobs, rising to as much as 4,500 feet above sea level, are not uncommon.

The climate in the basin is generally mild and humid. Rainfall is usually greater in the upper and lower areas than in the center. Major flood-producing storms usually occur in the winter or spring and last for several days. Floods in the upper basin tend to be sudden because of the hilly terrain and high runoff rates, while floods in the lower basin tend to rise more slowly and last longer because of the flatter land and more moderate slope of the streams.

The long growing season, abundant rainfall, and productive soils have made agriculture a major component of the basin's economy. However, the trend is toward fewer farms and larger farm units. Principal sources of farm income are poultry and poultry products in the region above Atlanta, and field crops, nuts and fruits in the upper Coastal Plain. Although forest products are important throughout the basin, they are of primary importance only in the lower reaches.

Altamaha River Basin

All 14,200 square miles of the Altamaha River basin are in the state of Georgia. The basin is 260 miles long, has a minimum width of about six miles at the lower end, a miximum width of about eighty miles, and an average width of fifty-five miles.

The headwaters of the river rise in the Piedmont along the base of the Chattahoochee Ridge between Atlanta and a point ten miles north-northeast of Gainesville. The two principle tributaries, the Ocmulgee and Oconee rivers, unite to form the Altamaha River. The confluence of these streams is known locally as The Forks near Hazlehurst.

The Altamaha River system has its headwaters and about 5,800 square miles of its drainage area in the central uplands of Georgia. The remaining 8,400 square miles of drainage area, which include that of the lower Ocmulgee, lower Oconee, and the Altamaha proper, lie in the Coastal Plain.

The headwaters of the Ocmulgee River are in the vicinity of Altanta at an elevation of about 1,000 feet above mean sea level (m.s.l.). The South and Yellow rivers join to form the Ocmulgee at a location within Jackson Lake, a reservoir with normal elevation 530 feet m.s.l. formed by the Lloyd Shoals Dam at about elevation 530 feet m.s.l. The Ocmulgee River flows in a generally narrow valley over rocky shoals about 43 miles and falls steeply to Macon, Georgia, where the river enters the Coastal Plain and the slope becomes gentle. The floodplain widens greatly below Macon and becomes a wooded swamp up to three miles wide in places.

The headwaters of the Oconee River rise at the base of the Chattahoochee Ridge. The North Oconee and Middle Oconee rivers join to form the Oconee River about six miles south of Athens. The Apalachee River enters the Oconee from the northeast at Carey. The Little River of Putnam County enters the Oconee at Lake Sinclair, a reservoir with normal elevation 340 feet m.s.l. that is formed by the Furman Shoals Dam of the Georgia Power Company just above Milledgeville. In this reach the Oconee has the characteristic rocky stream bed, shoals and pools of upland or mountain streams. The river valley is narrow and bordered by high hills. The northern portion of the Altamaha River basin to Lake Sinclair is described in this book. The Oconee River below Lake Sinclair's dam is described in a companion book, *Southern Georgia Canoeing: A Canoeing and Kayaking Guide to the Streams of the Western Piedmont, Coastal Plain, Georgia Coast, and Okefenokee Swamp.*

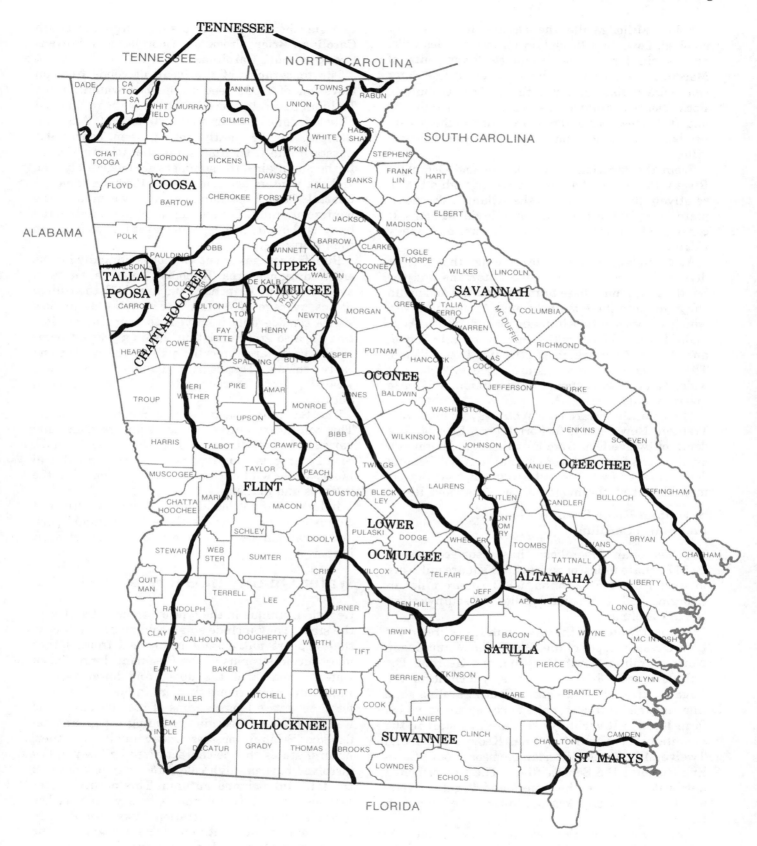

Figure 9: River Basins of Georgia

SOURCE: *Water Quality Monitoring Data for Georgia Streams, 1977.* Georgia Department of Natural Resources, Environmental Protection Division. Drawing by K. Jackson.

Below Milledgeville the Oconee River is very crooked, flows in a floodplain up to 4.5 miles wide, and is similar to the Ocmulgee River south of Macon. The materials in the banks of the low-water channel are also similar to those of the Ocmulgee. Rock shoals are numerous between river miles 73 and 105. A few rock outcrops are found in the stream bed below this reach and in the vicinity of Milledgeville.

From the junction of the Oconee and Ocmulgee Rivers, the Altamaha River flows through a broad, relatively flat floodplain to the Atlantic. The floodplain is typical of meandering, alluvial streams. It consists of swamps, hardwood forests, and sandy ridges.

At a point 22.8 miles above the mouth, the river divides into two branches, the Altamaha and the South Altamaha. These branches reunite and again subdivide into three mainstreams: Altamaha River, which empties into Altamaha Sound; South Altamaha River, which empties into Buttermilk Sound; and Darien River, which empties into Doboy Sound. These three delta streams are 1,000 to 2,000 feet wide. Tidal effects extend up the Altamaha River to about mile 39.

The Atlantic Intracoastal Waterway extends from Trenton, New Jersey, to Fort Pierce, Florida, at a depth of twelve feet, from Fort Pierce to Miami at a depth of ten feet; and from Miami to Key West at a depth of seven feet. The waterway traverses Buttermilk Sound at the mouth of the Altamaha River.

Savannah River Basin of Georgia and South Carolina

The Savannah River basin has a surface area of 10,577 square miles, of which 4,581 square miles are in western South Carolina, 5,821 square miles in Georgia, and 175 square miles in southwestern North Carolina.

The headwaters of the Savannah River are on the high forested slopes of the Blue Ridge Mountains in North Carolina, South Carolina, and Georgia. The Tallulah and Chattooga rivers, which form the Tugaloo River on the Georgia–South Carolina state line, and the Whitewater and Toxaway rivers, which form Keowee River in South Carolina, start in the mountains of North Carolina. Keowee River and Twelve Mile Creek join near Clemson, South Carolina, to form the Seneca River. The two principal headwater streams, the Seneca and Tugaloo rivers, join near Hartwell, Georgia, to form the Savannah River.

From this point, the Savannah flows about 300 miles south-southeastward to discharge into the Atlantic Ocean near Savannah, Georgia. Its major downstream tributaries include the Broad River in

Georgia, the two Little rivers in Georgia and South Carolina, Brier Creek in Georgia, and Stevens Creek in South Carolina.

The topography of the basin descends from an elevation of 5,500 feet at the headwaters of the Tallulah River, to about 1,000 feet in the rolling and hilly Piedmont, to around 200 feet at Augusta, Georgia, to the gently rolling then nearly flat Coastal Plain from Augusta to the Atlantic Ocean. In the mountains, the summers are moderately cool, and the winters are cold. In the Piedmont and the Coastal Plain, the summers are warm and the winters are mild. The average annual rainfall in the basin is about 53 inches. Snow cover is rare except in the mountains.

Runoff averages about 15 inches annually for the entire drainage area. Runoff at Augusta, Georgia, averages about 19 inches, compared with the United States average of 8 inches. The total streamflow varies considerably from year to year. In addition, there is also great variation within a year. Streams in the basin are typically high in the winter and early spring. During the summer and warm weather, flows recede and remain low through autumn.

The Savannah basin is predominantly forested. The wildlife resources of the basin are many and varied. Most of the land supports game animals. Small game is found principally on agricultural lands, while wild ducks and geese are found in the swamps and marshes.

Industry has settled along the Savannah River at Augusta, Georgia, where there is an inland port, and Savannah, Georgia, where there is a deep-draft harbor.

Water Quality in Georgia

Georgia is unique in the type of streams that flow in the state. They include small cold mountain brooks that support native and introduced trout, larger more turbid streams of the Piedmont, large "black water" streams of the upper and lower Coastal Plain, and short rivers that are influenced by tides for their entire length. Some of the streams of the Coastal Plain of Georgia (including the great Okefenokee Swamp) possess water quality in their natural states that is characterized by low pH, low dissolved oxygen, high color, and very low flows in the late summer and autumn. This natural water extends into some estuarine regions where very low dissolved oxygen concentrations may also occur in the summer and autumn. (The streams of the southern portion of the state are described in a companion book, *Southern Georgia Canoeing: A Canoeing and Kayaking Guide to the Streams of the*

Table 5: Estimated Natural Water Quality Levels

Estimated Natural Trend Monitoring Index Range	Location
90–100	Savannah River (above Augusta)
	Coosawattee River
	Etowah River
85–95	Chattahoochee River (above West Point)
	Oostanaula River
	Coosa River
	Oconee River
	Conasauga River
80–90	Chattooga River (Coosa Basin)

Western Piedmont, Coastal Plain, Georgia Coast and Okefenokee Swamp.)

No major streams in Georgia are grossly polluted for their entire lengths. The small Conasauga River is moderately polluted by treated industrial (primarily textile) and domestic wastewater downstream from Dalton to its confluence with the Coosawattee River. The Conasauga has a fauna characteristic of moderately polluted streams, and it influences its receiving stream, the Oostanaula River, which is further degraded by wastewater from Calhoun. The Oostanaula, with the Etowah, becomes the Coosa River. While none of these has been known to be anaerobic, all of them have fauna characteristic of streams that receive moderate amounts of organic and nonlethal inorganic materials. At the state line, the Coosa River shows a recovery from the total amount of wastes received. Another tributary, the Chattooga River of Chattooga County is severely degraded by residual industrial and municipal wastewaters. The Coosa River basin, considering its area, is the most heavily industrialized basin in Georgia.

Of the four areas of streams of the Tennessee River basin that flow through northern Georgia, only West Chickamauga Creek presently has water quality problems; however, TVA impoundments in two of the regions create adverse conditions for aquatic life.

The Ocmulgee River is degraded immediately below the Macon area by thermal, industrial, and domestic wastewater. Wastewater from Athens is detectable in the Oconee River; however, recovery occurs a short distance downstream. The Ocmulgee and Oconee rivers become the great Altamaha River downstream from their confluence. The Altamaha River has excellent quality water.

Of Georgia's many reservoirs, only one, Jackson Lake, is totally eutrophic ("dying"). Seven others, Allatoona, Sinclair, Walter F. George, Sidney Lan-

ier, Blackshear, High Falls, and Seminole have localized problems usually involving of one or two embayments, e.g., Lake Seminole has had a nuisance algal problem and high fecal coliform densities downstream from discharges of untreated wastewater from Bainbridge. The new Bainbridge wastewater treatment facility will improve water quality conditions in the upper part of Lake Seminole.

In summary, other streams and reaches of streams, apart from some small tributaries, have no serious wastewater problems. Of the many thousands of miles of streams in the state, only 500 miles have serious water quality problems and water quality standards that are being violated. These areas are basically downstream of publicly owned sewage systems. In the near future, it is expected that sections where violations occur will be substantially reduced.

Monitoring Trends in Georgia's Waters

The Georgia Environmental Protection Division operates a trend monitoring network in the streams, lakes, and estuaries of the ten river basins of the state. The trend monitoring network was established in 1967 and has been periodically expanded since that time to the 1977 total of 124 stations from which water samples are collected and analyzed on a routine basis. Most stations are sampled once every three months where specific site conditions do not require more frequent sampling. Each sample col-

Qualitative Description			
"Poor"	"Fair"	"Good"	"Excellent"
0	40	60	80

Trend Monitoring Index Value

Figure 10: The Water Quality Index Scale

lected is analyzed for chemical and fecal coliform bacterial content. Physical properties of the water are also measured.

The Trend Monitoring Index

Due to the complex nature of water quality evaluation and the large number of different parameters routinely used to evaluate water quality, it is helpful to define quality in simple terms that can be understood by everyone. To meet this need, a trend monitoring index is used to compare relative water quality trends throughout the state on a common basis. The trend monitoring index combines eight important physical, chemical, and microbiological measures of water quality in a single number. The index, adapted from a similar index developed by the National Sanitation Foundation, is not intended as a replacement for detailed scientific examination of water quality data, but as a means with which the division provides information on water quality to those without technical training. The trend monitoring index can range from 0 to 100 (see Figure 10), with higher numbers indicating better water quality conditions. The eight items included in the trend monitoring index are:

Dissolved Oxygen
Fecal Coliform Bacteria
pH
Biochemical Oxygen Demand
Ammonia
Nitrite plus Nitrate
Phosphorus
Turbidity

For each monitoring station, the trend monitoring index is computed for each sample collected throughout the year. The lowest and highest observed values for the index during the year represent the index range and the annual median index is that value for which one half of the observed index values are higher and the other half of the observed index values are lower. A larger annual index range is indicative of large variations in water quality conditions during the year while a small range indicates stable conditions. Long-term water quality trends are evaluated by comparisons of the annual median index values over several years of record at the same sampling location.

The trend monitoring index has been reported for seven years at selected trend monitoring stations in Georgia, although at some of those the index has been computed for as many as nine years.

The quality of all waters is changing with time as all streams experience seasonal changes according to natural weather patterns. In general, water quality is lowest when temperatures are high and streamflows are low as a result of minimal rainfall. Streams that are influenced by man's activities are subject to additional changes in water quality that are superimposed on the natural quality variations. Man-made influences on quality include runoff from farm lands and developed areas, the discharge of municipal and industrial wastewater, and the operation of stream impoundments.

Although most streams are influenced by man's activities, it is possible to estimate the probable natural limits for water quality at most locations on the basis of a detailed interpretation of available data. Table 5 shows that natural trend monitoring index values can range from 70 to 100 in Georgia. Although single values for the index have been found to run as high as 100, it is unlikely that any stream, natural or otherwise, could have a yearly median index greater than 95.

Water quality in 95 percent of Georgia's 20,000 miles of streams is in the good or excellent range and meets the federal "fishable, swimmable" requirements. Additionally, there are other near-natural streams that marginally meet the "fishable, swimmable" standard where growth and development in the future, without precaution, might trigger a decline in water quality.

Where the trend monitoring index was in the fair or poor range, the problems could usually be related to municipal or industrial wastewater discharges. However, non-point sources of pollution, such as urban area runoff, can reduce the index to the fair, or even poor, range for limited periods of time.

Note:Much of the information contained herein was provided by the Environmental Protection Division, Georgia Department of Natural Resources.

The Streams of Northern Georgia

Sock'em Dog, Chatooga River

Chapter 4

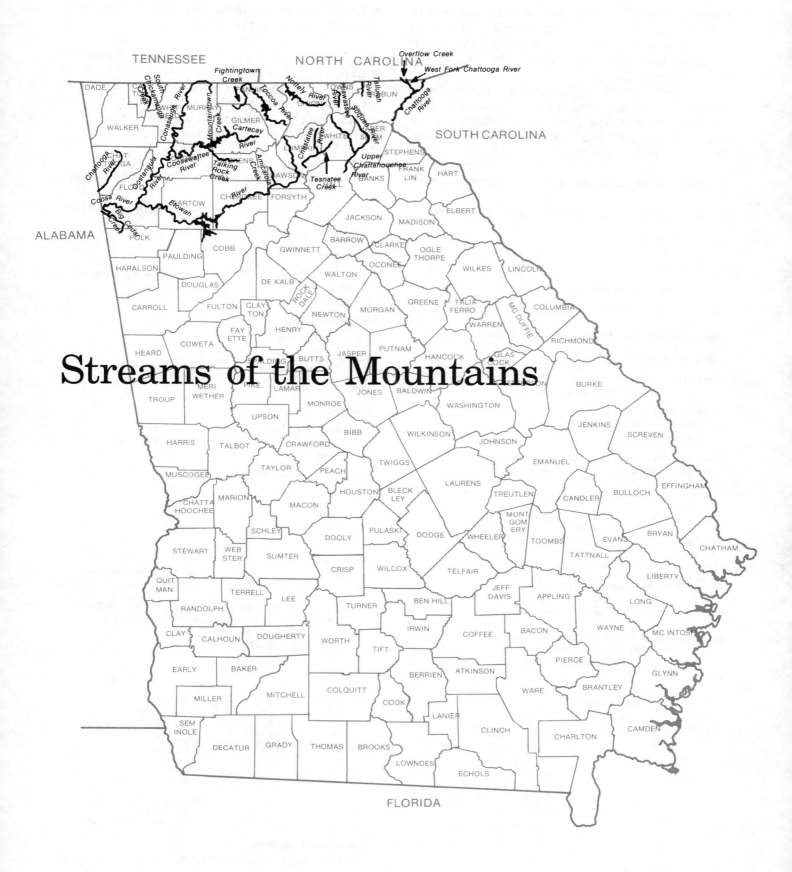

Streams of the Mountains

Overflow Creek

Overflow Creek is a high-water run for boaters with a high skill level and a little insanity. It is a Chattooga River tributary in Rabun County and is the major fork of the headwaters of the West Fork of the Chattooga River.

You might want to add a parachute to your list of safety gear for this one. In the four-mile section between Three Forks Road (Forest Service Road 86B) and where FS Road 86 crosses the West Fork, Overflow Creek drops 380 feet. Rapids of Class V+ difficulty are encountered. Scouting is frequently advisable, but it is very difficult due to the dense streamside foliage and nearly vertical banks. This is for experts only using all safety precautions. At least one highly skilled boater nearly lost his life on the creek recently.

Overflow Creek is a highly technical run. The stream is small but powerful when water is high. If Section IV of the Chattooga bores you, try Overflow Creek.

Section: USFS Rd. 86B to West Fork Overflow bridge

Counties: Rabun

Suitable For: Cruising

Appropriate For: Advanced

Months Runnable: March through June and after heavy rains

Interest Highlights: Scenery, wildlife, whitewater

Scenery: Spectacular

Difficulty: International Scale III-VI
Numerical Points 40

Average Width: 10-30 ft.
Velocity: Moderate to fast
Gradient: 158 ft./mi.

Runnable Water Level: Minimum 1.0 ft.
(Bridge over West Fork) Maximum 2.0 ft.

Hazards: Strainers, deadfalls, undercut rocks, difficult rapids
Scouting: All rapids and blind corners

Portages: As necessitated by water conditions and skill level
Rescue Index: Extremely remote

Mean Water Temperature (°F)

Jan 38	Feb 42	Mar 45	Apr 53	May 61	Jun 69
Jul 72	Aug 71	Sep 66	Oct 57	Nov 47	Dec 41

Source of Additional Information: Nantahala Outdoor Center (704) 488-2175; Southeastern Expeditions (706) 782-4331; Wildwater Ltd. (803) 647-5336

Access Point	Access Code	Access Key
AAA	2357	1 Paved Road
AA	2367	2 Unpaved Road
		3 Short Carry
		4 Long Carry
		5 Easy Grade
		6 Steep Incline
		7 Clear Trail
		8 Brush and Trees
		9 Launching Fee Charged
		10 Private Property, Need Permission
		11 No Access, Reference Only

Section: Overflow Creek Rd. bridge to Long Bottom Ford (off GA 28)

Counties: Rabun

Suitable For: Cruising

Appropriate For: Families, beginners, intermediates, advanced
Months Runnable: All

Interest Highlights: Scenery, wildlife, history

Scenery: Beautiful

Difficulty: International Scale I-II
Numerical Points 8

Average Width: 20-40 ft.
Velocity: Slow to moderate
Gradient: 10 ft./mi.

Runnable Water Level: Minimum 0.5 ft.
(GA 28 bridge Maximum 3.5 ft., open;
gauge) up to flood stage, decked

Hazards: Broken dams

Scouting: Dam sluice and big slide

Portages: None required

Rescue Index: Accessible

Mean Water Temperature (°F)

Jan 39	Feb 40	Mar 44	Apr 53	May 62	Jun 71
Jul 75	Aug 72	Sep 66	Oct 57	Nov 47	Dec 42

Source of Additional Information: U.S. Forest Service, Andrew Pickens Ranger District, Walhalla, S.C. (803) 638-9568; Chattooga Whitewater Shop (803) 647-9083

Access Point	Access Code	Access Key
AA	2367	1 Paved Road
BB	2357	2 Unpaved Road
CC	1357	3 Short Carry
A[1]	1357	4 Long Carry
B	1367	5 Easy Grade
		6 Steep Incline
		7 Clear Trail
		8 Brush and Trees
		9 Launching Fee Charged
		10 Private Property, Need Permission
		11 No Access, Reference Only

[1]On the Chattooga River
[2]To Russell bridge; 1.7 mi. to Long Bottom Ford

West Fork Chattooga River

The West Fork Chattooga River is a major tributary of the Chattooga River. It lies entirely within Rabun County and is formed where Big Creek, Overflow Creek and Holcomb Creek come together at Three Forks.

There are four miles of extremely scenic canoeing for the beginner from Overflow Creek Road bridge (access point AA) down to the junction with the main branch of the Chattooga River just two-tenths of a mile below Russell bridge on GA 28. This section is extremely popular for trout fishing also. Access point BB at the U.S. Forest Service campground is the most frequently used access. Parking is available at point BB, and the carry to the river is short.

Rapids are mostly Class I, but two rapids are designated Class II. The first of these is formed by the remains of an old dam one mile below access point CC, where Warwoman Road crosses the West Fork. The other Class II, Big Slide, is one and a half miles below the old dam and less than a half mile above the confluence with the main Chattooga.

There is no direct road access at the confluence of the West Fork and the main Chattooga. Take out at Russell bridge by paddling two-tenths of a mile up the main Chattooga or drift 1.7 miles downstream to Long Bottom Ford.

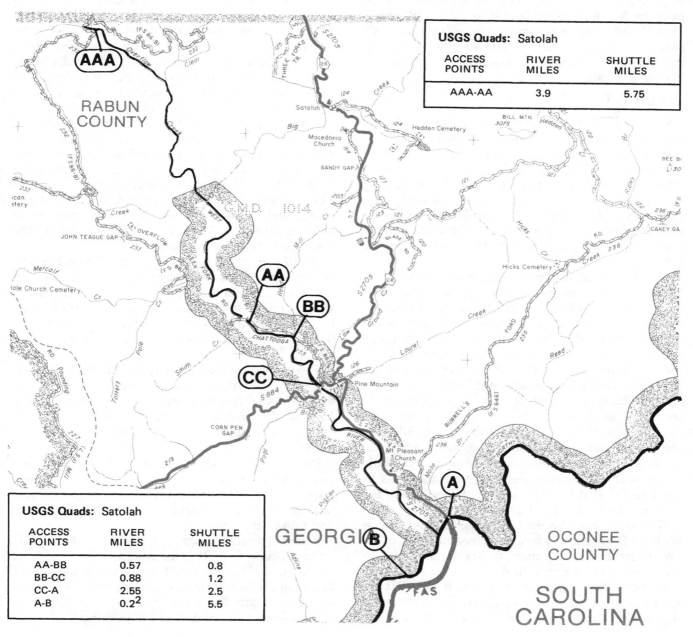

USGS Quads: Satolah		
ACCESS POINTS	RIVER MILES	SHUTTLE MILES
AAA-AA	3.9	5.75

USGS Quads: Satolah		
ACCESS POINTS	RIVER MILES	SHUTTLE MILES
AA-BB	0.57	0.8
BB-CC	0.88	1.2
CC-A	2.55	2.5
A-B	0.2^2	5.5

Chattooga River

The Chattooga River is now and will remain one of the nation's most popular rivers. It has something for everyone: from easy water suitable for beginners to raging Class V rapids for the whitewater crazies. The scenery is nothing short of spectacular for almost the entire length of the river. Its excellence rivals any river in this country.

The river flows from North Carolina to form the border between South Carolina and Georgia for approximately forty miles until it flows into Tugaloo Lake. Fortunately, the Chattooga is protected under the National Wild and Scenic Rivers Act and is managed by the U. S. Forest Service, Sumter National Forest, South Carolina. The Forest Service divides the river into four sections according to the major access points. Section I is from Burrells Ford near the North Carolina border to the GA 28 bridge. The Forest Service regulations state that "All boating is prohibited above Highway 28," so we will not consider Section I in this book. It is open for hiking and fishing.

Section II

Section II of the Chattooga begins at the GA 28 bridge (there is easy access and parking on the Georgia side of the bridge) and continues downriver to Earls Ford. This section is approximately seven miles long and is a good day trip for beginning boaters. Initially, the stream is shallow and rocky with only a slight gradient. Considerable volume is added when the West Fork of the Chattooga flows in from the right approximately 100 yards below the GA 28 bridge.

For these first few miles of Section II the Chattooga is a meandering, gentle valley stream. The valley through which it flows has a rich history. It was at one time the site of one of the largest Indian settlements in the Southeast. The settlement was called Chattooga Old Town. It became a major Indian trading center after white men came to the area. The valley was ideally suited for agriculture, and the land-lustful white men soon appropriated the valley as their own. It remained in agricultural use until recently. The Forest Service is allowing the land in its stewardship to return to a natural state. A large farm house owned by a Russell family is one of the few structures from the early agricultural period that is still standing. It lies just off the river on the South Carolina side.

This area was also visited by colonial naturalist William Bartram and was described in his *Travels*. The Bartram Trail, named in his honor, parallels the river down to Earls Ford.

Through the valley the river remains close to SC 28, and several seasonal dwellings in private ownership are scattered along the South Carolina shore.

Near the end of the valley is Long Bottom Ford. This is an alternate put-in for Section II and a take-out for a trip down the West Fork. Long Bottom Ford is easily reached from SC 28.

After reaching the end of the valley, the terrain begins to revert to a wilderness character. The river quickens its pace. Large hemlocks and white pines thrust from the rocky banks and small islands. (In the spring you will find a profusion of wild flowers and flowering shrubs, including the wild azaleas in flame orange and white.)

After passing several large islands in the stream, you will reach the long deep pool that preceeds Turn Hole Rapid, the first rapid that most paddlers deem worthy of a name. The rapid is not very difficult, but it can trick the unwary. The approach is through a shallow shoal area that has several possible routes. The main drop is usually entered near the left side. It calls for a quick turn to the right, which is necessary to avoid being pushed into the rocky bank. At average water levels, you can run near the center of the stream, straight across the main ledge, if you desire. The drop is about three feet.

Continuing downstream through another half mile or so of mild Class I and II rapids, you will round the bend to see a group of large boulders and rock slabs extending almost completely across the river. This is Big Shoals and it should be scouted. The approach to the rapid is blind due to the large rocks, and occasionally logs or entire trees have become lodged in the main chutes. Scout from the boulders to the right of center.

Big Shoals, rated a Class III by the Forest Service, is a veritable whitewater gymnasium—an excellent place for beginners to play and train. There are several routes to run and a large pool at the bottom for easy recovery. There is also a relatively simple portage back up and over the rocks if you wish to try again.

The easiest and most popular route at Big Shoals is next to the right bank. There is a nice tongue dropping swiftly into a small reversal wave at the head of the pool below. Other possible routes are over the curler in the right center and, at most water levels, the chute on the far left side.

Down to Earls Ford the river has many long, slow pools and a sprinkling of Class I and II whitewater. Look for wildlife in this section; many hawks nest near the stream, and deer are frequently seen early and late in the day.

You will easily recognize Earls Ford where Warwoman Creek, a fairly large stream, enters the river on the right. There is a well-trodden sand and gravel beach on the left. If you are getting out here, you are about to begin the worst part of your trip—the quarter-mile carry uphill to the parking lot.

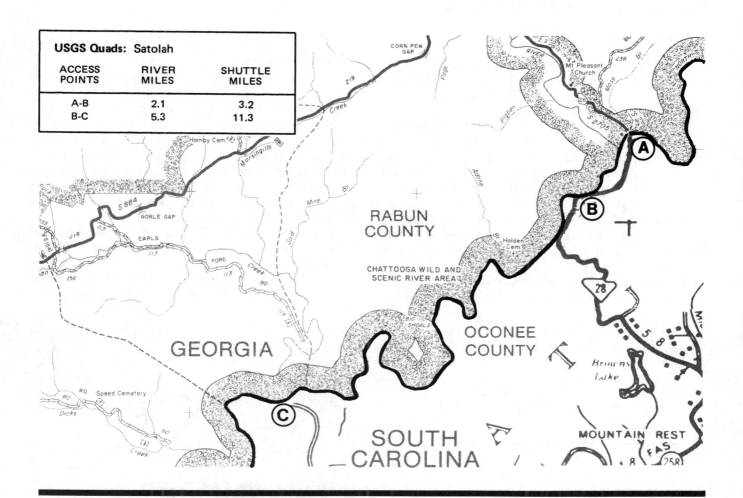

USGS Quads: Satolah

ACCESS POINTS	RIVER MILES	SHUTTLE MILES
A-B	2.1	3.2
B-C	5.3	11.3

Section: GA 28 to Earls Ford

Counties: Rabun (GA), Oconee (SC)

Suitable For: Cruising, camping, training

Appropriate For: Families, beginners, intermediates, advanced

Months Runnable: All

Interest Highlights: Scenery, wildlife, whitewater, local culture and industry, history, geology

Scenery: Exceptionally beautiful

Difficulty: International Scale I-II (III)
Numerical Points 12 (15)

Average Width: 30-60 ft.
Velocity: Slow to moderate
Gradient: 11.5 ft./mi.

Runnable Water Level: Minimum 0.8 ft.
(US 76 gauge) Maximum 3.5 ft.

Hazards: Strainers, deadfalls

Scouting: Big Shoals Rapid
Section
Portages: As conditions and skill level require

Rescue Index: Accessible but difficult

Mean Water Temperature (°F)

| Jan 38 | Feb 40 | Mar 45 | Apr 53 | May 62 | Jun 70 |
| Jul 74 | Aug 72 | Sep 66 | Oct 57 | Nov 48 | Dec 42 |

Source of Additional Information:
Chattooga Whitewater Shop (803) 647-9083

Access Point	Access Code	Access Key
A		1 Paved Road
B		2 Unpaved Road
C		3 Short Carry
		4 Long Carry
		5 Easy Grade
		6 Steep Incline
		7 Clear Trail
		8 Brush and Trees
		9 Launching Fee Charged
		10 Private Property, Need Permission
		11 No Access, Reference Only

35

Chattooga River—*Continued*

Section III

Earls Ford marks the beginning of Section III. Section III has been described by many as the ideal for open canoeists, and it is quite attractive to decked boaters as well. The scenery is nothing short of spectacular and rapids range in difficulty from Class I to Class IV+. I have been running this section for years, as a private boater and professional outfitter, and I have never become tired of it.

By the time it reaches Earls Ford, the volume of flow in the river has increased significantly and the average gradient to GA 76 is much steeper than that of Section II. The first rapid encountered is a fairly straight drop over a three-foot ledge. Drop over to the right of center.

From the large eddy and pool below this drop, look downstream and to the left for the entrance to

Warwoman Rapid. This tricky Class III should be entered on the left, heading toward the right. After the small initial drop, make a quick turn to the left and back downstream. There is a pillowed rock in the center of the chute. If you do not make your turn quickly, this one can pin your boat or capsize it.

The next noteworthy stretch of river is through the Rock Garden. This run is noted more for its scenic value than for the difficulty of its rapids. You weave between huge boulders and fingerlike slabs of granite that often overshadow the stream. The rapids are mild, but stay on your toes.

Three Rooster Tails Rapid is the next challenge. After a sharp bend in the river, the course narrows and spills over a series of funneling rocky ledges beneath overhanging rocks. Three pluming waves (the rooster tails) can be seen in the center of the

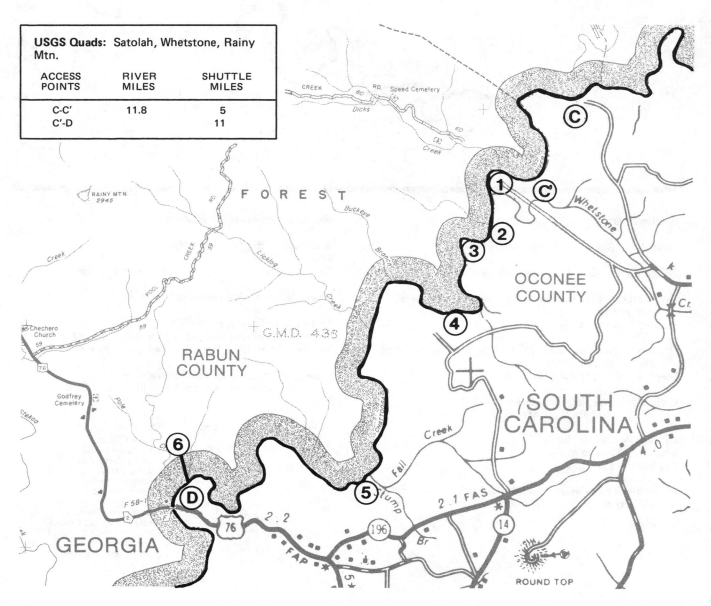

USGS Quads: Satolah, Whetstone, Rainy Mtn.		
ACCESS POINTS	RIVER MILES	SHUTTLE MILES
C-C′	11.8	5
C′-D		11

Section: Earls Ford to US 76 bridge

Counties: Rabun (GA), Oconee (SC)

Suitable For: Cruising, camping

Appropriate For: Intermediate and advanced paddlers

Months Runnable: All

Interest Highlights: Scenery, wildlife, whitewater, geology

Scenery: Spectacular

Difficulty: International Scale I-V
Numerical Points 24

Average Width: 5-65 ft.
Velocity: Moderate to fast
Gradient: 30 ft./mi.

Runnable Water Level: Minimum 0.8 ft.
(US 76 gauge) Maximum 3.5 ft. (above 2.0 ft. is considered dangerous)

Hazards: Strainers, deadfalls, rapids, undercut rocks, keeper hydraulics

Scouting: Dicks Creek Ledge, Narrows, Keyhole (Painted Rock) Rapid, Bull Sluice
Portages: Bull Sluice and others as conditions require

Rescue Index: Remote to extremely remote

Mean Water Temperature (°F)

| Jan 38 | Feb 40 | Mar 45 | Apr 53 | May 62 | Jun 70 |
| Jul 74 | Aug 72 | Sep 66 | Oct 57 | Nov 48 | Dec 42 |

Source of Additional Information:
Chattooga Whitewater Shop (803) 647-9083

Access Point	Access Code	Access Key
C	2467	1 Paved Road
C'	2467	2 Unpaved Road
D	1467	3 Short Carry
		4 Long Carry
		5 Easy Grade
		6 Steep Incline
		7 Clear Trail
		8 Brush and Trees
		9 Launching Fee Charged
		10 Private Property, Need Permission
		11 No Access, Reference Only

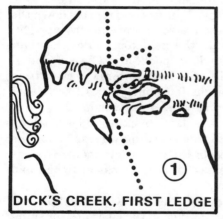

DICK'S CREEK, FIRST LEDGE ①

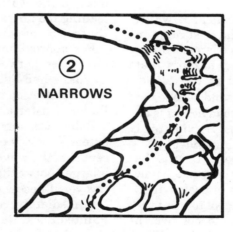

NARROWS ②

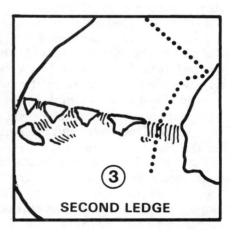

SECOND LEDGE ③

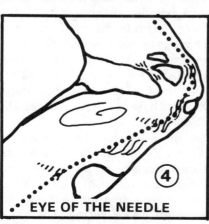

EYE OF THE NEEDLE ④

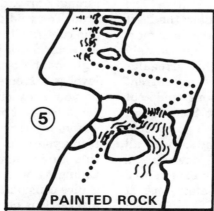

PAINTED ROCK ⑤

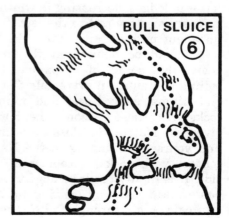

BULL SLUICE ⑥

Chattooga River—*Continued*

channel. The easiest run is just to the right of these pluming waves.

Just below this rapid the river widens and slows to relative tranquility. As you look far downstream you will see Dicks Creek (Five Finger) Falls coming into the river on the right. This is a picturesque waterfall where Dicks Creek cascades over a 50 to 60 foot drop into the river. Slightly upstream of this falls, on the Chattooga, is a low shelf of rock that forms part of a definite river horizon line. Stop on this shelf for a mandatory scouting of Dicks Creek Ledge.

Dicks Creek Ledge is given a Class IV rating in Forest Service literature. There are several possible routes; one of them is a portage over the rocks in the center. Most who run the rapid try to make the S turn over the two drops. Start the first drop heading toward the right, and be prepared to make an extreme cut back to the left at the bottom of the second drop. The S turn maneuver becomes increasingly difficult at higher water levels.

A short distance beyond Dicks Creek Ledge you will observe a large rocky island. Down the right side of this island is a series of Class III drops called Stairsteps Rapid. This is not one of the major rapids on Section III. If you are doing well at this point, selecting an appropriate course through the stairsteps should not be difficult.

Just below Stairsteps is another island, which announces Sandy Ford Rapid. The favored route in the past has been to the right of this island also, but downed trees have recently created hazards that now send most paddlers to the left of the island.

Sandy Ford is recognizable by the sand beaches on both sides of a pooled area. Gravel road access is on both sides of the river, but the Forest Service road on the South Carolina side is recommended.

The fabled Narrows of the Chattooga River is the next major rapid. As you round the bend below Sandy Ford you will come into a large pooled area. Get out on the lower left end of this pool to scout the entrance to the Narrows. The river drops over a series of ledges, decreasing in width as it drops. The biggest holes are just to the left of center; the least turbulent path is to the far right. Take your pick.

It should be noted that the area immediately below this series of drops has highly irregular boiling currents, an extremely fast moving current and strong eddy lines, and numerous undercut rocks. For these reasons, the Forest Service has given the Narrows a Class IV rating. If you should find yourself swimming in the Narrows, avoid all contact with rocks, except from the downstream side. It is highly recommended that an experienced boater lead the way, setting up a safety rope at strategic points through the Narrows.

Open canoes needing to bail and others needing a breather may eddy out on the left below the first series of drops. The river continues to narrow and drop until it's only a few feet wide, which creates some strangely turbulent currents. The final drop in the Narrows is around the right side of an undercut rock. Make a hard left turn very quickly as you drop, to avoid being forced into the rock face on the right.

The Narrows' combination of whitewater, high rock faces, and drooping ferns has made this a favorite spot on the river. If you brought your camera, this should be recorded on film.

One of the more dramatic rapids on Section III is not far downstream. Second Ledge is a breathtaking and heart-stopping six-foot vertical drop. It may be scouted from the left bank at any water level, and from the rocks in the center of the stream at lower levels. Most paddlers run straight over the top of this one. Keep your boat parallel to the current and maintain brisk speed. Be ready to brace firmly when you hit the aerated water at the bottom. Second Ledge is not extremely difficult, but it does get the adrenalin pumping.

Less than two miles from Second Ledge is Eye of the Needle, a Class III plunge. Most of the current is pushed against the left bank, down a narrow chute that cuts slightly back to the right. The current does most of the work for you in this rapid. Beware of leaning too far to the right as you progress down the chute. You may need a strong brace to stay upright.

For approximately the next four miles the river alternates between long pools and Class I and II rapids. When Fall Creek Falls enters the river from about 25 feet up on the left bank you will know that Roller Coaster and Keyhole are just ahead.

Roller Coaster is a fast, bucking ride down an extended series of large standing waves. Go for the center of the waves for the most excitement. There is a large pool at the base of Roller Coaster to bail and recover if necessary.

Immediately around the bend is Keyhole, or Painted Rock, Rapid. Much of the current is pushing strongly toward a huge boulder at the bottom of the drop. To avoid this rock, begin to the right of center and continue to work right as you descend. You may also run down the extreme left, but a move to the right of the boulder is still essential. If the water level is extremely low, the far left or far right may be your only choices. Keyhole is rated a Class IV rapid by the Forest Service.

Roughly three more miles of Class I and II water bring you to Bull Sluice. Even those who have run this rapid many times usually stop to scout it. Changing water levels alter the difficulty of Bull Sluice considerably and may also alter your plan of attack. It is often given a Class V rating. The total drop is over ten feet.

You will know when you have arrived at Bull Sluice because of the extremely large boulders extending from the Georgia side of the river that seem to block the entire stream. Pull out well above these rocks on the Georgia (right) side and walk down to do your scouting. Inexperienced paddlers and those unfamiliar with the sluice have been known to enter the Class III rapids just above the Bull only to find themselves committed to running the thundering lower drops against their will.

Bull Sluice has been run in an infinite variety of craft by an infinite variety of people. On any given day you will see examples of the worst and best whitewater technique at Bull Sluice. Unfortunately too many people have begun to take this rapid lightly. There have been fatalities here, and on several occasions people, both in and out of their boats, have been stuck in the upper hydraulic for uncomfortably long periods of time. The lower drop is much rockier beneath the surface than it appears. Look at it carefully before you decide to run it. The portage is on the right side over the boulders.

If you decide to run Bull Sluice, here is *one* of many possible routes. Follow the Class III entrance rapid down the South Carolina (left) side and hit the eddy on the left that is just above the major drop. If you are in an open canoe and have taken on very much water, this is the place to bail it out. It is a good spot for one to reconnoiter from river level what lies ahead. Peel out very high from this eddy and head straight over the first of the double drops just to the left of the center of the upper hole. The current will tend to push you to the left, so use it to your advantage to hit the second drop head on. Good luck!

A few hundred yards below Bull Sluice is the US 76 bridge. This marks the end of Section III and the beginning of Section IV. Boating access is from the large paved parking lot on the South Carolina side of the bridge. The US 76 bridge also provides a foot path access to Bull Sluice for those who may want to get a glimpse of the giant rapid without getting on the water.

Section IV

In spite of the myriad attractions of Section III, it is probably the reputation of Section IV as an ultimate whitewater experience that brings the throngs to the Chattooga. Skilled boaters from throughout the country try to make at least one pilgrimage to Section IV. Because of the greater difficulty and frequency of the rapids on this section, it should be attempted only by those with a high degree of competency. Since it is advisable that only advanced boaters attempt to paddle Section IV, this portion of the guidebook will give attention only to the more hazardous or unusual rapids.

Surfing Rapid, just around the first bend, is exactly what it sounds like—an excellent spot for surfing or playing the river. The best wave is to the far right.

Screaming Left Turn is located approximately 200 yards below Surfing Rapid. Large boulders direct the main stream to the far right. The river then flushes through an extremely sharp turn back to the left—almost all the way to the left bank. Head back across to the right for the best run of the lower part of this rapid. Screaming Left Turn is designated a Class IV by the Forest Service.

Approximately a half mile farther downstream you will reach a point where the river appears choked by large mounds of granite. This rapid is called Rock Jumble. Several routes are possible, but the best is probably to the left of center. Just below, the river calms into a pooled area known locally as Sutton's Hole. It is a popular swimming hole and a good rest stop.

At this point, you are not far from what is probably the most dangerous spot on the river, Woodall Shoals. When you see a granite shelf extending far into the river from the South Carolina (left) side, you are approaching Woodall. Stop on the rocks on the left side to scout. Do not be deceived by the way this rapid appears. The first drop creates a vicious recirculating hydraulic that has taken the lives of many people. Carry around over the rocks to the left and re-enter well below the hydraulic or take the route near the far right bank if the water is high enough. The rest of the river gives enough thrills so do not needlessly risk your neck at Woodall. Below the first drop, about 50 yards of Class III water takes you down into a large pool. There is a good dirt-road access (FS Road 757) on the South Carolina side if you wish to enter or leave the river from here.

Beyond the pool the river begins to narrow and drop swiftly. When the river appears to drop out of sight on the left, stop on the right and scout the next rapid—Seven Foot Falls. A large granite outcropping splits the stream with a sheer seven-foot drop on the left and a more gradual descent to the right. If you choose the left route, be quick with a right draw at the bottom or you will be literally smashed into the rock wall on the left. The right side is easier, but success is still not guaranteed.

The next few miles provide many Class II-III rapids with the first sizable series marked by Stekoa Creek cascading in from the Georgia side. The larger sheer drop of Long Creek Falls entering from the South Carolina side is not too far beyond and is an excellent place to stop for a break.

Chattooga River—*Continued*

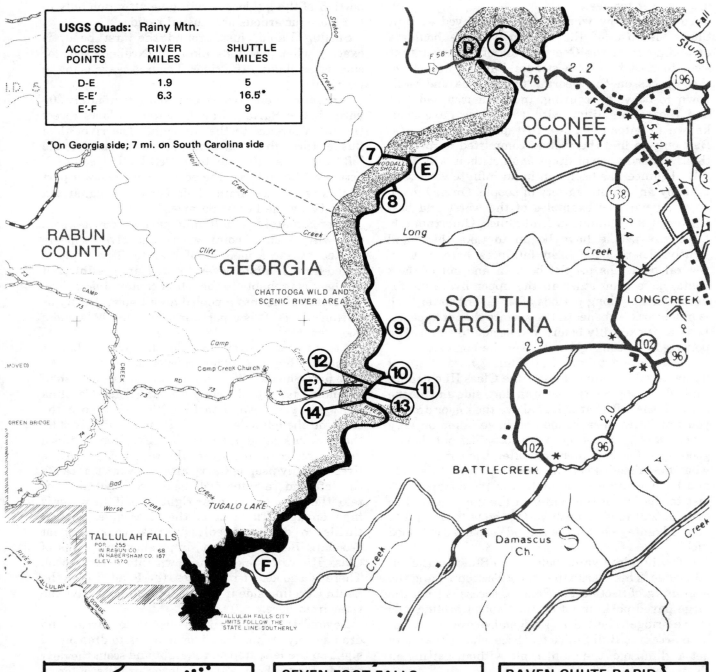

*On Georgia side; 7 mi. on South Carolina side

OCONEE COUNTY

RABUN COUNTY

GEORGIA

CHATTOOGA WILD AND SCENIC RIVER AREA

SOUTH CAROLINA

LONGCREEK

BATTLECREEK

Damascus Ch.

TUGALO LAKE

TALLULAH FALLS
POP. 255
IN RABUN CO. 68
IN HABERSHAM CO. 187
ELEV. 1570

TALLULAH FALLS CITY LIMITS FOLLOW THE STATE LINE SOUTHERLY

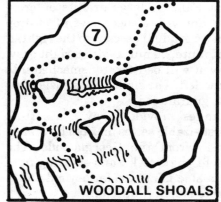

WOODALL SHOALS

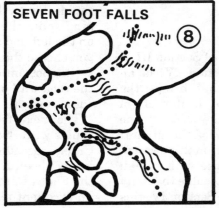

SEVEN FOOT FALLS

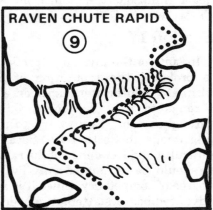

RAVEN CHUTE RAPID

Section: US 76 bridge to Tugaloo Lake

Counties: Rabun (GA), Oconee (SC)

Suitable For: Cruising, camping

Appropriate For: Advanced paddlers

Months Runnable: All

Interest Highlights: Scenery, wildlife, whitewater, geology

Scenery: Spectacular

Difficulty: International Scale I-V (VI)
Numerical Points   28+

Average Width: 10-60 ft.
Velocity: Moderate to fast
Gradient: 45 ft./mi.

Runnable Water Level: Minimum   0.8 ft.
(US 76 gauge)   Maximum   2.5 ft., open; 4.0 ft.,
decked expert; anything above
2.0 is considered dangerous

Hazards: Strainers, deadfalls, rapids, undercut rocks,
keeper hydraulics

Scouting: Woodall Shoals, Seven Foot Falls, Raven Rock,
Five Falls
Portages: Woodall Shoals, Five Falls, others as conditions
require
Rescue Index: Remote to extremely remote

Mean Water Temperature (°F)

| Jan 38 | Feb 40 | Mar 45 | Apr 53 | May 62 | Jun 70 |
| Jul 74 | Aug 72 | Sep 66 | Oct 57 | Nov 48 | Dec 42 |

Source of Additional Information:
Chattooga Whitewater Shop (803) 647-9083

Access Point	Access Code	Access Key
D	1467	1 Paved Road
E	2457	2 Unpaved Road
E'1	2467	3 Short Carry
F	2357	4 Long Carry
		5 Easy Grade
		6 Steep Incline
		7 Clear Trail
		8 Brush and Trees
		9 Launching Fee Charged
		10 Private Property, Need Permission
		11 No Access, Reference Only

[1] At Camp Creek, 2½ mi. below Woodall

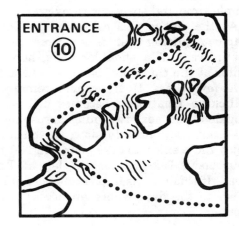

ENTRANCE ⑩

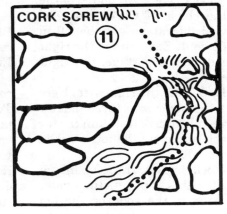

CORK SCREW ⑪

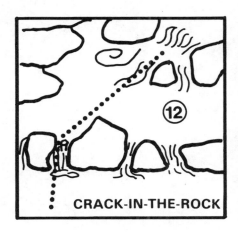

⑫ CRACK-IN-THE-ROCK

⑬ JAW BONE

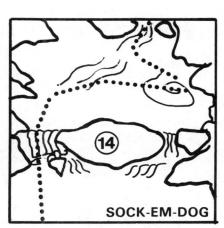

⑭ SOCK-EM-DOG

41

As you continue downstream, Deliverance Rock, a gargantuan boulder on the right, looms into view. It was so named because many of the scenes from the movie *Deliverance* were filmed there. Approach from the right side of the river above the rock. As you reach the rock make a sharp right turn around the left side of rock.

Raven Rock Rapid, also called Ravens Chute or Raven Cliff Rapid, is the next challenge and is easily recognized by the imposing cliffs seen below the rapid on the left side. Scouting should be done from the left shore. A good route starts on the left and follows the top of the long curling diagonal wave to the right. Then head back to the left again to the base of the cliff.

A mile or so of more moderate water brings you to Camp Creek Road, which can be discerned by a sandy beach on the right. Camp Creek Road, FS Road 511, is unpaved but it is the last opportunity for exit before the most formidable section of whitewater on the Chattooga—the Class III–V Five Falls.

All of the Five Falls should be scouted from the shore. First Fall, or Entrance Rapid, can be scouted from the right. Run this one down from the right but head quickly across to the left bank to scout the second fall, Corkscrew.

From the left bank you can get right on top of the drop and look into the chaos of Corkscrew. The bigger holes can be avoided by staying to the left in the first part of your descent. Eddy out on the right at the bottom. If you decide to portage, the right bank is slightly easier.

Scout Crack in the Rock from the right side. Here cracked boulders split the river into three narrow falls, each of which drops about five feet. Run the far right or the center crack but avoid the left crack at all costs. Portage on the left.

Below Crack in the Rock, ferry to the left bank for scouting Jawbone. Enter this rapid in the center pushing hard to get back to the eddy on the left below the first drop. Peel out high on the big curler and head toward the right and the safety of the eddy on the right side of the river above the large boulder in the center of the stream. This is Hydroelectric Rock. A large hole in the rock with water flushing through it resembles a pipe that funnels water down to hydroturbines in a dam. This hole is often lodged with debris and a swim into the hole could be your last. Ferry back to the left side of the stream below Hydroelectric Rock. The hazards present in Jawbone are magnified greatly by its proximity to Sock-Em-Dog. Frequently a swim in Jawbone becomes a continuing swim through Sock-Em-Dog.

Sock-Em-Dog, impressive at all water levels, is the last of the Five Falls. The Forest Service believes this one deserves a Class V rating. If you do not like the looks of Sock-Em-Dog, portage on the left. If you feel you must run the drop, start from the right as the current pushes strongly to the left. There is a smooth hump of water near the center of the top of the fall. This is sometimes referred to as the "launching pad." Keep up your speed and go over the top of the launching pad or just to the right of it. Cross currents are powerful. There is always the chance of landing at the bottom on rocks or in the hydraulic that can be a keeper at times. If you are unsuccessful, the large pool at the bottom gives ample time and space for recovery.

At the end of this calm area is Shoulder Bone Rapid. A jutting granite escarpment in the river is reminiscent of a shoulder bone, hence the name. Enter at the tip of the "bone" and head to the right.

A few Class II–III rapids remain before the rollicking Chattooga becomes dispassionate Lake Tugaloo. The next two miles across the lake to the take out are painfully slow, so you might as well enjoy the scenery to take your mind off the agony in your body. Take out on the left at Tugaloo Lake Road. If this road is impassable you must paddle on down to the dam where an access road is on the right.

Wildwater Raft at Corkscrew, Chatooga River

Hiawassee River

The Hiawassee River has its headwaters on the northern side of Unicoi Gap in Towns County. It flows from south to north and becomes the major feeder stream for Lake Chatuge near the town of Hiawassee.

The higher reaches of the Hiawassee roughly parallel GA 17/75. The stream is occasionally visible from the highway, but it is too small to be considered feasible for boaters. It is not until after Soapstone Creek and Corbin Creek have added their flow that the river becomes suitable for canoeing.

Access point A, at the junction with Corbin Creek, is on private property. Please ask for permission before launching your boat or leaving a vehicle here. The farm house is easy to find. This section down to the GA 17/75 crossing contains more rapids than the lower sections. It is runnable only if the water is fairly high, so exercise caution. None of the rapids is exceptionally formidable, but deadfalls and strainers may pose problems.

Below GA 17/75, the Hiawassee is a gentle valley river. There are no difficult rapids here, only rippling shoals. The surrounding area is mostly farmland. Streamside vegetation periodically opens for impressive vistas of the surrounding mountains. Take a picnic and take it easy. There are several acceptable access points to take out above Lake Chatuge.

The *Hiwassee* River, this same river as it flows through eastern Tennessee with a new spelling, is described in Chapter 6, "Steams of Special Mention."

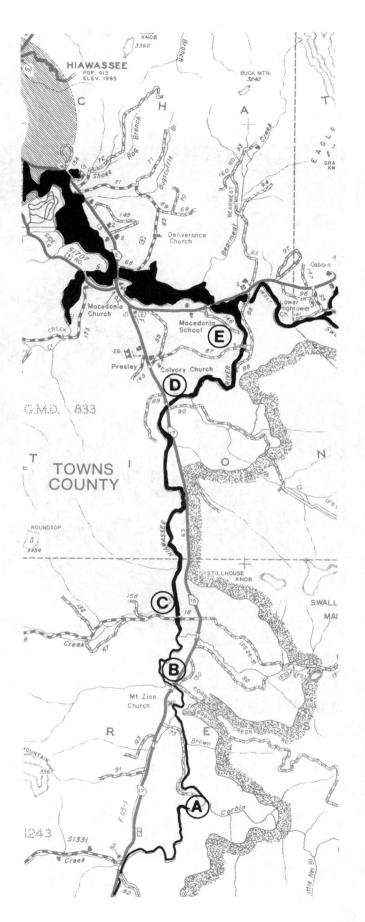

USGS Quads:	Tray Mtn, Macedonia	
ACCESS POINTS	RIVER MILES	SHUTTLE MILES
A-B	1.7	2
B-C	0.9	1.5
C-D	2.3	3.3
D-E	1.1	1.8

Section: Corbin Creek to Chatuge Lake

Counties: Towns

Suitable For: Cruising

Appropriate For: Beginners, intermediates, advanced

Months Runnable: January through July

Interest Highlights: Scenery, wildlife

Scenery: Beautiful

Difficulty: International Scale I-II
Numerical Points 10

Average Width: 20-30 ft.
Velocity: Slack to slow
Gradient: 5 ft./mi.

Runnable Water Level: Minimum 2.5 ft.
(Presley gauge)[1] Maximum 6 ft.

Hazards: Strainers, deadfalls

Scouting: None required

Portages: None required

Rescue Index: Accessible to accessible but difficult

Mean Water Temperature (°F)

Jan 43	Feb 44	Mar 49	Apr 54	May 60	Jun 66
Jul 69	Aug 67	Sep 62	Oct 55	Nov 50	Dec 45

Source of Additional Information: Dept. of Natural Resources Hiawassee River Area (706) 896-2505

Access Point	Access Code	Access Key
A	2357(10)	1 Paved Road
B	1357	2 Unpaved Road
C	1357	3 Short Carry
D	1357	4 Long Carry
E	2367	5 Easy Grade
		6 Steep Incline
		7 Clear Trail
		8 Brush and Trees
		9 Launching Fee Charged
		10 Private Property, Need Permission
		11 No Access, Reference Only

[1]On Hightower Creek near confluence with Hiawassee River

Talking Rock Creek.

Photo courtesy of *Brown's Guide to Georgia.*

Nottely River

The Nottely River is a small stream with its headwaters high in the mountains of Union County southeast of Blairsville. It flows northwestward across the county and is the major source stream for TVA's Nottely Lake. Nottely got its name from an early Cherokee Indian settlement on the stream near the current Georgia–North Carolina border.

The upper reaches of the river have excellent scenery but insufficient flow volume for boating. It is not until the Nottely has reached the valley at GA 180 that it is adequate for boating.

The moderate gradient creates no rapids above a Class II difficulty. There is a drop of forty feet over the first 2.2 miles below GA 180, but the remaining 7.7 miles down to the lake fall only 21 feet in elevation. A possible hazard is the remains of an old dam near the roadside park off US 129 at access point F.

Scenery is mountain farmland on both sides of the river with more woodland in the final two miles above the lake. The short section below Nottely Dam contains no rapids above Class I.

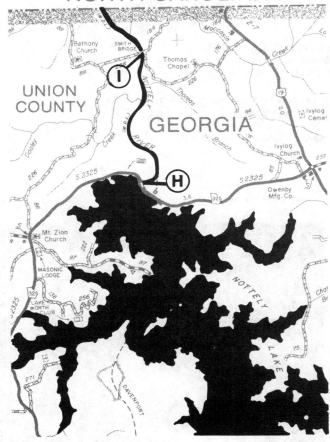

Section: GA 180 to North Carolina border

Counties: Union

Suitable For: Cruising

Appropriate For: Families, beginners, intermediates, advanced

Months Runnable: All; upper section best January through July

Interest Highlights: Scenery

Scenery: Pretty

Difficulty: International Scale I (II)
Numerical Points   7

Average Width: 20-40 ft.
Velocity: Moderate
Gradient: 10.3 ft./mi. (20+ ft./mi. in places)

Runnable Water Level: Minimum 2 ft.
 (Gauge near access E) Maximum 8 ft.

Hazards: Strainers, deadfalls

Scouting: Old dam site at access point F

Portages: Old dam site

Rescue Index: Accessible

Mean Water Temperature (°F)

| Jan 42 | Feb 44 | Mar 48 | Apr 55 | May 61 | Jun 66 |
| Jul 69 | Aug 68 | Sep 63 | Oct 56 | Nov 50 | Dec 45 |

Source of Additional Information: U.S. Forest Service, Blairsville (706) 745-6928

Access Point	Access Code	Access Key
A	1357	1 Paved Road
B	1357	2 Unpaved Road
C	1357	3 Short Carry
D	1357	4 Long Carry
E	1357	5 Easy Grade
F	1357	6 Steep Incline
G	1357	7 Clear Trail
H	1357	8 Brush and Trees
I	2357	9 Launching Fee Charged
		10 Private Property, Need Permission
		11 No Access, Reference Only

USGS Quads: Coosa Bald, Mulky Gap, Blairsville, Nottely Dam

ACCESS POINTS	RIVER MILES	SHUTTLE MILES
A-B	1.2	1.5
B-C	1	1
C-D	1.7	1.8
D-E	1.4	1.8
E-F	1.9	1.5
F-G	2.6	3.5
G-H	11.9	12.5
H-I	1.7	5.8

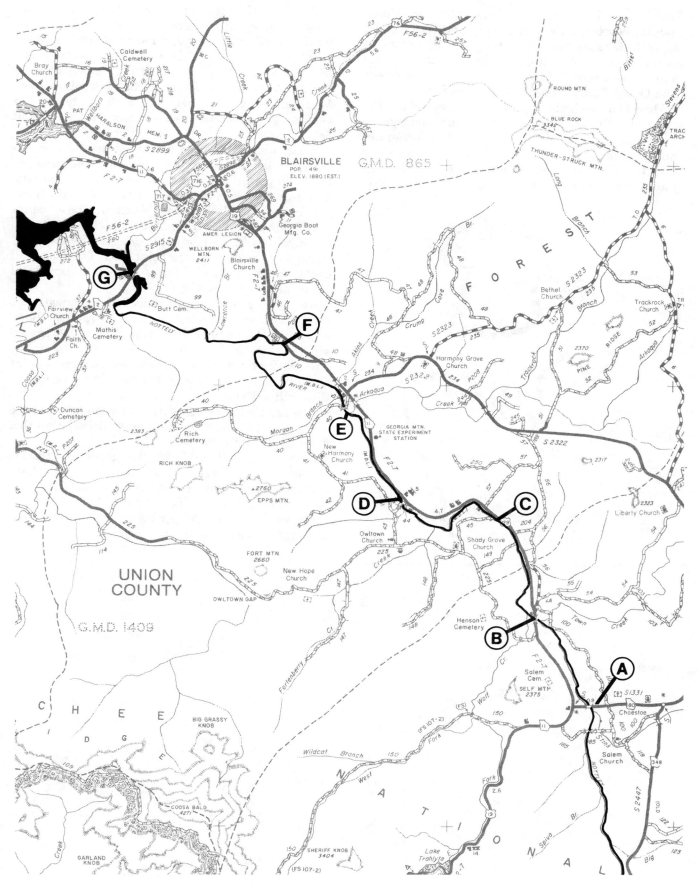

47

Toccoa River

The Toccoa River has its headwaters in Union County, flows into Fannin County and becomes the major feeder stream for Blue Ridge Lake. It resumes its flow below Blue Ridge Lake and travels into Tennessee where it is known as the Ocoee River. (The Ocoee River is described in Chapter 6.)

While it is navigable by canoe or kayak above the junction with Cooper Creek in Fannin County, the most popular access is at the U. S. Forest Service campground at Deep Hole on GA 60. Above Deep Hole the river at most times of the year is very shallow and rocky with few rapids. It offers little

seclusion as GA 60 closely follows the river corridor.

Below Deep Hole (access point B) the Toccoa traverses some farm land, some wood land and has a couple of brief skirmishes with roads (points C and D) before entering the national forest. Flowing through the national forest on the back side of Tooni Mountain, the river becomes a sheer delight for beginning canoeists, canoe campers, and trout fishermen.

Water quality is good and trout fishing is excellent. Add beautiful scenery and mild rapids and you have the perfect environment for an overnight trip. The only rapids of difficulty above low Class II are just below the Rock Creek junction. These rapids may reach low Class III in high-water situations. An Appalachian Trail loop trail crosses the river via suspension bridge at this point also. The loop trail could make a good hiking side trip up Tooni Mountain.

Although a few small rapids follow beneath the bridge, whitewater is not the main attraction. Relax and enjoy the scenery and fishing. The river gradually leaves forest seclusion and enters a valley environment again near Swan Bridge (access point E) and remains fairly pastoral the rest of the way to Blue Ridge Lake.

One final set of rapids offers a challenge just above access point I. The river is quickly stilled below this point as it enters the lake.

Below Blue Ridge Lake the gradient remains gentle. Signs of civilization are more prevalent. Railroad tracks parallel the river most of the way from Mineral Bluff to McCaysville. At McCaysville the river enters the Copper Basin area and becomes known as the Ocoee River.

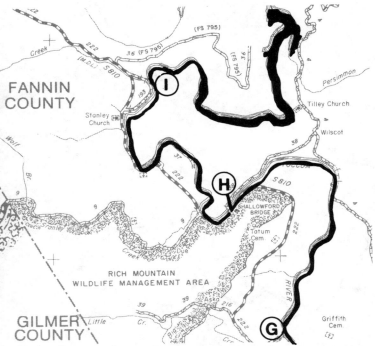

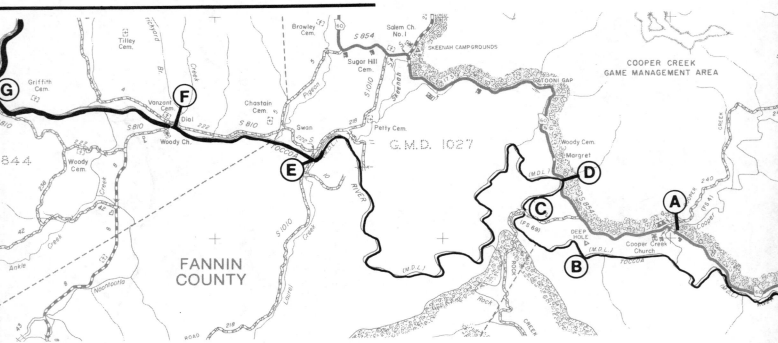

Section: Blueridge Dam to Tennessee

Counties: Fannin

Suitable For: Cruising, camping, training

Appropriate For: Families, beginners, intermediates, advanced

Months Runnable: All

Interest Highlights: Scenery, wildlife, trout fishing

Scenery: Moderate to exceptionally beautiful

Difficulty: International Scale I-II (III)
Numerical Points   1-8

Average Width: 20-50 ft.
Velocity: Moderate
Gradient: 18 ft./mi.

Runnable Water Level: Minimum 0.7 ft.
(Gauge between G   Maximum 6 ft.
and H)

Hazards: Small rapids, occasional deadfalls

Scouting: None

Portages: None

Rescue Index: Accessible to accessible but difficult

Mean Water Temperature (°F)

| Jan 42 | Feb 43 | Mar 47 | Apr 54 | May 62 | Jun 68 |
| Jul 70 | Aug 69 | Sep 64 | Oct 56 | Nov 50 | Dec 44 |

Source of Additional Information: Tennessee Valley Authority (615) 632-1606; Go With The Flow (404) 992-3200

Access Point	Access Code	Access Key
A	1357	1 Paved Road
B	1357	2 Unpaved Road
C	2357	3 Short Carry
D	1368	4 Long Carry
E	2357	5 Easy Grade
F	2357	6 Steep Incline
G	2357	7 Clear Trail
H	1357	8 Brush and Trees
I	2357	9 Launching Fee Charged
J	2357	10 Private Property, Need Permission
K	2357	11 No Access, Reference Only
L	1357	
M	2357	
N	1357	
O	1357	

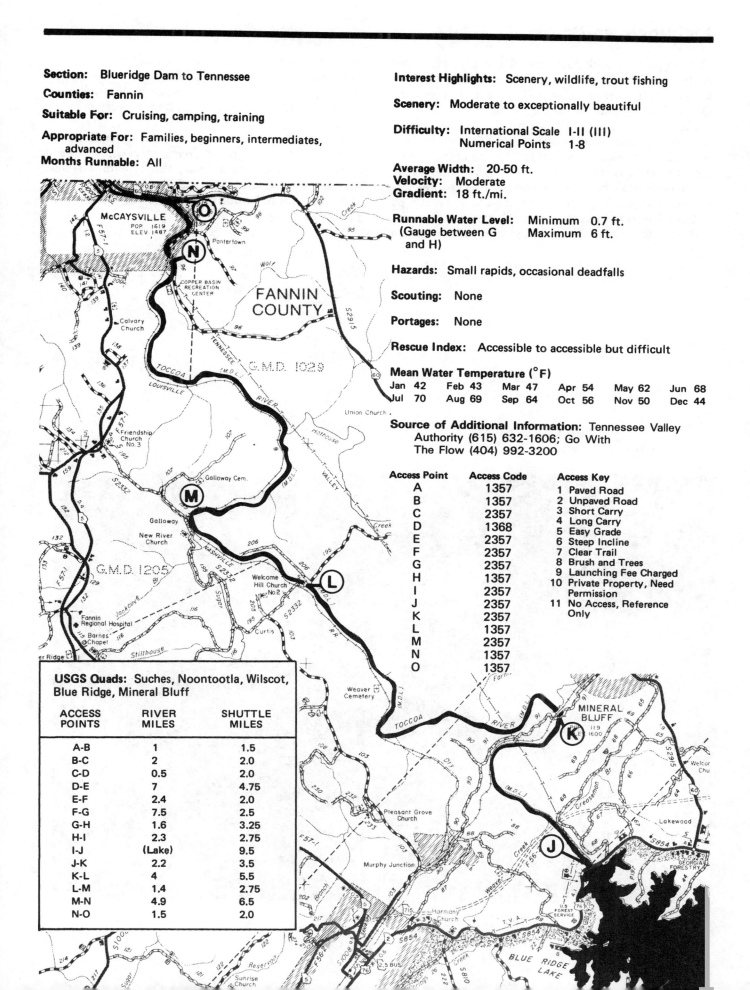

USGS Quads: Suches, Noontootla, Wilscot, Blue Ridge, Mineral Bluff

ACCESS POINTS	RIVER MILES	SHUTTLE MILES
A-B	1	1.5
B-C	2	2.0
C-D	0.5	2.0
D-E	7	4.75
E-F	2.4	2.0
F-G	7.5	2.5
G-H	1.6	3.25
H-I	2.3	2.75
I-J	(Lake)	9.5
J-K	2.2	3.5
K-L	4	5.5
L-M	1.4	2.75
M-N	4.9	6.5
N-O	1.5	2.0

Fightingtown Creek

Fightingtown Creek tumbles off the eastern slopes of the Cohutta Mountains in Gilmer County. It flows to the north across Fannin County and enters the Ocoee/Toccoa River in McCaysville.

Although it is small in its upper reaches, Fightingtown Creek gets sufficient rainfall in its watershed to make it suitable for canoeing many months of the year. Winter, spring, and early summer would be most dependable. The creek is usually no more than 20 to 30 feet wide and a canopy of trees keeps the paddler in nearly perpetual shade.

Road crossings are frequent, yet the stream has an aura of wild country. Current is swift, creating Class I–II rapids as it drops an average of twenty feet per mile. There are no heart-stopping drops, but the paddler must remain alert and maneuver precisely at times.

Hazards are mostly in the form of deadfalls and strainers. Boaters must frequently carry over or slide under trees that block the stream. Between access points C and D an old bridge has fallen into the creek; large beams and protruding spikes create potential danger.

Bull Sluice, Chattooga River.

Section: Cohutta Mountains to McCaysville

Counties: Fannin

Suitable For: Cruising

Appropriate For: Families, beginners, intermediates, advanced

Months Runnable: March through June and after heavy rains

Interest Highlights: Scenery, wildlife

Scenery: Beautiful in spots

Difficulty: International Scale   I-II
   Numerical Points   10

Average Width: 20-30 ft.
Velocity: Moderate to fast
Gradient: 20 ft./mi.

Runnable Water Level: Minimum 1.5 ft.
   (East Ellijay   Maximum 3.0 ft.
   gauge)
Hazards: Strainers, deadfalls, low bridges

Scouting: None required

Portages: As deadfalls and fallen bridge require

Rescue Index: Accessible but difficult

Mean Water Temperature (°F)

Jan 42	Feb 44	Mar 49	Apr 56	May 62	Jun 68
Jul 70	Aug 69	Sep 64	Oct 56	Nov 50	Dec 44

Source of Additional Information: Mountaintown Outfitters (706) 635-2524

Access Point	Access Code	Access Key
A	2357	1 Paved Road
B	1357	2 Unpaved Road
C	1357	3 Short Carry
D	1357	4 Long Carry
E	2357	5 Easy Grade
F	1357	6 Steep Incline
G	1357	7 Clear Trail
		8 Brush and Trees
		9 Launching Fee Charged
		10 Private Property, Need Permission
		11 No Access, Reference Only

USGS Quads: Cashes Valley, Epworth

ACCESS POINTS	RIVER MILES	SHUTTLE MILES
A-B	2.6	3.8
B-C	1.7	2
C-D	4.6	2.8
D-E	2.6	3
E-F	2.9	3
F-G	7.6	5.5

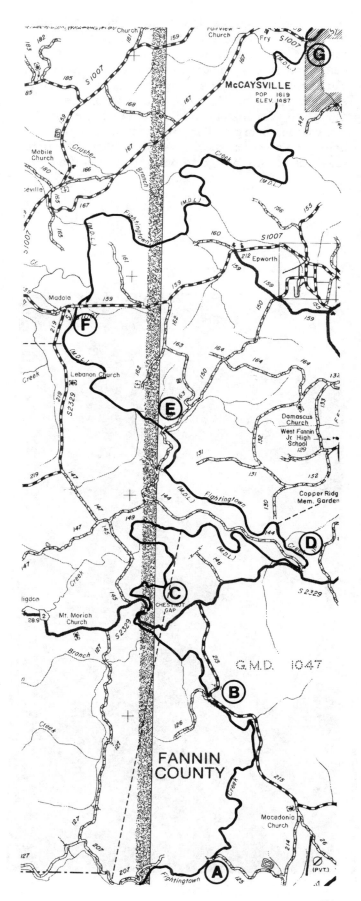

South Chickamauga Creek

South Chickamauga Creek is a long, winding, valley-floor stream. At lower levels, South Chickamauga Creek makes a placid, Class I float within easy access of the urban area of Chattanooga, Tennessee. Along the way you pass by caves, springs, sinks, bluffs, farm land, a wildlife sanctuary, Civil War history, and the old Swanson Mill at Graysville, Georgia. The mill dam is only 100 feet below the access at the Graysville bridge. Be sure to take out at this bridge to portage around the dam.

Upper Chattahoochee River near Helen.

Photo courtesy of *Brown's Guide to Georgia.*

Section: Ringgold to Brainerd Village Shopping Center

Counties: Catoosa (GA), Hamilton (TN)

Suitable For: Cruising

Appropriate For: Families, beginners, intermediates

Months Runnable: November through June

Interest Highlights: Scenery, wildlife, local culture and industry, history, geology
Scenery: Pretty

Difficulty: International Scale I
Numerical Points 6

Average Width: 40 ft.
Velocity: Slow
Gradient: 3.54 ft./mi.

Runnable Water Level: Minimum 180 cfs
Maximum Up to flood stage

Hazards: Deadfalls, strainers, dams, flashflooding

Scouting: None required

Portages: Mill dam at Graysville Rd.

Rescue Index: Accessible

Mean Water Temperature (°F)

Jan 47	Feb 49	Mar 54	Apr 63	May 66	Jun 74
Jul 77	Aug 75	Sep 71	Oct 63	Nov 51	Dec 50

Source of Additional Information: Tennessee Valley Authority (615) 745-1783

Access Point	Access Code	Access Key
A[1]	1357	1 Paved Road
B[2]	1357	2 Unpaved Road
C	1357	3 Short Carry
		4 Long Carry
		5 Easy Grade
		6 Steep Incline
		7 Clear Trail
		8 Brush and Trees
		9 Launching Fee Charged
		10 Private Property, Need Permission
		11 No Access, Reference Only

[1] GA 2 bridge
[2] Graysville bridge

USGS Quads: Ringgold, East Ridge, East Chattanooga		
ACCESS POINTS	RIVER MILES	SHUTTLE MILES
A-B	12.4	10.7
B-C	7.4	9

52

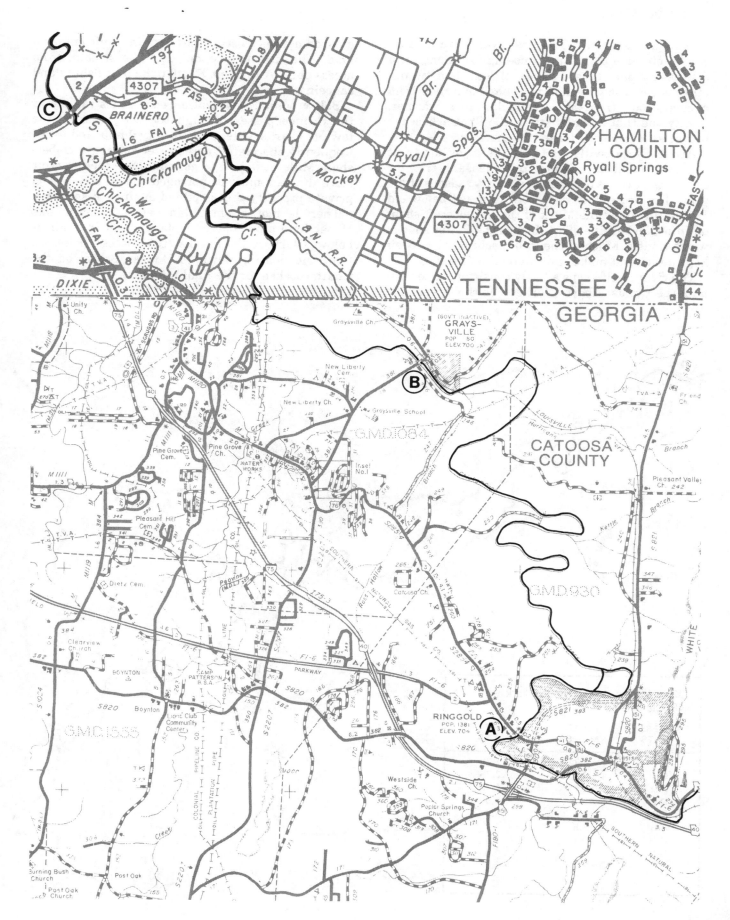

Soquee River

The Soquee is a Chattahoochee River tributary that can be either a delightful canoeing experience or a distressing one. In a distance of less than twenty miles one can see the metamorphosis of a river from a clear, cool, trout-supporting flow to a warmer, murky one that actually stains the Chattachoochee brown as it joins the larger stream.

Above Clarkesville, the river is a joy for trout fishermen and is a short but pleasant trip for canoeists at times other than very dry seasons of the year. The accessibility is good from just below old Watts Mill (now the Mark of the Potter craft shop) on into Clarkesville. The Mark of the Potter shop is worth a visit. Much of the mill machinery has been kept intact and makes an interesting display.

The river itself keeps a fairly consistent pace with no large rapids. Above Clarkesville the streamside environment is mostly forest with intermittent farm land. The first twelve miles of the stream, from access point A to point E, offer the best fishing and canoeing.

Below point E civilization encroaches rapidly as the Soquee passes through the congestion of the town of Clarkesville, past the city dump, and into a frequently chocolate-colored reservoir above Habersham Mills. It is best to get out above the reservoir since the dam must be portaged and all access is on private property that is posted against trespassing.

There is another small dam below the main Lake Habersham dam. The best place to put in again is below Clarkesville at GA 105 (access point J). Continue floating down to Duncan bridge on the Chattacoochee for the final take-out.

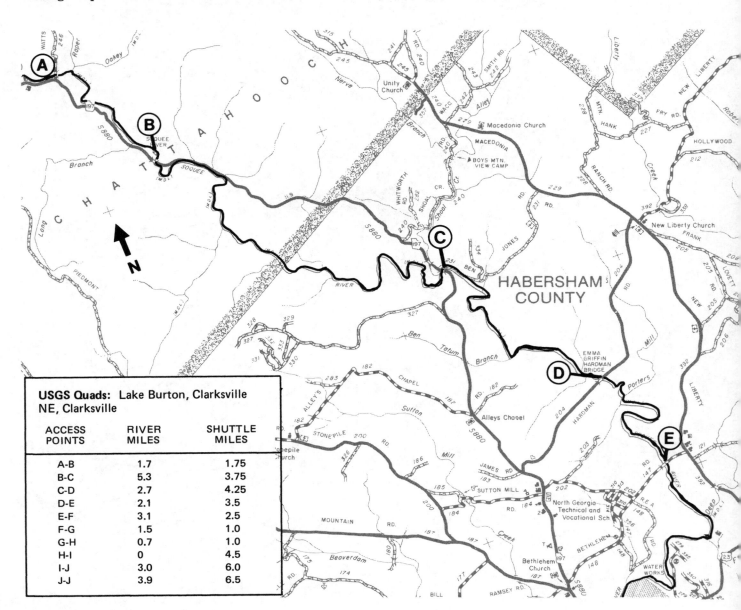

USGS Quads: Lake Burton, Clarksville NE, Clarksville

ACCESS POINTS	RIVER MILES	SHUTTLE MILES
A-B	1.7	1.75
B-C	5.3	3.75
C-D	2.7	4.25
D-E	2.1	3.5
E-F	3.1	2.5
F-G	1.5	1.0
G-H	0.7	1.0
H-I	0	4.5
I-J	3.0	6.0
J-J	3.9	6.5

Section: Watts Mills (Oakey Mountain Rd.) to
Chattahoochee River
Counties: Habersham

Suitable For: Cruising

Appropriate For: Families, beginners, intermediates,
advanced
Months Runnable: All except during dry spells

Interest Highlights: Scenery, wildlife, local culture and
industry, trout fishing
Scenery: Poor to beautiful

Difficulty: International Scale I-II
Numerical Points 8

Average Width: 20-30 ft.
Velocity: Slow to moderate
Gradient: 6-18 ft./mi.

Runnable Water Level: Minimum 1.5 ft.
(GA 115 gauge[1]) Maximum 6.0 ft.

Hazards: Strainers, deadfalls, dams

Scouting: None required

Portages: Dam at Habersham Mills

Rescue Index: Accessible to accessible but difficult

Mean Water Temperature (°F)

| Jan 42 | Feb 45 | Mar 50 | Apr 57 | May 65 | Jun 72 |
| Jul 76 | Aug 74 | Sep 69 | Oct 59 | Nov 50 | Dec 44 |

Source of Additional Information:
High Country (404) 391-9657

Access Point	Access Code	Access Key
A	1357	1 Paved Road
B	1357	2 Unpaved Road
C	1357	3 Short Carry
D	1357	4 Long Carry
E	1357	5 Easy Grade
F	1357	6 Steep Incline
G	1357	7 Clear Trail
H	1357	8 Brush and Trees
I	1357	9 Launching Fee Charged
J	1357	10 Private Property, Need Permission
J1	1357	11 No Access, Reference Only

[1] On the Chattahoochee River

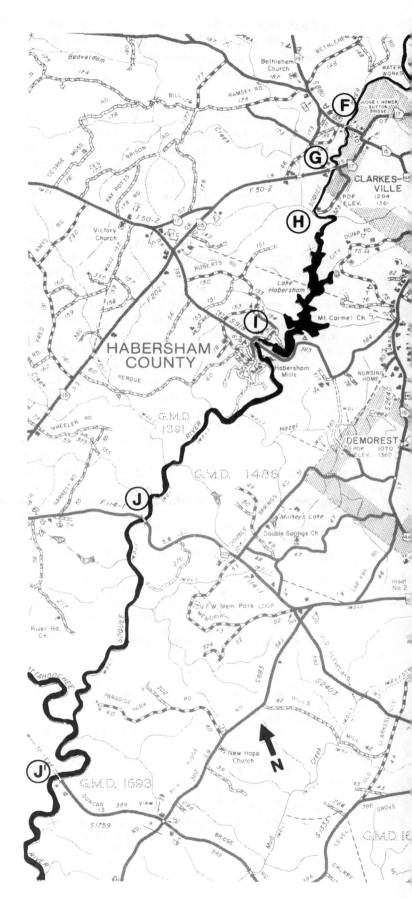

Upper Chattahoochee River

The Chattahoochee River is one of the major rivers draining the state of Georgia, and its remarkable diversity is an accurate reflection of Georgia topography. It is navigable by canoe or kayak from the dramatic mountain headwaters to the Florida border, where it becomes the Apalachicola, and remains navigable to the Gulf of Mexico. (The lower section of the Chattahoochee, below Buford Dam on Lake Sidney Lanier, is described in a companion book, *Southern Georgia Canoeing: A Canoeing and Kayaking Guide to the Streams of the Western Piedmont, Coastal Plain, Georgia Coast and Okefenokee Swamp.*)

There has been a metamorphosis of the river from an isolated crystalline mountain stream of a few decades ago to the overcrowded and abused stream of today. Increased construction of riverbank homes and businesses, lumbering scars, hordes of weekend paddlers, and the gradually increasing turbidity of the water itself have begun to take their toll on the Chattahoochee. Please treat it with care.

In spite of the changes, however, the Chattahoochee remains a sparkling jewel in Georgia's mountain crown. At higher water levels the headwaters above Robertstown and Helen are navigable by skilled boaters. The uppermost access is via unpaved U. S. Forest Service roads. The river is extremely small here, but the scenery and gradient combine to make a run that borders on the spectacular when the water level is right. The lower sections of the

USGS Quads: Jacks Gap, Cowrock, Helen, Leaf, Clarkesville, Lula		
ACCESS POINTS	RIVER MILES	SHUTTLE MILES
A-B	7.1	8
B-C	1.1	1.8
C-D	0.5	0.5
D-E	2	2
E-F	0.5	0.5
F-G	3.1	3
G-H	5.9	6.5

river must be approaching flood before a run on this section is feasible.

From FS Road 44 to Robertstown the river drops extremely fast through a rocky constricted channel bordered by hemlocks, mountain laurel, and rhododendron. There are many sections barely wide enough for a boat to pass through and occasional blind turns and drops. There is little margin for error. Scout as much of the river as possible from the road before putting in and scout all major drops while on the water. This seldom traveled section is a real treat for advanced boaters. Those who catch it when the water is right won't forget it.

On reaching the valley floor, the river calms into steady Class I riffles and remains that way through Helen. There are no obstacles except for one low wooden bridge near Robertstown that may present

---

Section: U.S. Forest Service Rd. 44 (52) to Lake Sidney Lanier

Counties: White, Habersham, Hall

Suitable For: Cruising, training (Helen to GA 115), camping below Sautee Creek

Appropriate For: Beginners, intermediates, advanced paddlers to GA 115; intermediate and advanced paddlers from GA 115 to Duncan Bridge Rd.

Months Runnable: All, in most sections

Interest Highlights: Scenery, wildlife, whitewater, local culture and industry (Helen), history

Scenery: Pretty to exceptionally beautiful

Difficulty: International Scale I-IV
Numerical Points 1-22 (in the upper reaches)

Average Width: 20-50 ft.
Velocity: Moderate
Gradient: 3 to 95+ ft./mi.

Runnable Water Level: Minimum 0.8 ft.
(GA 115 gauge)   Maximum 6 ft., for advanced paddlers only

Hazards: Strainers, deadfalls, difficult rapids, low bridges

Scouting: Entire section above Robertstown; Smith Island Rapid; Three Ledges; Horseshoe Rapid

Portages: Rapids, as necessary; Nora Mill dam

Rescue Index: Accessible to accessible but difficult

Mean Water Temperature (°F)

| Jan 42 | Feb 44 | Mar 49 | Apr 57 | May 65 | Jun 71 |
| Jul 75 | Aug 73 | Sep 68 | Oct 59 | Nov 51 | Dec 45 |

Source of Additional Information:
Wildewood Outpost (706) 865-4451

Access Point	Access Code	Access Key
A	2357	1 Paved Road
B	1357	2 Unpaved Road
C	1357	3 Short Carry
D	1357	4 Long Carry
E	1357	5 Easy Grade
F	1357	6 Steep Incline
G	1357	7 Clear Trail
		8 Brush and Trees
		9 Launching Fee Charged
		10 Private Property, Need Permission
		11 No Access, Reference Only

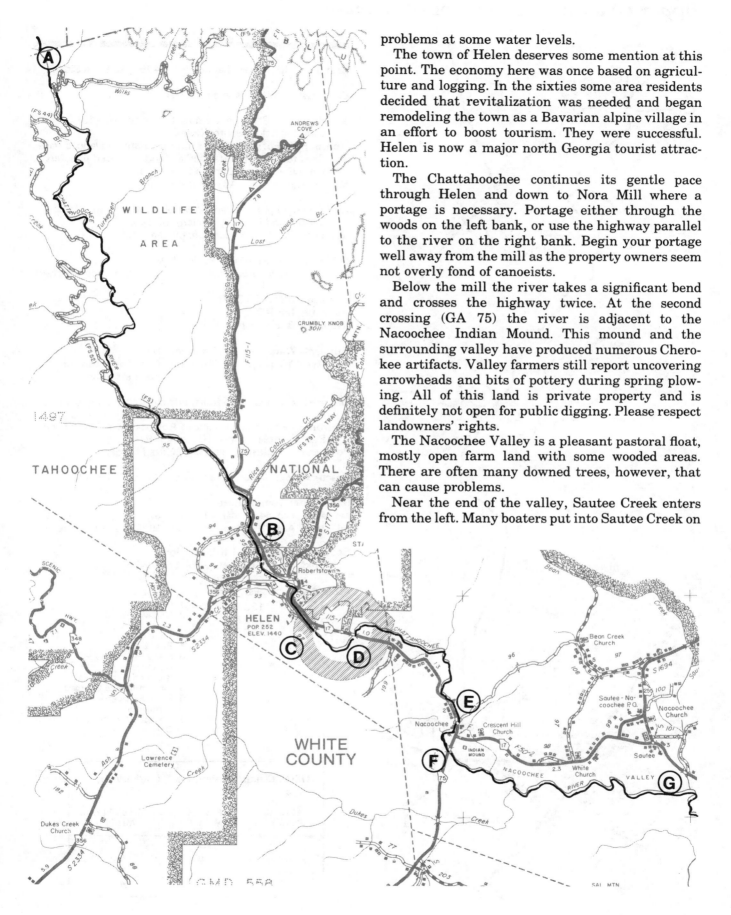

problems at some water levels.

The town of Helen deserves some mention at this point. The economy here was once based on agriculture and logging. In the sixties some area residents decided that revitalization was needed and began remodeling the town as a Bavarian alpine village in an effort to boost tourism. They were successful. Helen is now a major north Georgia tourist attraction.

The Chattahoochee continues its gentle pace through Helen and down to Nora Mill where a portage is necessary. Portage either through the woods on the left bank, or use the highway parallel to the river on the right bank. Begin your portage well away from the mill as the property owners seem not overly fond of canoeists.

Below the mill the river takes a significant bend and crosses the highway twice. At the second crossing (GA 75) the river is adjacent to the Nacoochee Indian Mound. This mound and the surrounding valley have produced numerous Cherokee artifacts. Valley farmers still report uncovering arrowheads and bits of pottery during spring plowing. All of this land is private property and is definitely not open for public digging. Please respect landowners' rights.

The Nacoochee Valley is a pleasant pastoral float, mostly open farm land with some wooded areas. There are often many downed trees, however, that can cause problems.

Near the end of the valley, Sautee Creek enters from the left. Many boaters put into Sautee Creek on

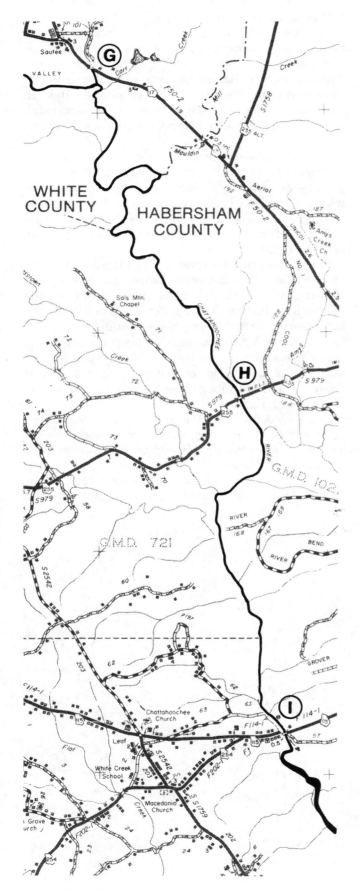

Section: U.S. Forest Service Rd. 44 (52) to Lake Sidney Lanier

Counties: White, Habersham, Hall

Suitable For: Cruising, training (Helen to GA 115), camping below Sautee Creek

Appropriate For: Beginners, intermediates, advanced paddlers to GA 115; intermediate and advanced paddlers from GA 115 to Duncan Bridge Rd.

Months Runnable: All, in most sections

Interest Highlights: Scenery, wildlife, whitewater, local culture and industry (Helen), history

Scenery: Pretty to exceptionally beautiful

Difficulty: International Scale I-IV
Numerical Points 1-22 (in the upper reaches)

Average Width: 20-50 ft.
Velocity: Moderate
Gradient: 3 to 95+ ft./mi.

Runnable Water Level: Minimum 0.8 ft.
(GA 115 gauge) Maximum 6 ft., for advanced paddlers only

Hazards: Strainers, deadfalls, difficult rapids, low bridges

Scouting: Entire section above Robertstown; Smith Island Rapid; Three Ledges; Horseshoe Rapid

Portages: Rapids, as necessary; Nora Mill dam

Rescue Index: Accessible to accessible but difficult

Mean Water Temperature (°F)

Jan 42	Feb 44	Mar 49	Apr 57	May 65	Jun 71
Jul 75	Aug 73	Sep 68	Oct 59	Nov 51	Dec 45

Source of Additional Information:
Wildewood Outpost (706) 865-4451

Access Point	Access Code	Access Key
G	1357	1 Paved Road
H	1367	2 Unpaved Road
I	1357 (11)	3 Short Carry
		4 Long Carry
		5 Easy Grade
		6 Steep Incline
		7 Clear Trail
		8 Brush and Trees
		9 Launching Fee Charged
		10 Private Property, Need Permission
		11 No Access, Reference Only

USGS Quads: Helen, Leaf, Clarkesville, Lula

ACCESS POINTS	RIVER MILES	SHUTTLE MILES
F-G	3.1	3
G-H	5.9	6.5
H-I	4.2	7
I-J	4	4

Lynch Mountain Road, an unpaved county road, next to the GA 17 bridge over the creek. The float down the creek is only a hundred yards to the main stream of the Chattahoochee.

From the Sautee creek junction down to GA 255 is one of the longest undisturbed stretches of the river. The terrain is heavily forested with large white pines and frequent rock outcroppings. The evidence of intrusion by man is less obvious than earlier, and a pleasant illusion of isolation settles in. This is a good section for camping. Rapids are fairly frequent but never go beyond a mild Class II category.

Access at the GA 255 bridge is on the left, or Habersham County, side of the river only. The property owner on the right side should not be disturbed. Use the public highway right-of-way.

This section begins with several Class I rapids and smooth pools. Then the river enters a long, slow area nicknamed the "Dead Sea" because its stillness offers a marked contrast to the rapids above and below. It is a beautiful area and should not be slighted. Large trees on either side form a cool green tunnel of vegetation that occasionally opens into rolling pastured vistas. The "Dead Sea" is partially formed by the natural damming effect of Smith Island and is the first warning sign that Smith Island rapid is near. The next indicator is a large, gently sloping granite face on the right bank and a small white house on the left.

Smith Island rapid is the first of the significant rapids on the upper Chattahoochee. It should be scouted by first timers or by anyone running the river at extreme water levels. Be sure not to scout from the island. It is very private. The left side of the island is the best route. It is a Class II at almost any water level, and at high water it becomes a solid Class III. Enter the rapid from the left side of the main stream at the tip of the island, and gradually work back to the right side (left bank of the island) for the final plunging chute. This chute ends in a fairly deep pool next to a large rock face. Recover on the island if necessary.
chute ends in a fairly deep pool next to a large rock face. Recover on the island if necessary.

The channel that goes to the right of the island may be scouted from the right bank of the river. It can be run at higher water levels (above three feet on the GA 115 gauge), but most of the time it is too shallow and rocky to be worthwhile. It does provide a nice view, however, if you look back upstream from below the island. Stay to the right of center for the best course below the island. Rapids are Class I.

There is no parking at GA 115. It is private, owned by Wildewood Outpost; however shuttles are available through this company—see Sources of Additional Information.

Whitewater buffs will find the section from the GA 115 bridge to Duncan bridge the most pleasant. None of the rapids is intimidating at normal water levels, but altogether they are frequent enough and challenging enough to keep you occupied.

Just below the bridge you will encounter a small, sloping drop into a long, wide, pooled area that disappears around the bend to the left. After rounding the bend, look downstream beyond the shallow shoals and you should be able to distinguish the tip of an island. The river has become quite wide here (over 100 feet) but is very shallow. The island you see marks the beginning of Buck Island Shoals, a fairly continuous quarter-mile section of Class II water. The best run is to the left of the first three small islands, then work back to the right center for the rest of the shoals. The gradient here is constant and fairly steep. This section has "eaten" experienced decked boaters at extremely high water levels when waves may exceed four feet in height. At low or average water levels one would encounter only minor technical problems.

After a series of Class I and pooling water, watch for a large granite outcropping on the right. This indicates the imminence of the Three Ledges. Many consider this to be the most fun or challenging series of rapids. Looking downstream to the left of center you will observe a large, low, flat rock protruding above water level. Run just to the left of this rock over the first ledge. Immediately ferry to the right of center for ledge number two, a more gradual slope that angles back to the left.

You are now approaching the third ledge, a straight drop of about three feet. Go straight over and you will do just fine. The hole at the base of this one is a great place to play.

The river then continues in a Class I and pool series, with the exception of one washboard series of small diagonal ledges that is interesting. After passing this, watch again for another long pool with granite outcroppings on the right. This denotes the approach to Horseshoe Rapid (Class II+). You can see a long, low ledge of rocks that the river hooks around, thus giving Horseshoe its name. Enter on the left, and be ready to cut hard back to the right.

Just below Horseshoe Rapid the Soquee River enters on the left followed shortly by a small creek falls that also enters on the left. You are now almost to the Duncan Bridge. Wildewood Outpost also owns the property at this access point. There is paid parking only.

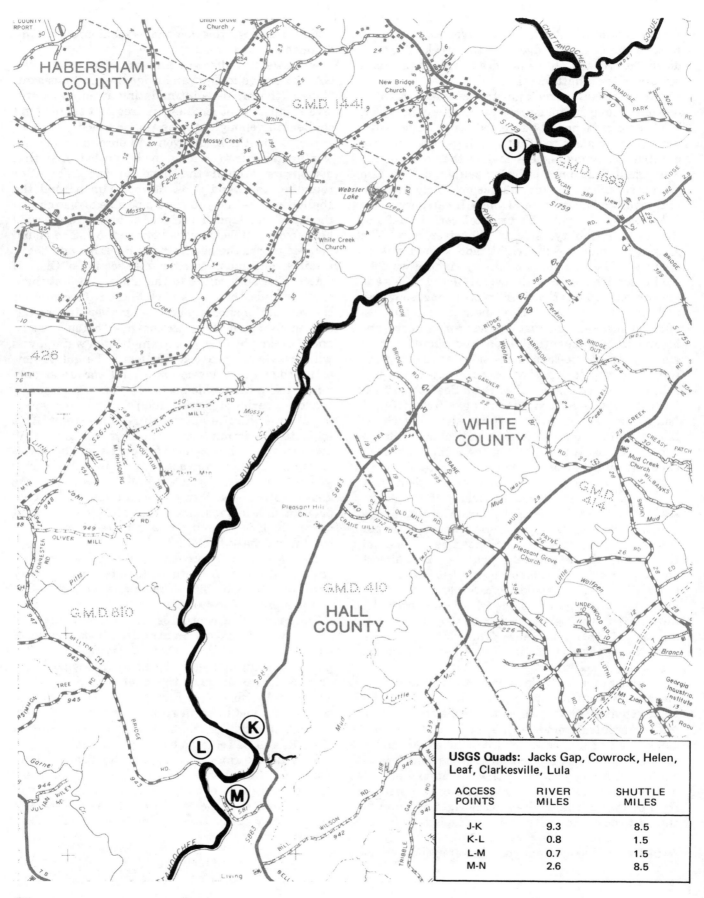

USGS Quads: Jacks Gap, Cowrock, Helen, Leaf, Clarkesville, Lula		
ACCESS POINTS	RIVER MILES	SHUTTLE MILES
J-K	9.3	8.5
K-L	0.8	1.5
L-M	0.7	1.5
M-N	2.6	8.5

The next reasonable access below Duncan bridge is Belton bridge on the backwaters of Lake Lanier. The scenery remains quite good, and there are a few Class I–II rapids left, but once you hit the backwaters of the lake forward progress becomes painful. Plan at least another half day to get to Belton bridge.

Section: U.S. Forest Service Rd. 44 (52) to Lake Sidney Lanier
Counties: White, Habersham, Hall

Suitable For: Cruising, training (Helen to GA 115), camping below Sautee Creek
Appropriate For: Beginners, intermediates, advanced paddlers to GA 115; intermediate and advanced paddlers from GA 115 to Duncan Bridge Rd.
Months Runnable: All, in most sections

Interest Highlights: Scenery, wildlife, whitewater, local culture and industry (Helen), history
Scenery: Pretty to exceptionally beautiful

Difficulty: International Scale I-IV
Numerical Points 1-22 (in the upper reaches)

Average Width: 20-50 ft.
Velocity: Moderate
Gradient: 3 to 95+ ft./mi.

Runnable Water Level: Minimum 0.8 ft.
(GA 115 gauge) Maximum 6 ft., for advanced paddlers only

Hazards: Strainers, deadfalls, difficult rapids, low bridges

Scouting: Entire section above Robertstown; Smith Island Rapid; Three Ledges; Horseshoe Rapid
Portages: Rapids, as necessary; Nora Mill dam

Rescue Index: Accessible to accessible but difficult

Mean Water Temperature (°F)

Jan 42	Feb 44	Mar 49	Apr 57	May 65	Jun 71
Jul 75	Aug 73	Sep 68	Oct 59	Nov 51	Dec 45

Source of Additional Information:
Wildewood Outpost (706) 845-4451

Access Point	Access Code	Access Key
J	1357 (9)	1 Paved Road
K	1357	2 Unpaved Road
L	2357	3 Short Carry
M	2357	4 Long Carry
N	1357	5 Easy Grade
		6 Steep Incline
		7 Clear Trail
		8 Brush and Trees
		9 Launching Fee Charged
		10 Private Property, Need Permission
		11 No Access, Reference Only

Tesnatee Creek

Tesnatee creek is a tributary of the Chestatee River. It provides an excellent day trip when water conditions are favorable. Starting near Cleveland, Georgia, only about seven miles of the stream are navigable. The average gradient, however, is over twenty-three feet per mile, so the pace is usually lively.

While the scenery could not be termed dramatic, it is quite nice. Draping hemlocks hang over the stream in places, and occasional 20- to 30-foot-high rock faces help create some good picture-taking spots.

Rapids do not exceed a Class II difficulty at normal water levels. There is one man-made hazard, however, that presents slight problems and necessitates a portage. A dam, which remains from an abandoned hydroelectric power project, is located approximately one mile above access point C and two and one-half miles below point B. Some of the buildings associated with the power plant are still standing but have been gutted by vandals and the effects of the elements. Local people have nicknamed this area "Hobbit Land" because of the bizarre landscape it creates. The easier portage around the dam is on the right.

An excellent take-out point for a trip on Tesnatee Creek is located on the Chestatee River approximately two miles beyond the point where the two streams meet. Chestatee access point E is located just below Copper Mine Rapid, a moderate Class III drop. Copper Mine Rapid is described in the following section about the Chestatee River.

Section: County Rd. 5976 near Cleveland to Old Copper Mine Road

Counties: White, Lumpkin

Suitable For: Cruising

Appropriate For: Beginners, intermediates, advanced

Months Runnable: March through June

Interest Highlights: Scenery, wildlife, whitewater, history

Scenery: Beautiful

Difficulty: International Scale I-III
Numerical Points 16

Average Width: 20-30 ft.
Velocity: Slow to moderate
Gradient: 23 ft./mi. (30 ft./mi. A-B)

Runnable Water Level: Minimum 1.2 ft.
Maximum 5.0 ft., open; up to flood stage, decked

Hazards: Strainers, deadfalls, dams

Scouting: At rapids, as needed

Portages: Dam and falls at "Hobbitt Land"

Rescue Index: Accessible to accessible but difficult

Mean Water Temperature (°F)

| Jan 42 | Feb 43 | Mar 46 | Apr 53 | May 62 | Jun 67 |
| Jul 71 | Aug 70 | Sep 66 | Oct 59 | Nov 51 | Dec 45 |

Source of Additional Information:
High Country (404) 391-9657

Access Point	Access Code	Access Key
A	1357	1 Paved Road
B	1357	2 Unpaved Road
C	2357	3 Short Carry
E[1]	1357	4 Long Carry
		5 Easy Grade
		6 Steep Incline
		7 Clear Trail
		8 Brush and Trees
		9 Launching Fee Charged
		10 Private Property, Need Permission
		11 No Access, Reference Only

[1] On the Chestatee River

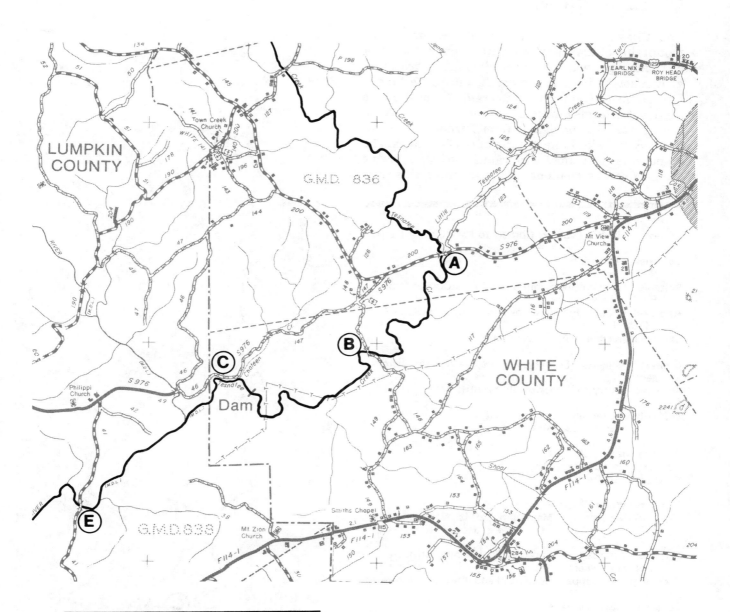

USGS Quads:	Cleveland, Dahlonega	
ACCESS POINTS	RIVER MILES	SHUTTLE MILES
A-B	2.1	1.75
B-C	2.6	2.75
C-E	2.2	3.25

Chestatee River

The Chestatee River has its headwaters in the mountains of northern Lumpkin County, northeast of Dahlonega, which was the site of America's first gold rush. It flows to the south, into Lake Sidney Lanier, near Gainesville, Georgia. At medium to high water levels (above 1.5 on the gauge at GA 53) the Chestatee is navigable from Turners Corner all the way to Lake Lanier, a distance of 32 miles. The scenery is beautiful, and rapids on some of the sections can be challenging, but running this river

---

Section: US 129 (Turners Corner) to Lake Sidney Lanier

Counties: Lumpkin

Suitable For: Cruising, camping, training (Copper Mine Rapid to lake)

Appropriate For: Families,[1] beginners, intermediates, advanced

Months Runnable: All (lower sections)

Interest Highlights: Scenery, wildlife, whitewater, history, geology

Scenery: Pretty to exceptionally beautiful

Difficulty: International Scale   I-III
                 Numerical Points   17

Average Width: 20-45 ft.
Velocity: Moderate to fast
Gradient: 5-40+ ft./mi.

Runnable Water Level: Minimum   1 ft.
  (GA 52 gauge)   Maximum   3.0 ft., open; up to
                                flood stage, decked

Hazards: Strainers, deadfalls, difficult rapids, difficult property owners
Scouting: At Copper Mine Rapid and elsewhere as needed

Portages: Grindle Falls

Rescue Index: Remote to accessible

Mean Water Temperature (°F)

Jan 42	Feb 43	Mar 47	Apr 54	May 62	Jun 68
Jul 71	Aug 69	Sep 66	Oct 58	Nov 51	Dec 45

Source of Additional Information:
  Appalachian Outfitters (706) 864-7117

Access Point	Access Code	Access Key
A	1367	1 Paved Road
B	1367	2 Unpaved Road
C	1367	3 Short Carry
D	1357	4 Long Carry
E	1357	5 Easy Grade
F	1367	6 Steep Incline
G	1357	7 Clear Trail
H	1357	8 Brush and Trees
I	2357	9 Launching Fee Charged
		10 Private Property, Need Permission
		11 No Access, Reference Only

[1] Below GA 60

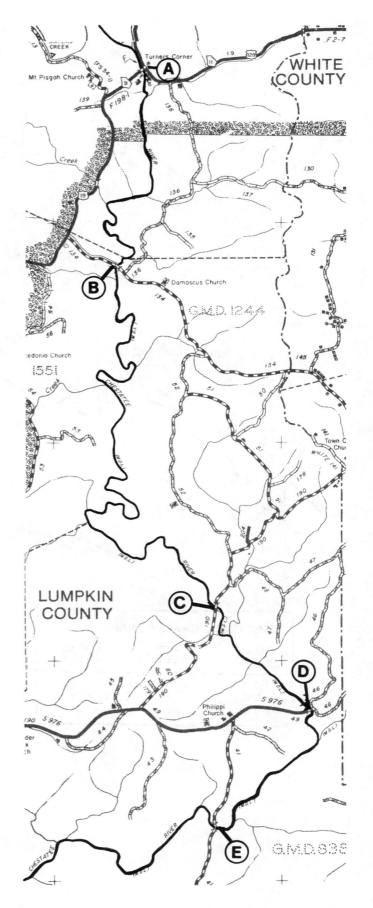

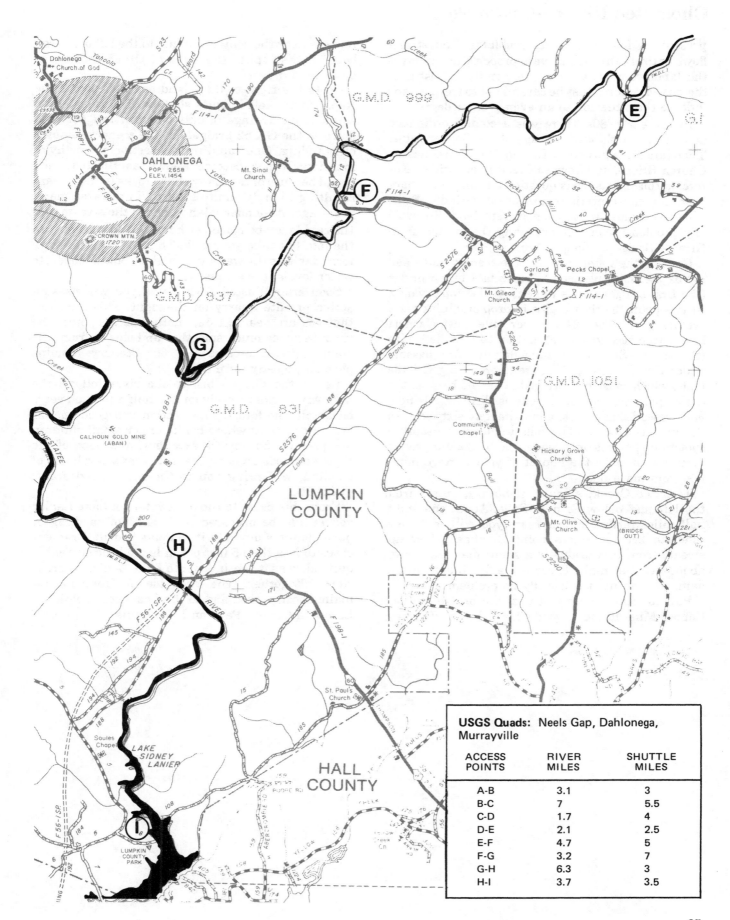

Chestatee River—*Continued*

presents a few frustrating problems. The stream flows entirely through private property and many of the landowners have been unfriendly to hostile in the past. Boaters must be careful not to trespass and inflame the situation to an even greater degree.

In the early '80s, there was a county ordinance passed that prohibited floating above Copper Mine. There are signs posted at Turners Corner, Damascus Church Bridge, and Townes Creek Road Bridge. Enforcing this ordinance is questionable and there have been no confrontations except at Grindle Falls, where you must portage on private land. To avoid any problems, consider excluding the stretch from Grindle Bridge to Copper Mine.

Once on the water, however, the scenery and small rapids are quite pleasant. Damascus Church bridge (the first bridge) marks the end of the upper valley. At this point the river begins to drop at a brisk pace, averaging just over 24 feet per mile, past Garnett bridge (the second bridge) and on to Grindle bridge (the third). Slow down immediately after passing under Grindle bridge. You are approaching Grindle Falls, which must be portaged. The left bank is the easier portage, but either side is difficult. Grindle Falls cascades in stages, approximately sixty feet, to the river bed below. The falls would be a beautiful spot to linger, but once again, the banks are private property, so make the impact of your portage minimal, and move on.

Tesnatee Creek, a major tributary, enters from the left just below Grindle Falls. About one and a half miles farther downstream you will see a new concrete bridge (access point E) ahead. Just upstream from this bridge is a small man-made dam about two feet high. There are a few breaks in the dam, so running it is usually no problem.

Pull to either shore just past the bridge to scout Copper Mine Rapid, a good Class III drop. The best route is near the center and just to the left of a large boulder that splits the stream. Other routes are possible, however.

Go to the right of the island below Copper Mine Rapid as the left is quite shallow. The river's drop slows to an average of only thirteen feet per mile down to the GA 52 bridge, but the scenery remains outstanding. One rapid in this section is worthy of mention. It has become known as Blasted Rock Rapid because of the many sharp rocks in the stream resulting from dynamite blasting in the area many years ago. A slender island divides the stream and the rapid may be run on either side. Most people run the left, but take your pick. This one becomes more formidable as the water gets higher, but at moderate water levels it is a Class II.

Soon after Blasted Rock Rapid you will pass an active granite quarry on the right. This indicates that you are near GA 52, another access point. The river becomes much smoother and slower from this point until it crosses GA 60. Scenery remains pleasant, mostly farm land.

Below the GA 60 bridge the river follows the highway corridor closely for one-half mile then veers back into the forest. This section is a good one for family day trips where beginners or small children are present. Scenery is excellent, and none of the rapids exceeds an easy Class II. Just a few hours of paddling will bring you to the next paved access (point H).

From this point to the backwaters of Lake Lanier you should be prepared to do a lot of paddling or have plenty of daylight if you plan to drift. Gradient eases to less than 5 feet per mile, and the current is quite slow as it continues into Lake Lanier where it stops altogether. The riverside environment remains mostly woodland to the final access, which is Lumpkin County Park on Lake Lanier.

Amicalola Creek

The Amicalola, which gets its name from the Cherokee phrase for tumbling water, is called a creek on most maps, but if it is merely a creek, it is an awesome one. The scenery is spectacular, the rapids are sometimes stupendous. It is hard to describe this stream without superlatives, so if it is a creek, it is simply the best whitewater creek in the state.

Located entirely in Dawson County, its upper east fork, Little Amicalola Creek, contains the famous Amicalola Falls. Amicalola Falls State Park encompasses the southern end of the Appalachian Trail, which stretches from there to Mount Katahdin in Maine.

The stream does not become navigable until below the junction of the Little Amicalola with the main Amicalola. The small wooden bridges near Afton mark the highest normal put-in point. These are small county roads surrounded by private property. Please be extremely courteous and respectful of the rights of landowners in this area.

Check the gauge for this section first. It is in the pool just upstream of the GA 53 bridge, toward the east bank. With 0.8 feet or more, the upper section has enough water to be a comfortable run. For the most part it provides easy floating, quiet beauty, and a few small rapids. It is possible to encounter deadfalls above 6-mile put-in. Then the stream turns east and comes to a shallow and rocky series of Class II ledges. In mid-run, Cochrane Creek enters on the left and increases stream volume considerably. In the next half mile are three good rapids that

may require scouting. The first is a wide, five-foot ledge. Look for a little chute into a pool just left of the downstream island. The next rapid is more complex; from a right-side approach several routes are possible. The third rapid is a three-and-a-half-foot ledge that can be sneaked through on the extreme right; the main route left of center can be a boat-buster. The remaining miles provide easy floating through forest damaged recently by a tornado.

By the time it reaches Devils Elbow (access point D), the Amicalola has a more respectable volume. A covered bridge here was burned by vandals in the mid-seventies, but some timbers are still visible along the banks and, unfortunately, in the stream bed. The three and a half miles from the covered bridge ruins to the GA 53 bridge is an excellent afternoon trip. The mountain flora so common on the first section continues, and there are more frequent rock outcroppings. Because it starts flat and builds gradually to several Class II rapids, this section has proved to be an excellent training course for beginners. The last Class II rapid, just a quarter mile from the bridge, has a feisty little hole at the bottom that creates a good surfing wave. There is a good recovery pool if upsets occur.

Below GA 53 the Amicalola is for experienced boaters only. Here the rapids crescendo to Class IV+ heights when the water is high and even at low water rate a solid Class III. It is runnable from a level of 0.6 at the GA 53 gauge, but if the level is above 1.2, all boaters should be very competent. The

Edge of the World Rapid, Amicalola Creek.

Amicalola Creek—*Continued*

USGS Quads: Amicalola, Nelson, Juno, Matt

ACCESS POINTS	RIVER MILES	SHUTTLE MILES
A-B	0.3	0.5
B-C	4.0	4.0
C-D	3.7	4.0
D-E	2.3	4.2
E-K	10	8.5

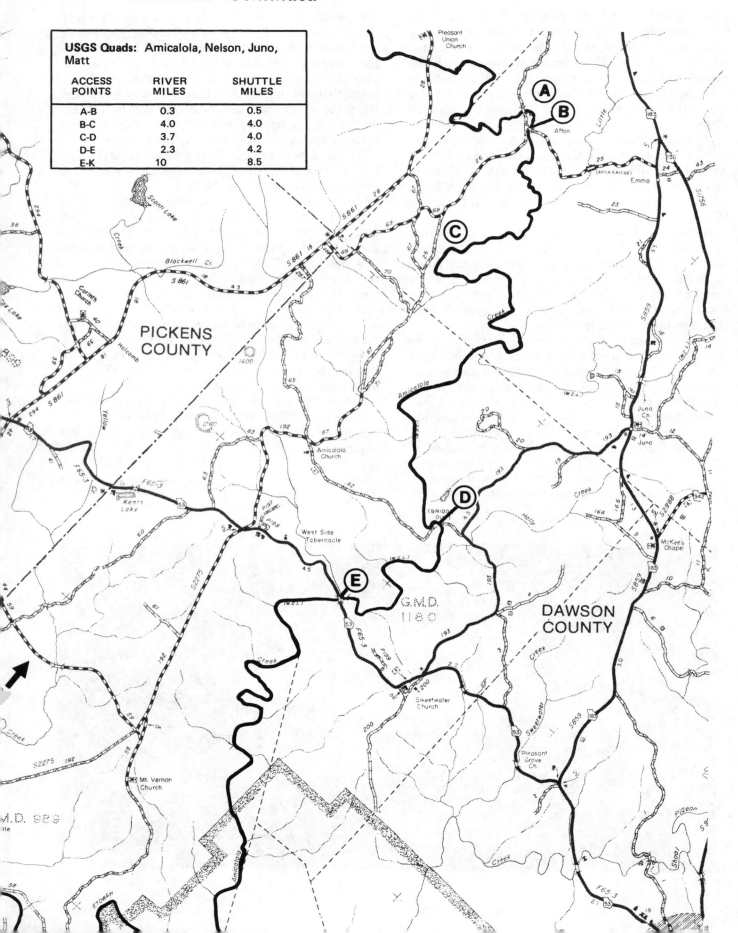

Section: Goshen Rd. (Afton) to Etowah River

Counties: Dawson

Suitable For: Cruising, camping, training[1]

Appropriate For: Beginners, intermediates, advanced above GA 53; intermediate and advanced paddlers from GA 53 to the Etowah River

Months Runnable: March through July

Interest Highlights: Scenery, wildlife, whitewater

Scenery: Exceptionally beautiful to spectacular

Difficulty: International Scale I-IV (V)
Numerical Points   5-29

Average Width: 30-40 ft.
Velocity: Fast
Gradient: 5-80 ft./mi.

Runnable Water Level: Minimum   0.8 ft. above GA 53;
0.6 ft. below GA 53
Maximum   2.5 ft., open; 3.5 ft., decked

Hazards: Strainers, deadfalls, undercut rocks, difficult rapids

Scouting: At major rapids below GA 53

Portages: As required by water level

Rescue Index: Accessible to extremely remote

Mean Water Temperature (°F)

Jan 42	Feb 44	Mar 49	Apr 56	May 62	Jun 68
Jul 72	Aug 70	Sep 64	Oct 55	Nov 50	Dec 44

Source of Additional Information:
Appalachian Outfitters (706) 864-7117

Access Point	Access Code	Access Key
A	2357	1 Paved Road
B	2357	2 Unpaved Road
C	2358	3 Short Carry
D	2357	4 Long Carry
E	1367	5 Easy Grade
K[2]	2357	6 Steep Incline
		7 Clear Trail
		8 Brush and Trees
		9 Launching Fee Charged
		10 Private Property, Need Permission
		11 No Access, Reference Only

[1]Above GA 53
[2]On the Etowah River

first two miles below the highway average over 80 feet per mile drop. The first mile is almost continuous rapids so be adept at self-rescue.

The Edge of the World is the name given the first set of rapids below the bridge. The boater will see a definite rocky horizon line all across the river. A large log jam in the center of the stream provides a good vantage point for scouting. The Edge is composed of two large drops of 5 to 6 feet each with several small drops interspersed. Begin on the left side for the first drop and work all the way across to the right side over the smaller ledges. The second large drop is a straight shot near the right bank.

The Class II-III action continues for another half mile of maneuvering before slowing to any sizeable pool. Pools interspersed with Class II rapids continue for another half mile to Off the Wall Rapid.

Off the Wall can be recognized by the steep sloping granite face on the right bank. A large portion of the stream flow is diverted by boulders into a narrow channel on the right. Here the water rebounds off the granite face and makes a quick drop. Draw to the left of the protruding rock at the bottom of the chute.

Scenery surpasses the expectations of most travelers on their first descent. Lacy hemlocks and towering pines jut out from rocky precipices. Sheer walls occasionally rise several hundred feet above water level. Tributary streams cascade into the crystalline Amicalola and the influences of nearby civilization are seldom evident. Savor it.

Class I-II rapids are abundant and quickly bring you to Split Rock Rapid. Here the stream divides into three channels with the center channel seemingly splitting a large boulder. The left channel is blocked by large fallen trees, but the center and right channels are runnable; the center channel is preferable.

The action begins to moderate, but streamside environment remains extraordinary. Just about the time you think the Amicalola has shown you all of its thrills, you reach Roostertail Rapid. The stream drops steeply with good routes along the left (the roostertail) and the far right. The center is usually too shallow and rocky.

The intense whitewater is now ended and the stream begins to change character altogether. Rapids become less frequent and the current is almost slack. The Etowah River merges from the left a few miles below Roostertail Rapid, increasing the volume but not velocity of the flow. Relax and enjoy this section in contrast to the adrenalin rush of the upper, or stroke hard if the day is waning. It always takes longer than you think it will. The take-out is on the right bank and might be bypassed if you do not have a watchful eye.

Etowah River

The Etowah River is a stream of striking beauty suitable for beginners during most seasons of the year. It is navigable from Hightower Road northwest of Dahlonega to Rome, Georgia, where it merges with the Oostanaula River to form the Coosa River.

At Hightower Road, an unpaved county road, the river is quite small and there is a relatively large amount of deadfall. Its volume increases rapidly, however, due to the many feeder streams that enter as the river slips around the western side of Campbell Mountain. The scenery here is quite pleasant with dense thickets of mountain laurel, rhododendron, and hemlock crowding the shoreline. At normal water levels a few small ledges create rapids of Class II difficulty. Some of these become borderline Class III at higher water levels. Trout fishing on this upper section is good, and a canoe provides easy access since roads to this section are infrequent and primitive.

After rounding Campbell Mountain, the river enters a small valley. The gradient remains reasonably constant and gentle from this valley past GA 52 and on to US 19. Access at US 19 is good. Enter or exit next to the North Georgia College Farm property on the south side of the bridge.

Just below US 19 the environment changes back to primitive woodland from the farm land of the valley. High rock bluffs often rise above the river and rapids become more frequent. Of particular interest are Chuck Shoals and Etowah Falls. Chuck Shoals is approximately three-quarters of a mile below the US 19 bridge. It is usually run from the left, angling back toward the center chute. It can be scouted from the right side by those who so desire.

Although there are many calm pools, the river generally moves at a steady and brisk pace down to Etowah Falls. The falls can be easily recognized if you look for the distinct horizon line all the way across the stream, and *listen* for the sound. The falls are approximately four miles below the US 19 bridge. Pull out on the large rocks on the right side to admire the view. And portage; the drop is at least ten vertical feet. These falls have been run successfully by many people, but it is not recommended. This is a good area for taking pictures, having lunch, and swimming (below the falls).

Continuing its lively flow, the Etowah creates several more Class II rapids before Castleberry bridge. Move to the right of the small islands encountered a short distance above the bridge. At the bridge there is good access on the right bank. The section of the Etowah between US 19 and Auraria's Castleberry bridge is the most popular section of the Etowah and possibly the most scenic.

The Dahlonega–Auraria area was the site of the first gold rush in the United States. In 1837 a

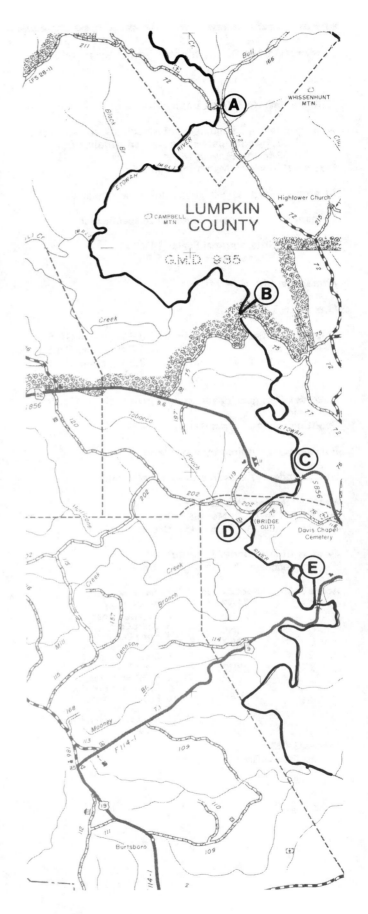

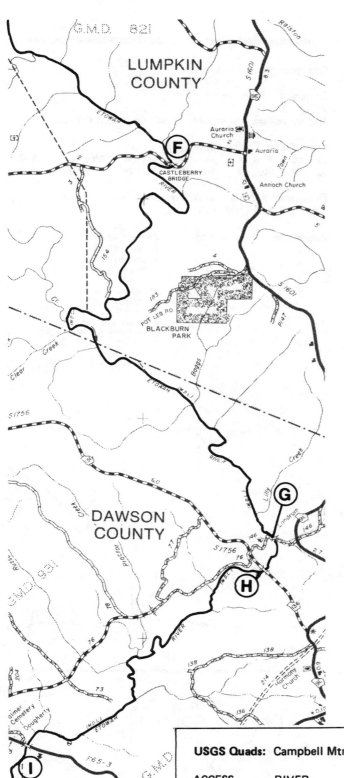

Section: Hightower Rd. bridge (near Campbell Mountain) to US 19 (south of Dawsonville)
Counties: Lumpkin, Dawson

Suitable For: Cruising, camping, training

Appropriate For: Families, beginners, intermediates, advanced
Months Runnable: All, in most sections

Interest Highlights: Scenery, wildlife, whitewater, geology, history
Scenery: Beautiful

Difficulty: International Scale I-II (III)
　　　　　　　Numerical Points　9

Average Width: 15-40 ft.
Velocity: Slow to fast
Gradient: 12.3 ft./mi.

Runnable Water Level: Minimum 0.9 ft.
　(GA 9 gauge)　Maximum 6 ft.

Hazards: Strainers, deadfalls, Etowah Falls, mine tunnel

Scouting: At Etowah Falls and mine tunnel

Portages: Etowah Falls

Rescue Index: Accessible to accessible but difficult

Mean Water Temperature (°F)

| Jan 45 | Feb 46 | Mar 50 | Apr 58 | May 66 | Jun 72 |
| Jul 76 | Aug 75 | Sep 71 | Oct 63 | Nov 56 | Dec 49 |

Source of Additional Information: Appalachian Outfitters (706) 864-7117; Go With The Flow (404) 992-3200

Access Point	Access Code	Access Key
A	2357	1 Paved Road
B	1357	2 Unpaved Road
C	1357	3 Short Carry
D	2357	4 Long Carry
E	1357	5 Easy Grade
F	1357	6 Steep Incline
G	2457	7 Clear Trail
H	1357 (11)	8 Brush and Trees
I	1357	9 Launching Fee Charged
		10 Private Property, Need Permission
		11 No Access, Reference Only

USGS Quads: Campbell Mtn., Dawsonville, Coal Mtn.

ACCESS POINTS	RIVER MILES	SHUTTLE MILES			
A-B	5.5	4.8			
B-C	2.7	4.5	F-G	7.4	6.5
C-D	0.6	1.8	G-H	0.8	1
D-E	1.7	3	H-I	3.6	5.5
E-F	5.9	7.5	I-J	4.3	4.5

Etowah River—*Continued*

Section: US 19 (south of Dawsonville) to Allatoona Reservoir

Counties: Dawson, Forsythe, Cherokee

Suitable For: Cruising, camping

Appropriate For: Families, beginners, intermediates, advanced

Months Runnable: All

Interest Highlights: Scenery

Scenery: Beautiful

Difficulty: International Scale I-II
Numerical Points 4-8

Average Width: 30-70 ft.
Velocity: Slack to slow
Gradient: 3.63 ft./mi.

Runnable Water Level: Minimum Not applicable
Maximum Up to flood stage

Hazards: Strainers, deadfalls

Scouting: None required

Portages: None required

Rescue Index: Accessible to accessible but difficult

Mean Water Temperature (°F)

| Jan 45 | Feb 46 | Mar 50 | Apr 58 | May 66 | Jun 72 |
| Jul 76 | Aug 75 | Sep 71 | Oct 63 | Nov 56 | Dec 49 |

Source of Additional Information: Appalachian Outfitters (706) 864-7117

Access Point	Access Code	Access Key
J	1357	1 Paved Road
K	2357	2 Unpaved Road
L	2357	3 Short Carry
M	1357	4 Long Carry
N	1357	5 Easy Grade
O	1357	6 Steep Incline
		7 Clear Trail
		8 Brush and Trees
		9 Launching Fee Charged
		10 Private Property, Need Permission
		11 No Access, Reference Only

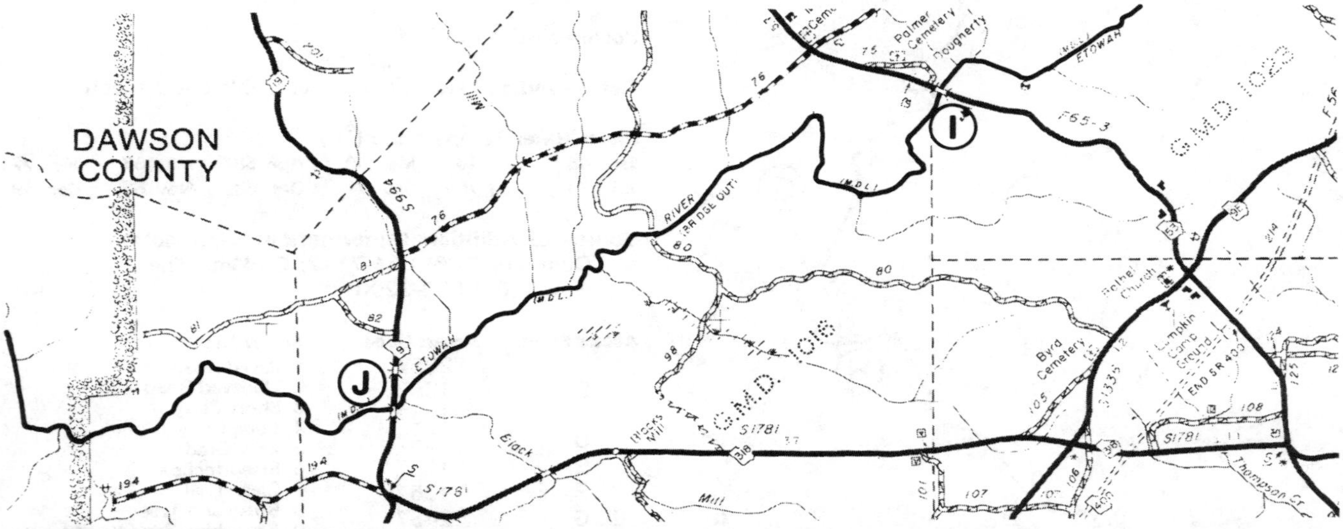

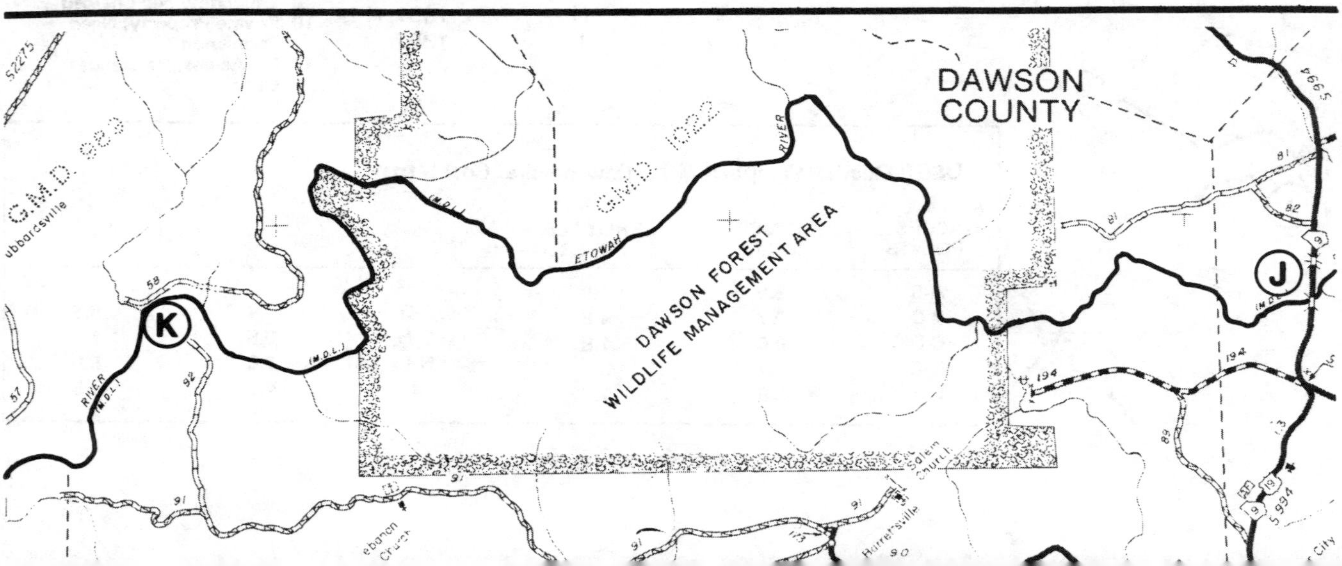

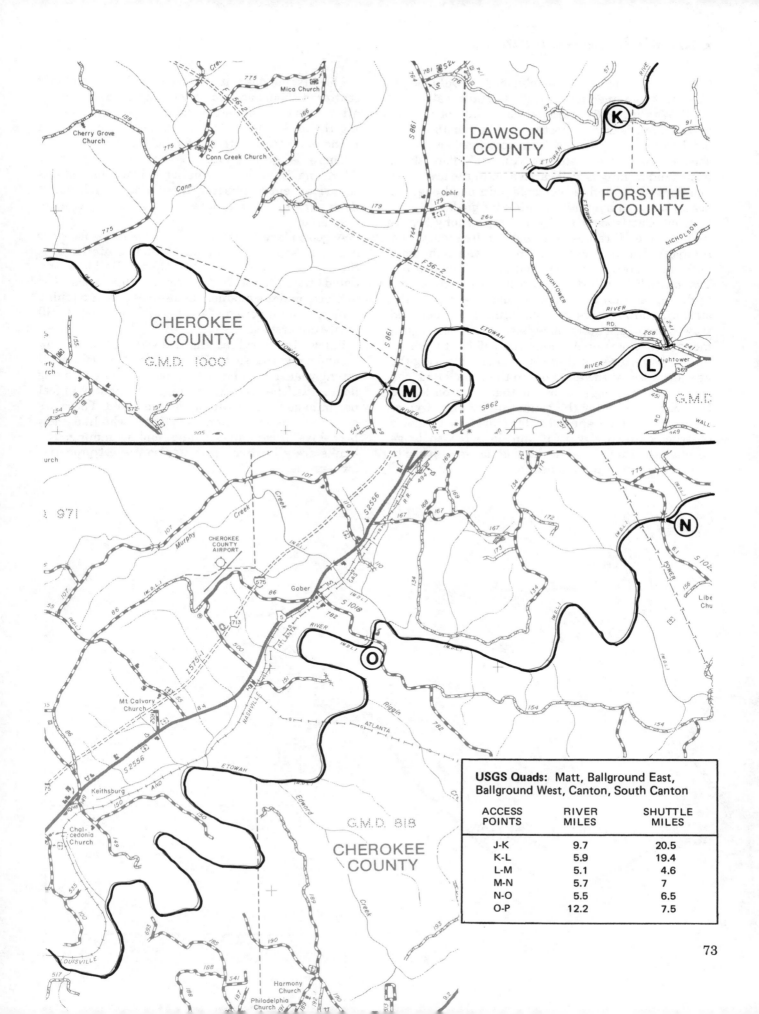

USGS Quads: Matt, Ballground East, Ballground West, Canton, South Canton

ACCESS POINTS	RIVER MILES	SHUTTLE MILES
J-K	9.7	20.5
K-L	5.9	19.4
L-M	5.1	4.6
M-N	5.7	7
N-O	5.5	6.5
O-P	12.2	7.5

73

Etowah River—*Continued*

United States mint was established in Dahlonega. The mint remained active until the outbreak of the Civil War in 1861. Auraria was a hub of mining activity, but is now a ghost town. The remains of an old hotel and a Georgia historical marker are all that remain as evidence of Auraria's flourishing past. Gold mining is still carried on in the area, and paddlers may find a portable mining dredge in operation or individuals panning for gold.

Below Castleberry bridge the topography begins to flatten and rapids diminish in frequency and intensity. But this portion of the Etowah is far from dull and contains a unique and mysterious feature. Two miles below Castleberry bridge the river seems to disappear into the earth. A major portion of the stream's flow enters an old mining tunnel and travels approximately one-quarter mile through a mountain. The tunnel can be run safely at medium to low water levels if there is no debris blocking the passage. Stop at the entrance to the tunnel and look closely for any logs or brush that may be lodged inside. Do not enter the tunnel under any circumstances if the daylight at the far end of the tunnel is obstructed in any way. If you do not wish to go through the tunnel, follow the original stream bed to the right around the mountain.

The river's descent remains mellow with only scattered shoals and no serious rapids. The scenery alternates between forest and farm land until reaching the backwaters of Lake Allatoona. The Etowah is the main feeder stream for Lake Allatoona.

There is good access to the river just below Allatoona Dam, but a smaller private dam blocks the river approximately three and a half miles downstream, so the lower access may be more desirable.

A good place to visit and another possible river access is at Etowah Indian Mounds State Historic Site near Cartersville. The Mound Builders predated the Cherokee Indians in this area. The artifacts and the mounds themselves give intriguing glimpes into a period of Georgia history that is still dimly understood.

Below Cartersville, the Etowah takes a slow meandering course to Rome. The flow volume is strong year round and gives opportunity for relaxing float trips. The gradient averages less than four feet per mile so no difficult rapids are found. There are good sections for beginners or those who like a few lazy days of camping, fishing, and swimming. The banks are all private property so respect property-owners' rights.

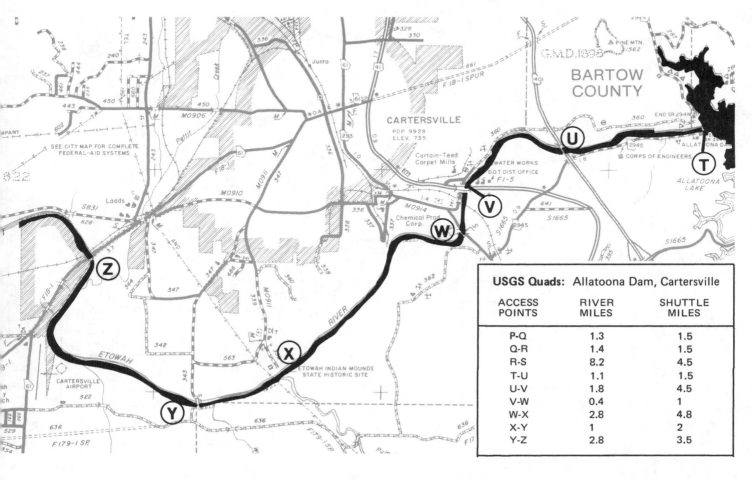

USGS Quads:	Allatoona Dam,	Cartersville
ACCESS POINTS	RIVER MILES	SHUTTLE MILES
P-Q	1.3	1.5
Q-R	1.4	1.5
R-S	8.2	4.5
T-U	1.1	1.5
U-V	1.8	4.5
V-W	0.4	1
W-X	2.8	4.8
X-Y	1	2
Y-Z	2.8	3.5

Section: Allatoona Dam to GA 113 (near Cartersville)

Counties: Bartow

Suitable For: Cruising, camping

Appropriate For: Families, beginners, intermediates, advanced

Months Runnable: All

Interest Highlights: Scenery, history

Scenery: Unattractive to beautiful

Difficulty: International Scale I (II)
Numerical Points 4-8

Average Width: 30-90 ft.
Velocity: Slow to moderate
Gradient: 4.1 ft./mi.

Runnable Water Level: Minimum Not applicable
Maximum Up to flood stage

Hazards: Strainers, deadfalls, dams

Scouting: None required

Portages: Dam at Allatoona and small dam three miles below Allatoona Dam
Rescue Index: Accessible to accessible but difficult

Mean Water Temperature (°F)

Jan 45	Feb 46	Mar 50	Apr 58	May 66	Jun 72
Jul 76	Aug 75	Sep 71	Oct 63	Nov 56	Dec 49

Access Point	Access Code	Access Key
P	1358	1 Paved Road
Q	1357	2 Unpaved Road
R	1357	3 Short Carry
S	1367	4 Long Carry
T	13571[1]	5 Easy Grade
U	(11)	6 Steep Incline
V	1357	7 Clear Trail
W	1357	8 Brush and Trees
X	1357(11)[2]	9 Launching Fee Charged
Y	1357	10 Private Property, Need Permission
Z	1357	11 No Access, Reference Only

[1] Not recommended; next portage too close
[2] Etowah Indian Mounds State Historic Site. Not always open; check first for hours gates are not locked.

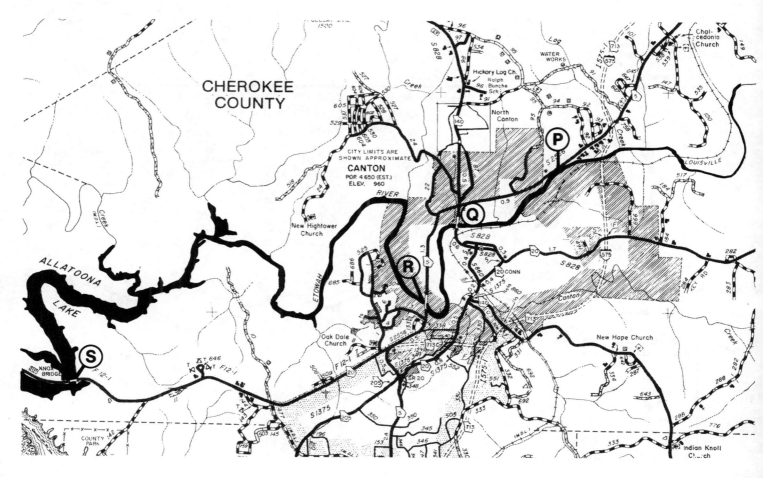

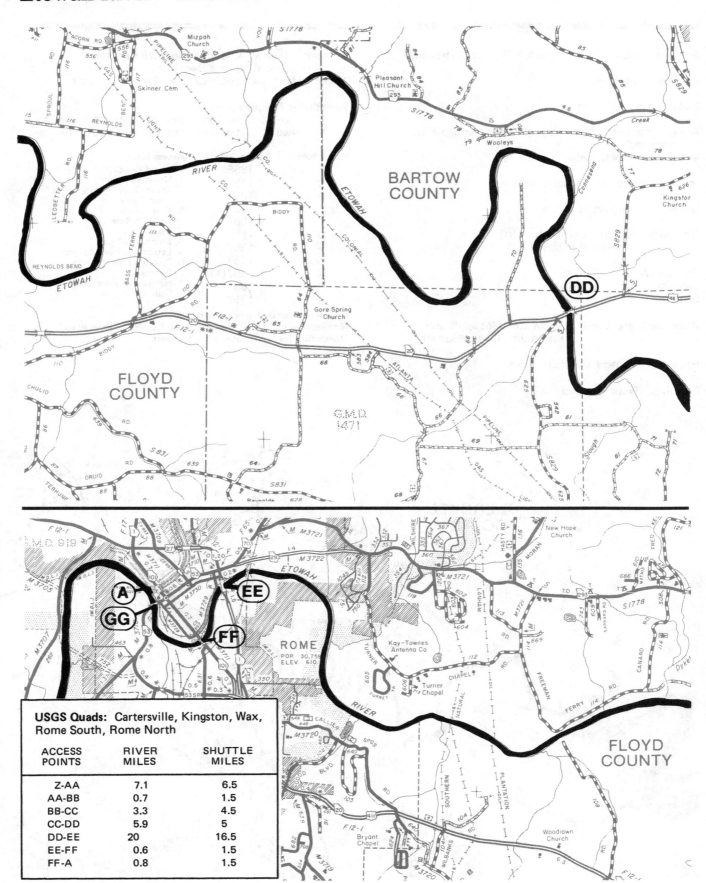

USGS Quads: Cartersville, Kingston, Wax, Rome South, Rome North

ACCESS POINTS	RIVER MILES	SHUTTLE MILES
Z-AA	7.1	6.5
AA-BB	0.7	1.5
BB-CC	3.3	4.5
CC-DD	5.9	5
DD-EE	20	16.5
EE-FF	0.6	1.5
FF-A	0.8	1.5

Section: GA 113 (near Cartersville) to Rome

Counties: Bartow, Floyd

Suitable For: Cruising, camping

Appropriate For: Families, beginners, intermediates, advanced

Months Runnable: All

Interest Highlights: Scenery, history

Scenery: Beautiful to unattractive

Difficulty: International Scale I
Numerical Points 4

Average Width: 50-90 ft.
Velocity: Slow to moderate
Gradient: 3.6 ft./mi.

Runnable Water Level: Minimum Not applicable
Maximum Up to flood stage

Hazards: None

Scouting: None required

Portages: None required

Rescue Index: Accessible to accessible but difficult

Mean Water Temperature (°F)

| Jan 45 | Feb 46 | Mar 50 | Apr 58 | May 66 | Jun 72 |
| Jul 76 | Aug 75 | Sep 71 | Oct 63 | Nov 56 | Dec 49 |

Access Point	Access Code	Access Key
Z	1357	1 Paved Road
AA	1357	2 Unpaved Road
BB	1357	3 Short Carry
CC	1357	4 Long Carry
DD	(11)	5 Easy Grade
EE	(11)	6 Steep Incline
FF	(11)	7 Clear Trail
A[1]	1357	8 Brush and Trees
		9 Launching Fee Charged
		10 Private Property, Need Permission
		11 No Access, Reference Only

[1]On the Coosa River

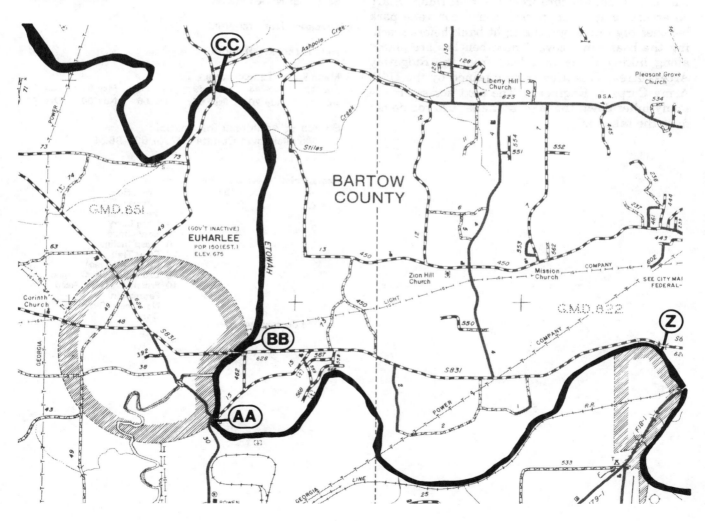

Mountaintown Creek

Mountaintown Creek is a tributary of the Coosawattee River. It flows approximately six miles from GA 282 west of Ellijay to its junction with the Coosawattee. In addition to these six miles, paddling Mountaintown Creek commits a boater to an additional mile of easy whitewater on the Coosawattee, and a three-and-one-half-mile paddle across Carters Lake to the nearest take-out point.

After an inauspicious beginning through an automobile junkyard and past several riverside dwellings, the scenery reverts to primitive woodland below the GA 282 bridge. The rapids are frequent, and pooled areas are small. Difficulty ranges from Class I to easy Class II. The steady pace on Mountaintown Creek makes forward progress seem so easy that the paddler becomes spoiled, making the trip across Carters Lake seem torturously slow.

The take-out is at the Ridgeway Boat Ramp, which is approximately three and one-half miles from the point where flat water silences the rapids of the Coosawattee. The boat ramp is not visible from the main channel. You must look to the right shore for a long cove that bends back to the right. A small island lies just offshore from the boat ramp. Sharp observers may first notice some concrete park benches high up along the right bank before reaching the boat ramp cove. These benches are placed along hiking trails that lead from the Ridgeway Access Area. This area is maintained by the U. S. Army Corps of Engineers. The next access area is many miles down the lake, so make sure you do not miss the take-out.

Section: GA 282 to Ridgeway Park (Carters Lake)

Counties: Gilmer

Suitable For: Cruising

Appropriate For: Beginners, intermediates, advanced

Months Runnable: January through July

Interest Highlights: Scenery, whitewater

Scenery: Exceptionally beautiful except for junkyard near GA 282

Difficulty: International Scale I-II
Numerical Points 12

Average Width: 20-35 ft.
Velocity: Moderate to fast
Gradient: 20 ft./mi.

Runnable Water Level: Minimum 2.0 ft.
(East Ellijay gauge) Maximum 3.5 ft.

Hazards: Strainers, deadfalls

Scouting: None required

Portages: None required

Rescue Index: Remote

Mean Water Temperature (°F)

| Jan 42 | Feb 44 | Mar 49 | Apr 56 | May 61 | Jun 68 |
| Jul 71 | Aug 70 | Sep 65 | Oct 56 | Nov 50 | Dec 44 |

Source of Additional Information:
Mountaintown Outfitters (706) 635-2524

Access Point	Access Code	Access Key
A	1357	1 Paved Road
C[1]	2367	2 Unpaved Road
		3 Short Carry
		4 Long Carry
		5 Easy Grade
		6 Steep Incline
		7 Clear Trail
		8 Brush and Trees
		9 Launching Fee Charged
		10 Private Property, Need Permission
		11 No Access, Reference Only

[1] On the Coosawattee River

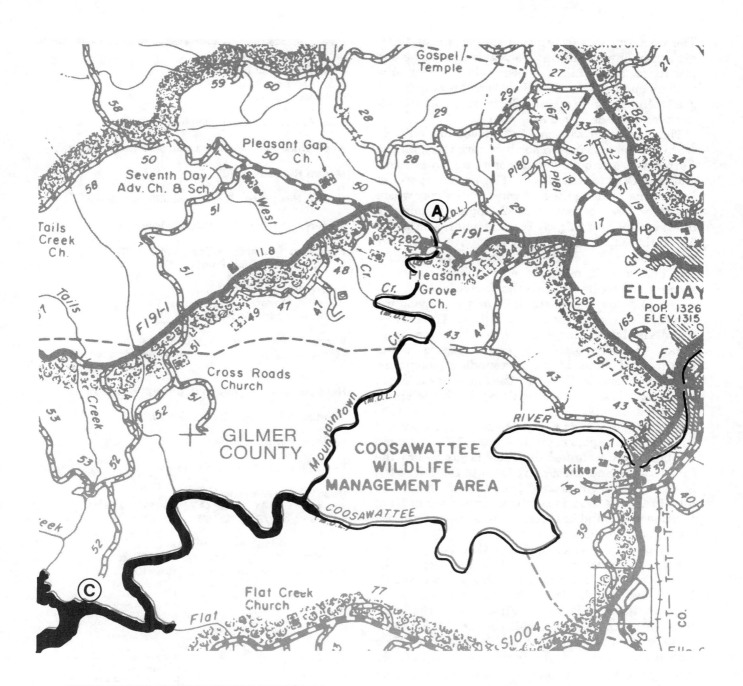

USGS Quads: Dyer Gap, Webb		
ACCESS POINTS	RIVER MILES	SHUTTLE MILES
A-C	8.8	8

Cartecay River

The Cartecay was for years a sleeper among Georgia's many fine whitewater streams. It rolled along unnoticed near Ellijay, known only to a few area anglers and local boaters. However, this situation is gradually changing and the Cartecay is now attracting some well-deserved attention.

The navigable section of the river lies entirely within Gilmer County in northwestern Georgia. The Cartecay is a tributary of the once mighty but now dammed Coosawattee River. The usual uppermost launch site is along the highway right-of-way where the river flows beneath GA 52, approximately five miles east of East Ellijay. The take-out is also on GA 52 at the city limits of East Ellijay. A short, five mile, thoroughly paved shuttle sets up the boater for ten and a half miles of outstanding mountain scenery and whitewater on the Cartecay.

The first few miles are slow and easy paddling through a scenic mountain valley. Thickets of mountain laurel, large pines, and various hardwoods will often suddenly part to expose rolling pasture and views of the surrounding mountains. The flow here is Class I. The only hazards are occasional downed trees that may block the entire narrow stream bed.

As the valley ends the gradient gets steeper and easy Class II rapids begin to appear. The first rapid of significant technical difficulty is just below the first large island encountered. Go to the left of the island and scout if desired from the left shore. The terrain in this area is reminiscent of Section III of the Chattooga and has often been called a miniature version of the Narrows.

A long pool breaks up the action, but this pool serves as a warning for the first big drop on the river. The drop is at the end of this pool and should be scouted on the left. Although not technically difficult itself, this rapid, First Fall, looks quite impressive and a very small pool is all that separates it from several tight rapids just below. First Fall may be run straight down the center over the pluming wave in the main chute. Be ready to brace and recover for the technical turns that follow.

The Cartecay, like the Chattooga, is a drop-and-pool stream, with rapids coming in sudden bursts interrupted by long, nearly placid stretches. This pattern continues as the river caroms along until a series of small islands is reached. At the bottom of this series, pull out on the left to scout the second major drop, Clear Creek Falls. At normal water levels run near the left bank. At higher water levels (above three feet) a potentially hazardous hydraulic reversal develops at the base of the falls. Portage is easiest on the right.

Clear Creek Falls is the last large drop on the river, but the pace remains brisk with some interest-

Section: GA 52 to East Ellijay

Counties: Gilmer

Suitable For: Cruising, camping

Appropriate For: Intermediates, advanced paddlers

Months Runnable: All

Interest Highlights: Scenery, wildlife, whitewater

Scenery: Pretty to exceptionally beautiful

Difficulty: International Scale I-III
Numerical Points 20

Average Width: 20-40 ft.
Velocity: Moderate
Gradient: 10 to 40+ ft./mi.

Runnable Water Level: Minimum 1.0 ft.
(East Ellijay gauge) Maximum 4.0 ft., open; up to flood stage, decked

Hazards: Strainers, deadfalls, difficult rapids

Scouting: First Fall, Clear Creek Falls

Portages: None required

Rescue Index: Accessible to remote

Mean Water Temperature (°F)

| Jan 43 | Feb 44 | Mar 48 | Apr 55 | May 61 | Jun 68 |
| Jul 70 | Aug 69 | Sep 65 | Oct 57 | Nov 51 | Dec 46 |

Source of Additional Information:
Mountaintown Outfitters (706) 635-2524

Access Point	Access Code	Access Key
A	1357	1 Paved Road
B	2367	2 Unpaved Road
C	1357	3 Short Carry
		4 Long Carry
		5 Easy Grade
		6 Steep Incline
		7 Clear Trail
		8 Brush and Trees
		9 Launching Fee Charged
		10 Private Property, Need Permission
		11 No Access, Reference Only

ing Class II ripples before reaching the lower valley. Here the river slows almost to a halt and signs of civilization reappear in abundance. Highway noises filter through the woods. Riverside homes and pastures are again noticeable and a mobile-home park marks the end of all seclusion. A Class II rapid just above the river gauging station on the right bank denotes the end of the trip. Take out on the highway right-of-way on the right bank.

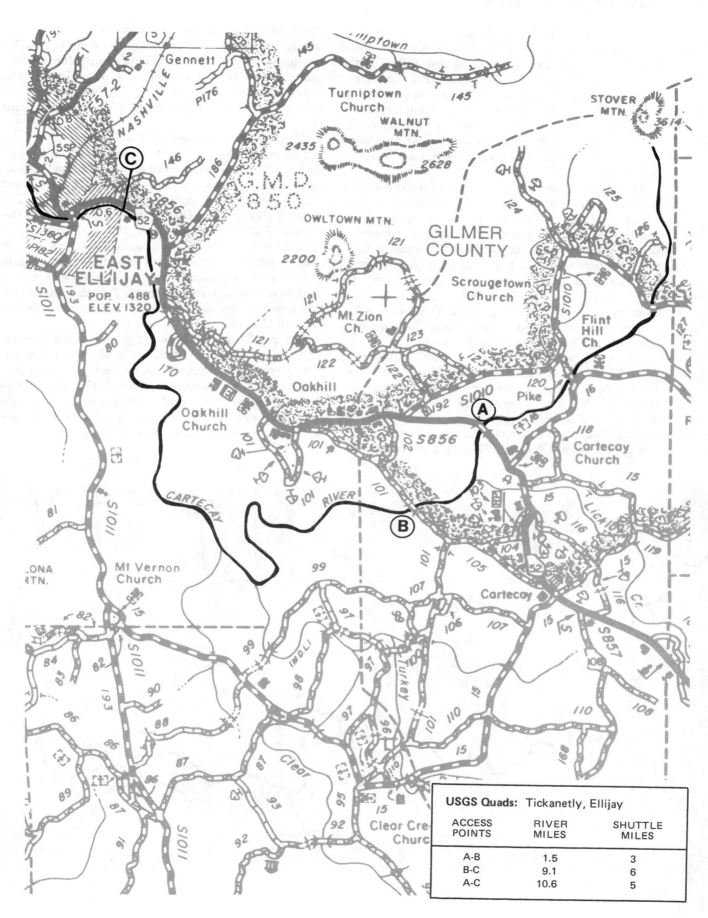

USGS Quads:	Tickanetly, Ellijay	
ACCESS POINTS	RIVER MILES	SHUTTLE MILES
A-B	1.5	3
B-C	9.1	6
A-C	10.6	5

Talking Rock Creek

Talking Rock Creek is navigable from GA 5 in Pickens County to GA 136 (in some places marked GA 156) in Murray County. A few miles of the stream are in southwestern Gilmer County, but there is no road access to this portion of the stream. Approximately the last two miles of paddling prior to reaching the access at GA 136 (156) are across the Carters Lake reregulation reservoir. At this point Talking Rock Creek has merged with the Coosawattee River.

At the upper access at GA 5 (point A), the stream is quite small and flows through a valley almost the entire distance to county road 198 (point B), a distance of almost three miles. Although this section is scenic and pleasant to paddle when water is high, most boaters prefer to put in at point B or point C.

Below point B the streamside environment becomes much steeper and flow volume is more conducive to easy floating since Town Creek has entered just above the bridge. Shoals become more frequent but are not extremely difficult.

GA 136 (point C) provides easy access to a splendid canoeing experience. Talking Rock Creek here enters a gorge environment of beauty and isolation. Terrain is extremely rugged and sheer walls often rise one hundred feet or more above the stream. There are many rapids, some quite long but few pass beyond Class II difficulty. Numerous deep, quiet pools give ample opportunity for swimming, fishing, or just relaxing. This is an excellent area for camping, and this section is long enough for two full, relaxed days. It may be traversed in one day, but the boater should allow maximum daylight time. There is no good access until reaching the highway at point D.

Of particular interest is the scenery along the entire route. At low water levels there are many small islands of river grasses and flowers in midstream that create a maze for canoeists. Sheer rock walls often will be on the sides of the stream. The name Talking Rock Creek probably came from the echoes that reverberate from the cliffs when any loud noise is made. One imposing bluff on the right side about two thirds of the way down this section contains what appears to be the entrance to a cave that is well above stream level. The gorge area also holds one of the last stands of virgin timber in the state of Georgia.

Talking Rock Creek is subject to rapid fluctuations in water level, and the difficulty of navigation is appreciably increased in extreme high water. Due to the lack of easy access and the incumbent difficulty of evacuation if problems arise, inexperienced boaters are advised to float this section only when the water is moderate to low.

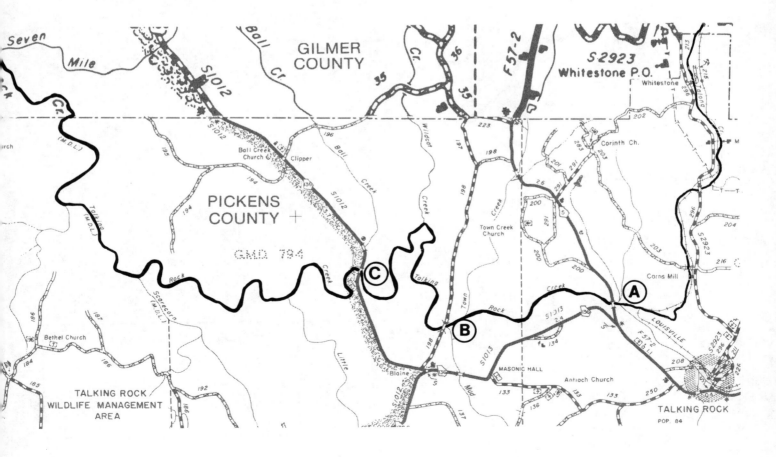

Section: Blaine to Carters Lake Reregulation Reservoir

Counties: Pickens, Gilmer, Gordon, Murray

Suitable For: Cruising, camping

Appropriate For: Intermediates and advanced paddlers; all may run with precautions

Months Runnable: January through July

Interest Highlights: Scenery, wildlife, whitewater

Scenery: Beautiful to spectacular

Difficulty: International Scale I-III
Numerical Points 16

Average Width: 20-45 ft.
Velocity: Moderate
Gradient: 19 (30+) ft./mi.

Runnable Water Level: Minimum 1.5 ft.
Maximum 4.0 ft., open;
6.0 ft., decked

Hazards: Strainers, deadfalls, difficult rapids, powerboat traffic

Scouting: Rapids as required by ability level

Portages: None required

Rescue Index: Accessible but difficult to remote

Mean Water Temperature (°F)

Jan 42	Feb 44	Mar 48	Apr 55	May 63	Jun 69
Jul 73	Aug 71	Sep 65	Oct 56	Nov 50	Dec 45

Source of Additional Information:
Mountaintown Outfitters (706) 635-2524

Access Point	Access Code	Access Key
A	1357	1 Paved Road
B	2357	2 Unpaved Road
C	1357	3 Short Carry
D	1357	4 Long Carry
		5 Easy Grade
		6 Steep Incline
		7 Clear Trail
		8 Brush and Trees
		9 Launching Fee Charged
		10 Private Property, Need Permission
		11 No Access, Reference Only

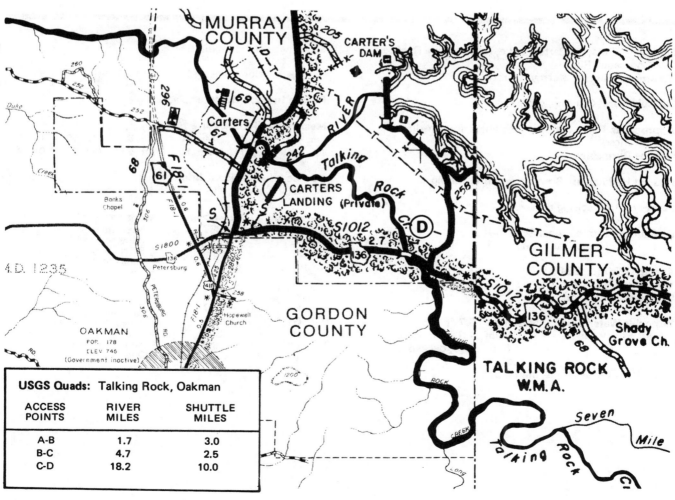

USGS Quads: Talking Rock, Oakman		
ACCESS POINTS	RIVER MILES	SHUTTLE MILES
A-B	1.7	3.0
B-C	4.7	2.5
C-D	18.2	10.0

Coosawattee River

The Coosawattee River is formed by the union of the Cartecay and Ellijay rivers in Gilmer County near Ellijay, Georgia. What was at one time one of northern Georgia's most magnificent whitewater streams is now partially inundated by Carters Lake to the southwest of Ellijay. Below Carters Lake the Coosawattee snakes along a sedate course across Gordon County where it merges with the Conasauga River and becomes the Oostanaula River.

A sense of what the Coosawattee was and what it has become is masterfully conveyed by James Dickey's poem "On the Coosawattee." It has been suggested that Dickey's experiences on the Coosawattee before it was dammed were a major influence on his writing of the novel *Deliverance* and that the Coosawattee was as dramatic as the now-famous Chattooga River. The best whitewater of the Coosawattee is forever drowned by Carters Lake, however.

Below Ellijay the scenery is still breathtaking at times, but rapids never get above a Class II level under normal conditions. Soon after passing through Ellijay, the boater finds several fish weirs that supposedly date back to the Cherokees. These create small ledges but no real hazard to navigation.

The miles to the backwaters of Carters Lake are not dull. Scenery is excellent and fishing is good for those who care to try their luck. A state record trout was taken from the Coosawattee a few years ago. There are many long, pooled sections, but enough Class I and II rapids intervene to keep one from becoming too complacent.

Rapids become more frequent below the junction with Mountaintown Creek from the right and flow volume is significantly increased.

Soon after the rapids begin to hold the boater's interest they come to an abrupt end in the backwaters of the lake. The lake is a pretty one and powerboat traffic is usually light, but one should allow several hours of paddling time to reach the first available access point at Ridgeway Boat Ramp.

Below Carters Lake the Coosawattee is very sluggish and flows through more populated areas. Farm land, industrial plants, and some woodland make up the streamside environment. The Coosawattee merges with the Conasauga near Resaca and is thereafter called the Oostanaula River.

Section: Ellijay to Carters Lake; Carters Lake Dam to Conasauga River
Counties: Gilmer, Murray, Gordon

Suitable For: Cruising, camping

Appropriate For: Families, beginners, intermediates, advanced
Months Runnable: All

Interest Highlights: Scenery, wildlife, fishing

Scenery: Uninspiring to beautiful

Difficulty: International Scale I-II
Numerical Points 12

Average Width: 20-65 ft.
Velocity: Moderate
Gradient: 21 ft./mi.

Runnable Water Level: Minimum 0.7 ft.
(East Ellijay gauge) Maximum 4.0 ft., open; up to flood stage, decked

Hazards: Few deadfalls, mild rapids

Scouting: None required

Portages: None required

Rescue Index: Remote to accessible

Mean Water Temperature (°F)

| Jan 43 | Feb 45 | Mar 50 | Apr 58 | May 68 | Jun 74 |
| Jul 77 | Aug 74 | Sep 69 | Oct 60 | Nov 52 | Dec 46 |

Source of Additional Information:
High Country (404) 391-9657

Access Point	Access Code	Access Key
A	1357	1 Paved Road
B	2357	2 Unpaved Road
C	2367	3 Short Carry
(Lake)		4 Long Carry
D	1357	5 Easy Grade
E	1357	6 Steep Incline
F	2367	7 Clear Trail
G	2357	8 Brush and Trees
H	1357	9 Launching Fee Charged
I	1357	10 Private Property, Need Permission
J	1357	11 No Access, Reference Only
K	1357	

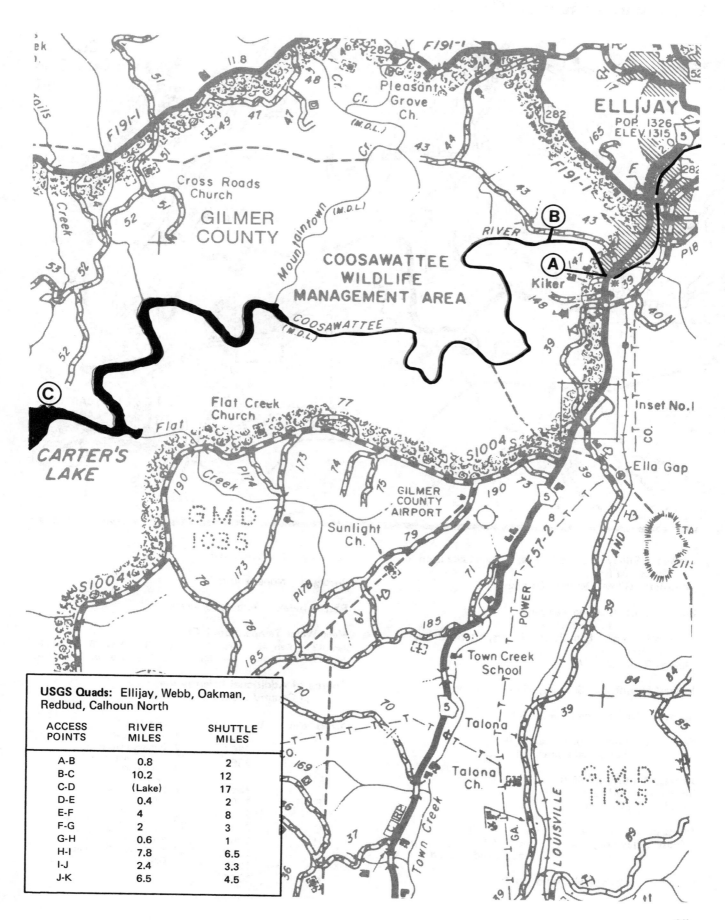

USGS Quads: Ellijay, Webb, Oakman, Redbud, Calhoun North

ACCESS POINTS	RIVER MILES	SHUTTLE MILES
A-B	0.8	2
B-C	10.2	12
C-D	(Lake)	17
D-E	0.4	2
E-F	4	8
F-G	2	3
G-H	0.6	1
H-I	7.8	6.5
I-J	2.4	3.3
J-K	6.5	4.5

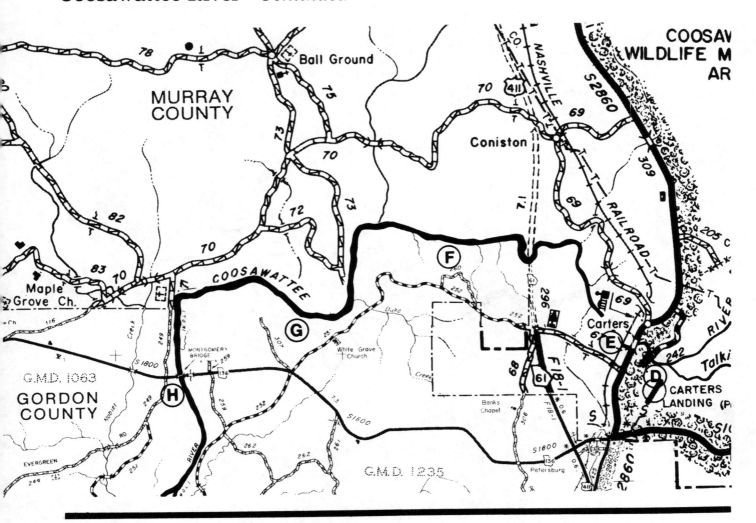

Section: Ellijay to Carters Lake; Carters Lake Dam to Conasauga River

Counties: Gilmer, Murray, Gordon

Suitable For: Cruising, camping

Appropriate For: Families, beginners, intermediates, advanced

Months Runnable: All

Interest Highlights: Scenery, wildlife, fishing

Scenery: Uninspiring to beautiful

Difficulty: International Scale I-II
Numerical Points 12

Average Width: 20-65 ft.
Velocity: Moderate
Gradient: 21 ft./mi.

Runnable Water Level: Minimum 0.7 ft.
(East Ellijay gauge) Maximum 4.0 ft., open; up to flood stage, decked

Hazards: Few deadfalls, mild rapids

Scouting: None required

Portages: None required

Rescue Index: Remote to accessible

Mean Water Temperature (°F)

Jan 43	Feb 45	Mar 50	Apr 58	May 68	Jun 74
Jul 77	Aug 74	Sep 69	Oct 60	Nov 52	Dec 46

Source of Additional Information:
High Country (404) 391-9657

Access Point	Access Code	Access Key
A	1357	1 Paved Road
B	2357	2 Unpaved Road
C	2367	3 Short Carry
(Lake)		4 Long Carry
D	1357	5 Easy Grade
E	1357	6 Steep Incline
F	2367	7 Clear Trail
G	2357	8 Brush and Trees
H	1357	9 Launching Fee Charged
I	1357	10 Private Property, Need Permission
J	1357	11 No Access, Reference Only
K	1357	

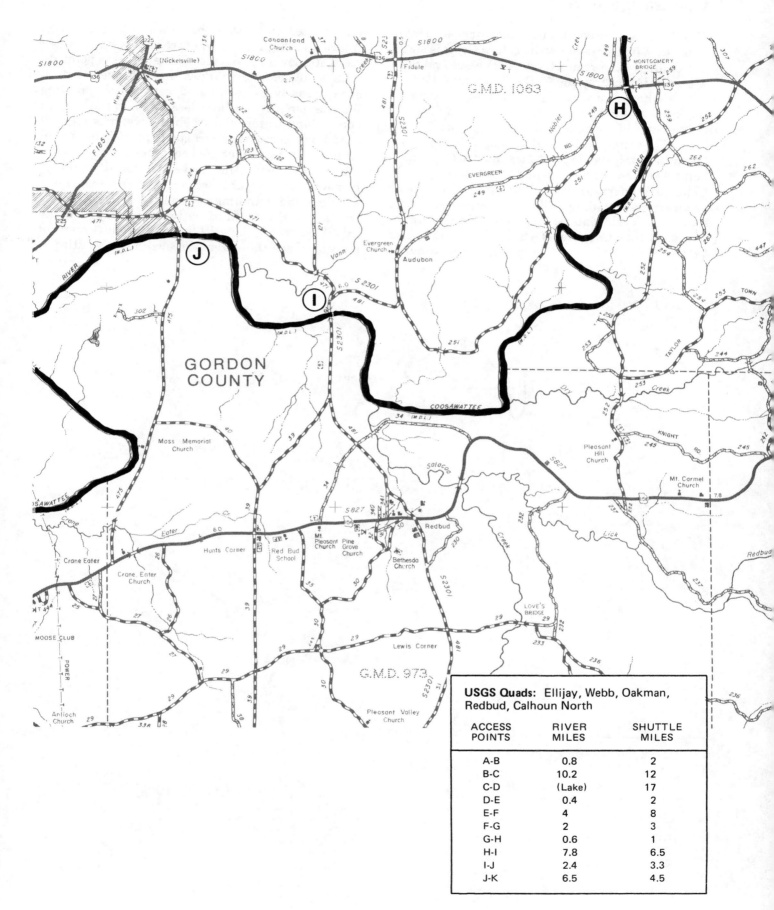

USGS Quads: Ellijay, Webb, Oakman, Redbud, Calhoun North		
ACCESS POINTS	RIVER MILES	SHUTTLE MILES
A-B	0.8	2
B-C	10.2	12
C-D	(Lake)	17
D-E	0.4	2
E-F	4	8
F-G	2	3
G-H	0.6	1
H-I	7.8	6.5
I-J	2.4	3.3
J-K	6.5	4.5

87

Conasauga River

The Conasauga River has its headwaters deep in the Cohutta Wilderness in northwestern Georgia's Fannin County. It flows north into Tennessee and takes a serpentine course along the Tennessee–Georgia border then loops south back into Georgia. It combines with the Coosawattee River to form the Oostanaula River near Calhoun.

In high-water periods, experienced boaters may begin their trip as high as Chicken Coop Gap (access point A) off Forest Service Road 17 at the edge of the Cohutta Wilderness Area. Putting in at this point requires map reading skills, determination, and a high skill level. Map reading skills are required to locate Chicken Coop Gap. Determination is required to get your boat and equipment approximately

one-quarter mile straight down into the gorge. Above all a high skill level is require to successfully navigate down to Alaculsy Valley (access point B). This is rugged and wild terrain. The river drops in some areas over one hundred feet per mile, creating intense, lengthy rapids (Class IV+). It can only be run in high water, and when the water is high all conditions combine to create a potentially lethal situation. It is no place for beginners.

For those with the above-mentioned qualities, however, the rewards are great. The scenery is pristine and stunningly beautiful. The water is crystalline and contains native trout. Rapids range in difficulty to Class IV+ and the quick rate of descent keeps the adrenalin level high. Scouting is

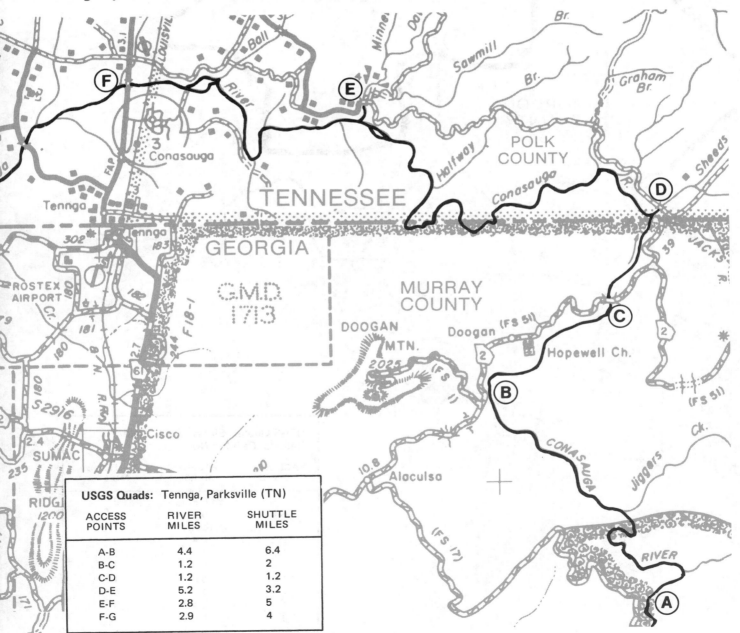

USGS Quads: Tennga, Parksville (TN)		
ACCESS POINTS	RIVER MILES	SHUTTLE MILES
A-B	4.4	6.4
B-C	1.2	2
C-D	1.2	1.2
D-E	5.2	3.2
E-F	2.8	5
F-G	2.9	4

frequently necessary around blind drops and turns. All rapids on this section have been run, but portages may be prudent at certain times.

Below access point B the river remains in the Alaculsy Valley until the Jacks River junction. The Valley is pretty but in comparison to the upper section, it might produce either ennui or welcome relief to the paddler.

The most popular section of the Conasauga for boaters, campers, and anglers begins at the Jacks River junction. The added flow of the Jacks doubles the volume of the stream and makes boating practical over a greater portion of the year. Access is much easier as a well-maintained Forest Service road goes right to this point. This is also an entrance to Cohutta Wilderness backpacking trails.

The river returns to a character similar to the upper section, but gradient and therefore rapids are greatly moderated. Most remain in the Class I to Class II category. One series locally known as simply The Falls is generally considered a Class III. Get out on the right above the rapid and follow the trail if scouting is desired. Portage on the right also if it appears too difficult. Many of the remaining

Section: Chicken Coop Gap to US 411 (in Tennessee)

Counties: Murray (GA); Polk, Bradley (TN)

Suitable For: Cruising, camping, training (below Jacks River)

Appropriate For: Families, beginners, intermediates, advanced, lower sections; advanced paddlers only Section A-B

Months Runnable: Section A-B, January through July; lower sections, December through March

Interest Highlights: Scenery, wildlife, whitewater

Scenery: Beautiful to spectacular

Difficulty: International Scale I-IV+ above access point B; I-III below access point B
Numerical Points 15-30

Average Width: 15-40 ft.
Velocity: Moderate to fast
Gradient: 40 ft./mi. (A-C, 125 ft./mi.)

Runnable Water Level: Minimum Unknown
No gauge   Maximum Unknown

Hazards: Strainers, deadfalls, difficult rapids, keeper hydraulics
Scouting: All rapids in section A-B; falls in B-C section

Portages: Rapids, as necessary

Rescue Index: Accessible to extremely remote

Mean Water Temperature (°F)

Jan 42	Feb 44	Mar 50	Apr 59	May 68	Jun 75
Jul 78	Aug 74	Sep 68	Oct 59	Nov 50	Dec 44

Source of Additional Information:
High Country (404) 391-9657

Access Point	Access Code	Access Key
A	2468	1 Paved Road
B	2357	2 Unpaved Road
C	2357	3 Short Carry
D	2357	4 Long Carry
E	2357	5 Easy Grade
F	1357	6 Steep Incline
G	1357	7 Clear Trail
		8 Brush and Trees
		9 Launching Fee Charged
		10 Private Property, Need Permission
		11 No Access, Reference Only

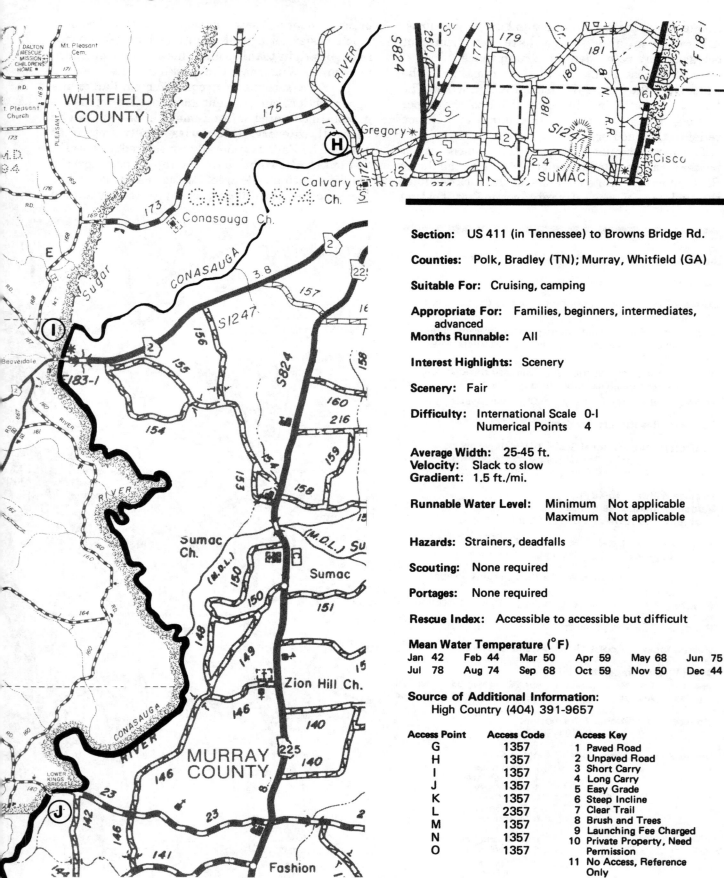

Section: US 411 (in Tennessee) to Browns Bridge Rd.

Counties: Polk, Bradley (TN); Murray, Whitfield (GA)

Suitable For: Cruising, camping

Appropriate For: Families, beginners, intermediates, advanced

Months Runnable: All

Interest Highlights: Scenery

Scenery: Fair

Difficulty: International Scale 0-I
Numerical Points 4

Average Width: 25-45 ft.
Velocity: Slack to slow
Gradient: 1.5 ft./mi.

Runnable Water Level: Minimum Not applicable
Maximum Not applicable

Hazards: Strainers, deadfalls

Scouting: None required

Portages: None required

Rescue Index: Accessible to accessible but difficult

Mean Water Temperature (°F)

Jan 42	Feb 44	Mar 50	Apr 59	May 68	Jun 75
Jul 78	Aug 74	Sep 68	Oct 59	Nov 50	Dec 44

Source of Additional Information:
High Country (404) 391-9657

Access Point	Access Code	Access Key
G	1357	1 Paved Road
H	1357	2 Unpaved Road
I	1357	3 Short Carry
J	1357	4 Long Carry
K	1357	5 Easy Grade
L	2357	6 Steep Incline
M	1357	7 Clear Trail
N	1357	8 Brush and Trees
O	1357	9 Launching Fee Charged
		10 Private Property, Need Permission
		11 No Access, Reference Only

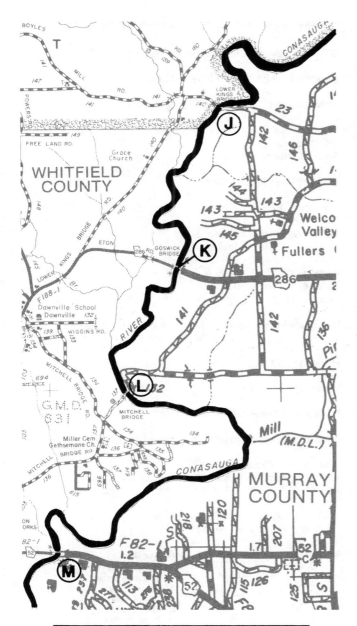

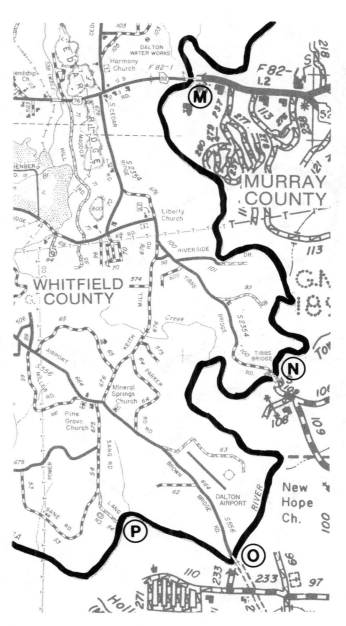

rapids are challenging but none is as tricky as The Falls.

The scenery alone makes this trip worthwhile. Many camping spots beckon the boater. Even though this section can be easily done in one day, it is a pleasant area in which to linger.

Class I-II rapids sporadically appear until the valley is reached a few miles above US 411. From this point on down to the Coosawattee River junction near Calhoun, the Conasauga is definitely a pastoral stream. Rapids have disappeared and the presence of man becomes more prevalent. Some attractive wooded sections remain, but all pale in comparison to the delights of the mountainous region.

Conasauga River—*Continued*

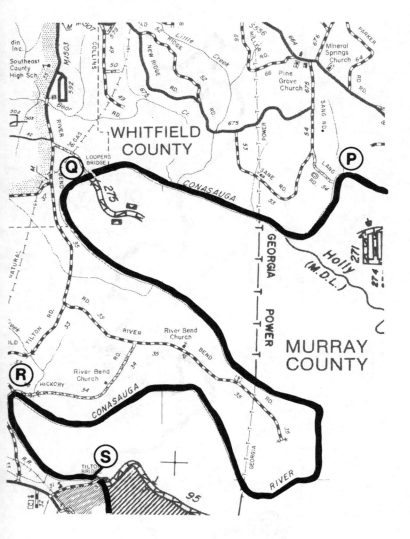

Section: Browns Bridge Rd. to Resaca

Counties: Murray, Whitfield, Gordon

Suitable For: Cruising, camping

Appropriate For: Families, beginners, intermediates, advanced

Months Runnable: All

Interest Highlights: Scenery

Scenery: Fair

Difficulty: International Scale 0-I
Numerical Points 4

Average Width: 25-45 ft.
Velocity: Slack to slow
Gradient: 1.5 ft./mi.

Runnable Water Level: Minimum Not applicable
Maximum Not applicable

Hazards: Strainers, deadfalls

Scouting: None required

Portages: None required

Rescue Index: Accessible to accessible but difficult

Mean Water Temperature (°F)

| Jan 42 | Feb 44 | Mar 50 | Apr 59 | May 68 | Jun 75 |
| Jul 78 | Aug 74 | Sep 68 | Oct 59 | Nov 50 | Dec 44 |

Source of Additional Information:
High Country (404) 391-9657

Access Point	Access Code	Access Key
O	1357	1 Paved Road
P	2357	2 Unpaved Road
Q	2357	3 Short Carry
R	1358	4 Long Carry
S	1357	5 Easy Grade
T	2357	6 Steep Incline
U	1357	7 Clear Trail
K[1]	1357	8 Brush and Trees
A[2]	1357	9 Launching Fee Charged
		10 Private Property, Need Permission
		11 No Access, Reference Only

[1] On the Coosawattee River
[2] On the Oostanaula River

USGS Quads: Calhoun NE, Dalton S, Calhoun N

ACCESS POINTS	RIVER MILES	SHUTTLE MILES
O-P	1	3.5
P-Q	3.4	6.2
Q-R	9	4
R-S	1.2	1.8
S-T	2.6	3.7
T-U	3.8	3.4
U-K	5.3	5.4
K-A	4.1	4

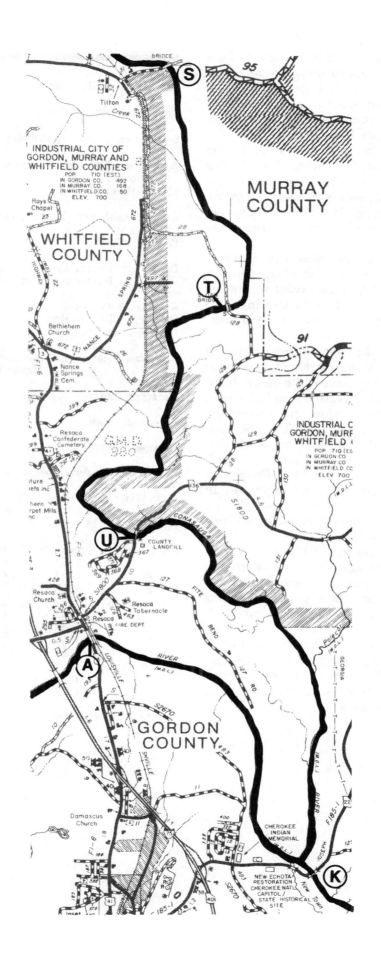

Oostanaula River

The Oostanaula River is created by the union of the Coosawattee and Conasauga rivers just northeast of Calhoun in Gordon County. It loops lazily to the southwest across Gordon County and into Floyd County. In Rome, the Oostanaula and Etowah rivers combine to form the Coosa River.

The name Oostanaula is a derivation of the Cherokee Indian phrase for "Shoal River." The Cherokees who gave the river this name must have had active imaginations, however, since the gradient of the stream averages less than one foot per mile. The stream occasionally ripples, but rapids are nonexistent.

Current is slow and downstream momentum is dependent on the will and stamina of the paddler. Streamside environment is agricultural with some woodland. The area is well suited for farming since it is part of Georgia's Great Valley in the northwestern corner of the state.

The Oostanaula River has figured prominently in Georgia history. It was a major artery for trade for the Cherokee Indians long before white men entered the territory. The Cherokee Nation's capital was at the head of the Oostanaula where the Conasauga and the Coosawattee come together. The town was known as New Echota. It was the center of government and culture for the Cherokees. In 1826, Sequoyah began printing the *Cherokee Phoenix,* a newspaper printed in the Cherokee alphabet, in New Echota. New Echota is now the city of Calhoun. The Cherokee presence is memorialized in the New Echota Restoration State Historical site.

Farther downstream the city of Rome grew from the Cherokee trading village of Chiaha, where the Oostanaula meets the Etowah. Rome is also the home of Berry College and Academy. The campus and surrounding acreage are beautiful and well worth a visit.

Navigation of the river is uncomplicated. Some of the scenery is interesting, but the river begins and ends in urban areas. The man-made flood control levees in Rome block some of the city's evidence and create a parklike atmosphere.

Section: GA 255 in Gordon Co. to Rome

Counties: Gordon, Floyd

Suitable For: Cruising, camping

Appropriate For: Families, beginners, intermediates, advanced

Months Runnable: All

Interest Highlights: Scenery, levees in Rome, Cherokee history

Scenery: Fair

Difficulty: International Scale I
Numerical Points 4

Average Width: 50-70 ft.
Velocity: Slack to slow
Gradient: 1 ft./mi.

Runnable Water Level: Minimum Not applicable
Maximum Not applicable

Hazards: Strainers, deadfalls

Scouting: None

Portages: None

Rescue Index: Accessible to accessible but difficult

Mean Water Temperature (°F)

Jan 42	Feb 43	Mar 49	Apr 57	May 66	Jun 75
Jul 78	Aug 76	Sep 72	Oct 63	Nov 54	Dec 46

Access Point	Access Code	Access Key
K[1]	1357	1 Paved Road
A	1357	2 Unpaved Road
B	1358(11)	3 Short Carry
C	1357	4 Long Carry
D	1357	5 Easy Grade
E	1357	6 Steep Incline
F	1357	7 Clear Trail
G	1357	8 Brush and Trees
H	1357	9 Launching Fee Charged
I	1357	10 Private Property, Need Permission
J	1357	11 No Access, Reference Only

[1]On the Coosawattee River

USGS Quads: Calhoun N, Sugar Valley, Calhoun S, Plainville, Armuchee, Shannon, Rome N

ACCESS POINTS	RIVER MILES	SHUTTLE MILES
K-A	4.1	4.5
A-B	0.6	1.5
B-C	6.6	6.5
C-D	6.9	4.5
D-E	6.3	4.5
E-F	11.3	10.0
F-G	12.5	11.5
G-H	1.2	1.0
H-I	0.2	1.0
I-J	0.4	1.0

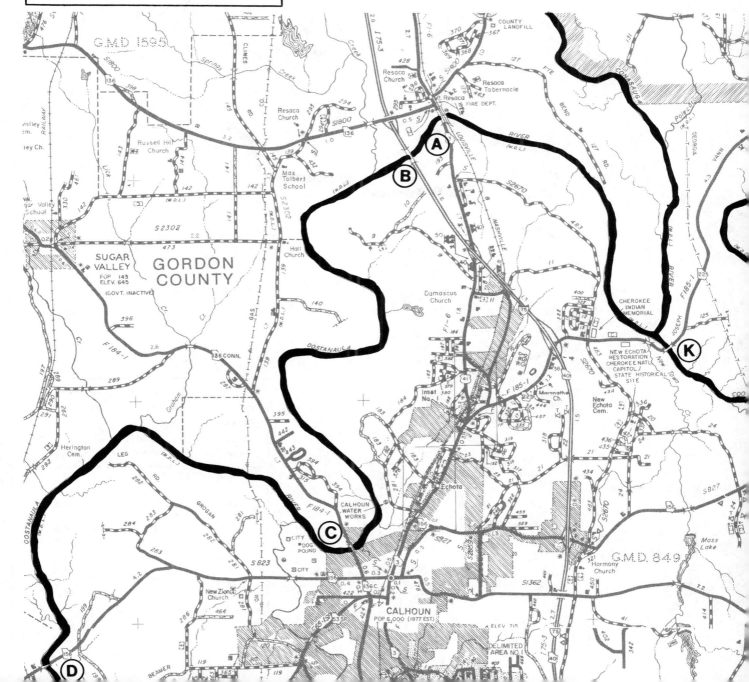

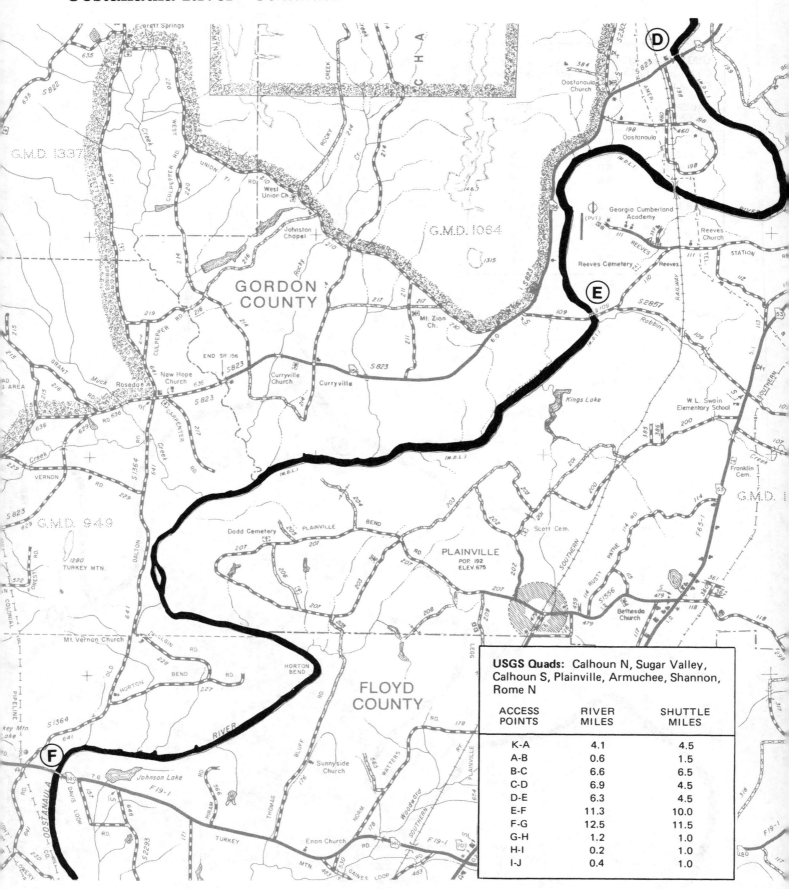

USGS Quads:	Calhoun N, Sugar Valley, Calhoun S, Plainville, Armuchee, Shannon, Rome N	
ACCESS POINTS	RIVER MILES	SHUTTLE MILES
K-A	4.1	4.5
A-B	0.6	1.5
B-C	6.6	6.5
C-D	6.9	4.5
D-E	6.3	4.5
E-F	11.3	10.0
F-G	12.5	11.5
G-H	1.2	1.0
H-I	0.2	1.0
I-J	0.4	1.0

Section: GA 255 in Gordon Co. to Rome

Counties: Gordon, Floyd

Suitable For: Cruising, camping

Appropriate For: Families, beginners, intermediates, advanced

Months Runnable: All

Interest Highlights: Scenery, levees in Rome, Cherokee history

Scenery: Fair

Difficulty: International Scale I
Numerical Points 4

Average Width: 50-70 ft.
Velocity: Slack to slow
Gradient: 1 ft./mi.

Runnable Water Level: Minimum Not applicable
Maximum Not applicable

Hazards: Strainers, deadfalls

Scouting: None

Portages: None

Rescue Index: Accessible to accessible but difficult

Mean Water Temperature (°F)

| Jan 42 | Feb 43 | Mar 49 | Apr 57 | May 66 | Jun 75 |
| Jul 78 | Aug 76 | Sep 72 | Oct 63 | Nov 54 | Dec 46 |

Access Point	Access Code	Access Key
K[1]	1357	1 Paved Road
A	1357	2 Unpaved Road
B	1358(11)	3 Short Carry
C	1357	4 Long Carry
D	1357	5 Easy Grade
E	1357	6 Steep Incline
F	1357	7 Clear Trail
G	1357	8 Brush and Trees
H	1357	9 Launching Fee Charged
I	1357	10 Private Property, Need Permission
J	1357	11 No Access, Reference Only

[1] On the Coosawattee River

Big Cedar Creek

Big Cedar Creek is a Coosa River tributary. Its headwaters are near Cedartown in Polk County. It flows northwestward out of Polk County and across Floyd County into Weiss Lake on the Georgia–Alabama border. The Coosa River is the feeder stream for Weiss Lake.

The creek got its name from the glades of large eastern red cedar that at one time were plentiful in the area. The vegetation and topography are similar to central Tennessee. Unfortunately most of the large cedar trees are gone. Longleaf pines and mixed hardwoods now are dominant.

Boaters may begin their trip on GA 100 in Polk County (access point A). This is good, easy public access for those who wish to float the upper section. Access point B, Kings bridge, is on a gravel road on private property. Ask for permission before launching, exiting, or parking a vehicle near here.

The gradient along the entire course of the stream consistently averages ten feet per mile. There are no large rapids on the creek, only Class I-II shoals. The water level changes dramatically from season to season with high-water periods over fifteen feet above the normal summer flows. Debris from flood periods is jammed under most bridge trusses, so exercise caution if the water is up. The gauge is just below access point A. If the level is above ten feet, passing under bridges may be hazardous.

Fish are abundant in Big Cedar Creek and are often visible if the boater is cautious. Current is slow enough to make fishing from the boat practical.

Below the point where GA 100 crosses the creek for the second time (access point F), current becomes slack and progress will be much slower. Scenery is still pleasant and mostly woodland. Almost two miles of paddling across Weiss Lake are required to reach the final take-out at access point D.

Section: GA 100 to Weiss Lake

Counties: Polk, Floyd

Suitable For: Cruising

Appropriate For: Families, beginners, intermediates, advanced

Months Runnable: All except during drought; January through July best

Interest Highlights: Scenery, fishing

Scenery: Pretty

Difficulty: International Scale I-II
Numerical Points 9

Average Width: 20-30 ft.
Velocity: Slack to moderate
Gradient: 9 ft./mi.

Runnable Water Level: Minimum Unknown
(GA 100 gauge) Maximum 10 ft.

Hazards: Strainers, deadfalls

Scouting: None required

Portages: None required

Rescue Index: Accessible to accessible but difficult

Mean Water Temperature (°F)

Jan 47	Feb 50	Mar 54	Apr 59	May 66	Jun 71
Jul 73	Aug 72	Sep 67	Oct 61	Nov 54	Dec 50

Source of Additional Information: City of Cedartown (706) 748-3220

Access Point	Access Code	Access Key
A	1357	1 Paved Road
B	2357(10)	2 Unpaved Road
C	1357	3 Short Carry
D	1357	4 Long Carry
E	1367	5 Easy Grade
F	1357	6 Steep Incline
G	1357	7 Clear Trail
D¹	1357	8 Brush and Trees
		9 Launching Fee Charged
		10 Private Property, Need Permission
		11 No Access, Reference Only

¹On the Coosa River

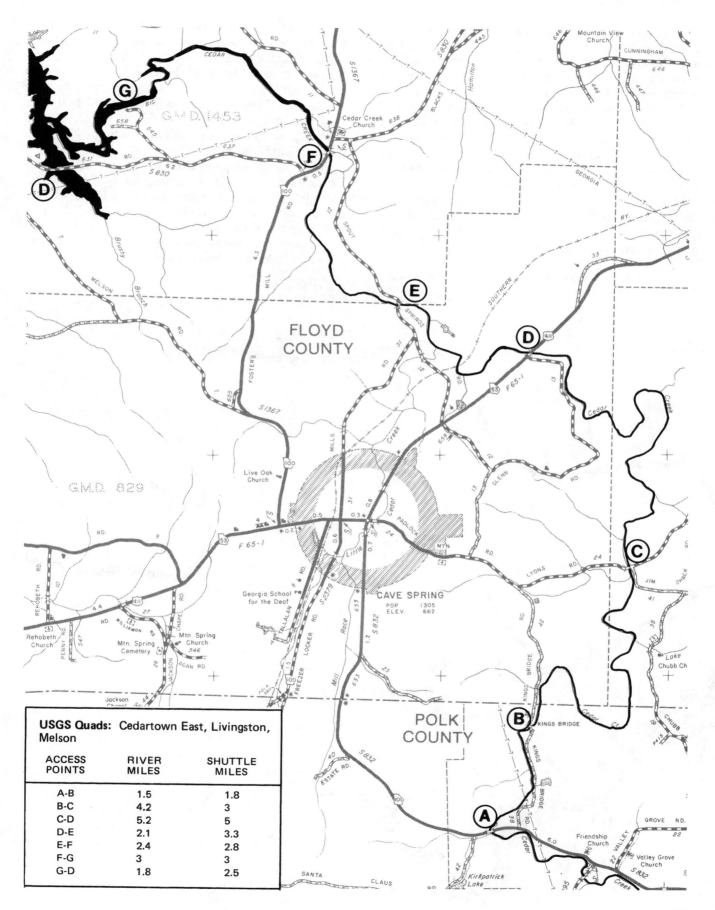

USGS Quads:	Cedartown East, Livingston, Melson	
ACCESS POINTS	RIVER MILES	SHUTTLE MILES
A-B	1.5	1.8
B-C	4.2	3
C-D	5.2	5
D-E	2.1	3.3
E-F	2.4	2.8
F-G	3	3
G-D	1.8	2.5

Coosa River

The Coosa River is formed in Floyd County in downtown Rome by the merger of the Oostanaula and Etowah rivers. It is a large river and has been used for commercial navigation. It is the major feeder stream for Weiss Lake.

The first few miles flow through an industrial area of Rome, but the boater is sometimes visually separated from this by grassy, man-made levees. Mayos lock and dam (access point B) is now inoperative, but it is still an interesting place to investigate. Portage on the left.

The flow of the river is extremely sluggish even before reaching Weiss Lake backwaters. The gradient averages less than two feet per mile. There are no rapids. Its character is similar to that of a Coastal Plains stream.

Of particular interest is the area around Fosters Bend just above Weiss Lake. Here a large oxbow lake and swamp are formed. A small population of cottonmouth (water mocassins) is here. This snake is usually found only in the Coastal Plain and no other populations of the snake are known to be near this area. There are also many plants found here that are indigenous to the Coastal Plains. On the higher ground near the oxbow, evidence has been found of early Indian settlements.

The final access point is on Weiss Lake (Big Cedar Creek access point H). Reaching it requires approximately three miles of paddling below Fosters Bend. For those who wish to visit Fosters Bend without paddling the upper part of the Coosa, put in on the lake access and paddle back up. A navigational map of Weiss Lake may be helpful.

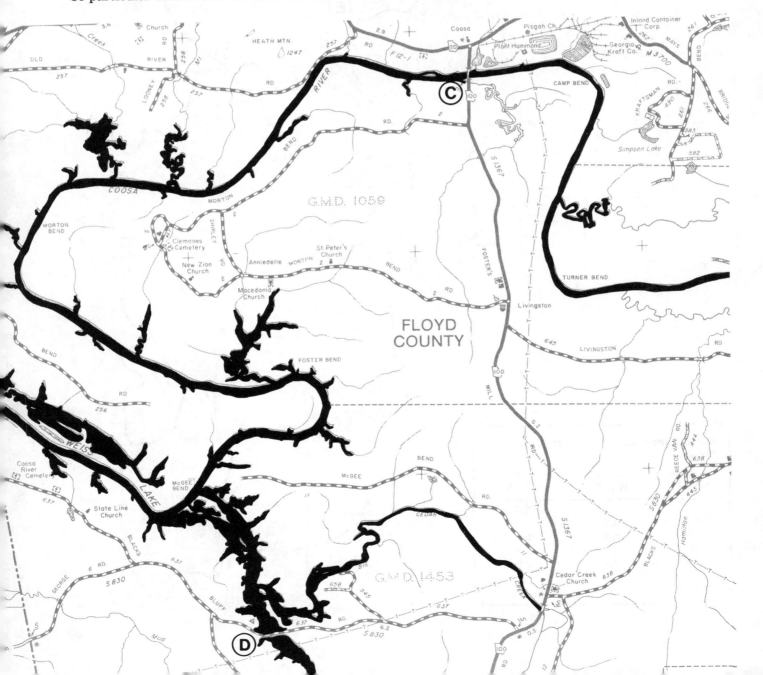

Section: Rome to Georgia–Alabama border

Counties: Floyd

Suitable For: Cruising

Appropriate For: Families, beginners, intermediates, advanced

Months Runnable: All

Interest Highlights: Scenery, wildlife, levees in Rome, history

Scenery: Uninspiring to pretty

Difficulty: International Scale   I
Numerical Points   4

Average Width: 30-70 ft.
Velocity: Slack to slow
Gradient: 1.2 ft./mi.

Runnable Water Level: Minimum   8.0 ft.
(Mayos Lock gauge)   Maximum   14.0 ft., open; up to flood stage, decked

Hazards: Strainers, powerboats

Scouting: None required

Portages: Mayos Lock and Dam (Rome)

Rescue Index: Accessible to accessible but difficult

Mean Water Temperature (°F)

| Jan 45 | Feb 46 | Mar 50 | Apr 56 | May 66 | Jun 73 |
| Jul 76 | Aug 75 | Sep 72 | Oct 65 | Nov 56 | Dec 49 |

Access Point	Access Code	Access Key
A	1357	1 Paved Road
B	1357	2 Unpaved Road
C	1357	3 Short Carry
D	1357	4 Long Carry
		5 Easy Grade
		6 Steep Incline
		7 Clear Trail
		8 Brush and Trees
		9 Launching Fee Charged
		10 Private Property, Need Permission
		11 No Access, Reference Only

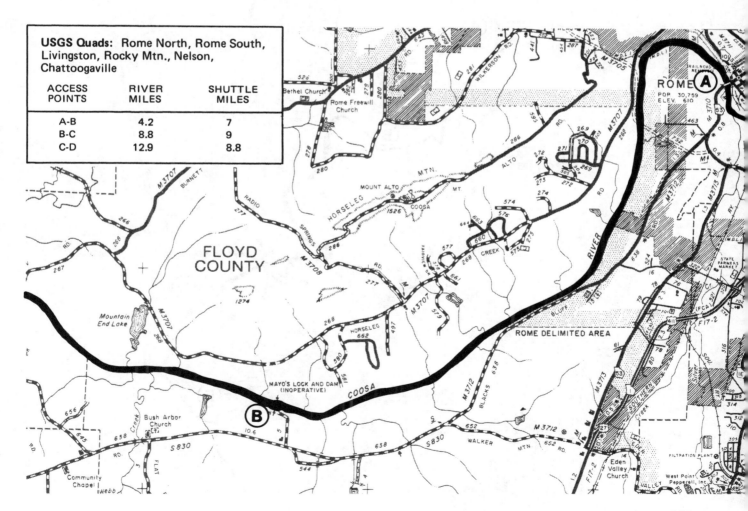

USGS Quads: Rome North, Rome South, Livingston, Rocky Mtn., Nelson, Chattoogaville

ACCESS POINTS	RIVER MILES	SHUTTLE MILES
A-B	4.2	7
B-C	8.8	9
C-D	12.9	8.8

Chattooga River of Chattooga County

There are two Chattooga Rivers in Georgia. One is a splendid wilderness whitewater stream; it forms the border between Georgia and South Carolina in the extreme northeastern corner of the state. The other Chattooga River gurgles gently in northwestern Georgia in Chattooga County.

The only thing the northwestern Chattooga River has in common with the northeastern Chattooga River is the name. The northwestern Chattooga flows through the towns of Trion, Summerville, and Lyerly. Although sandstone ridges like Dirtseller Mountain and Taylor Ridge rise on either side of the river, it has a docile gradient average of four feet per mile. There are no significant rapids.

Access to the river is good. Roads cross every two to five miles in the 27.9-mile course from just north of Trion (access point A) to Holland Chattoogaville Road (access point J). The Chattooga flows from there into Alabama. It is a major feeder for Weiss Lake.

USGS Quads: Trion, Summerville, Chattoogaville, Lyerly		
ACCESS POINTS	RIVER MILES	SHUTTLE MILES
A-B	2.1	2.25
B-C	3.5	3.25
C-D	0.7	2
D-E	2.0	2
E-F	4.6	6
F-G	2.9	4
G-H	4.8	5.5
H-I	1.7	2.25
I-J	5.6	6

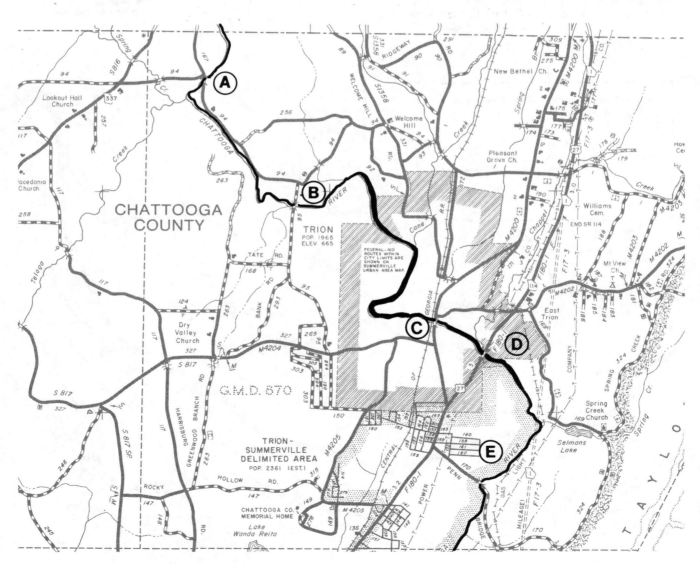

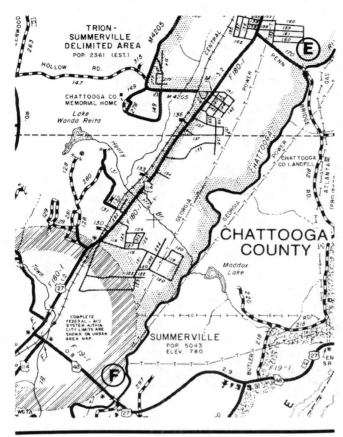

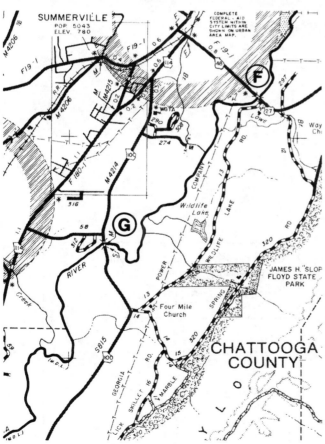

Section: Walker County line to Georgia–Alabama border

Counties: Chattooga

Suitable For: Cruising

Appropriate For: Families, beginners, intermediates, advanced

Months Runnable: All

Interest Highlights: Scenery

Scenery: Pleasant

Difficulty: International Scale   I
Numerical Points   3

Average Width: 20-40 ft.
Velocity: Slack
Gradient: 3.5 ft./mi.

Runnable Water Level Minimum 2.0 ft.
(US 27 gauge) Maximum 5.0 ft.

Hazards: Strainers, deadfalls

Scouting: None required

Portages: None required

Rescue Index: Accessible to accessible but difficult

Mean Water Temperature (°F)

Jan 47	Feb 49	Mar 52	Apr 58	May 65	Jun 70
Jul 73	Aug 72	Sep 68	Oct 60	Nov 53	Dec 50

Access Point	Access Code	Access Key
A	1357	1 Paved Road
B	1357	2 Unpaved Road
C	1357	3 Short Carry
D	1357	4 Long Carry
E	1357	5 Easy Grade
F	1357	6 Steep Incline
G	1357	7 Clear Trail
H	1357	8 Brush and Trees
I	1357	9 Launching Fee Charged
J	1357	10 Private Property, Need Permission
		11 No Access, Reference Only

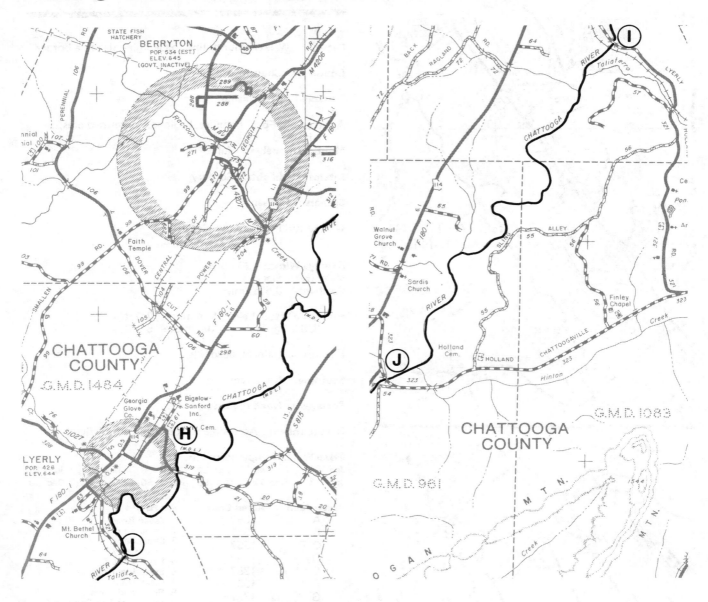

USGS Quads: Trion, Summerville, Chattoogaville, Lyerly		
ACCESS POINTS	RIVER MILES	SHUTTLE MILES
A-B	2.1	2.25
B-C	3.5	3.25
C-D	0.7	2
D-E	2.0	2
E-F	4.6	6
F-G	2.9	4
G-H	4.8	5.5
H-I	1.7	2.25
I-J	5.6	6

Section: Walker County line to Georgia–Alabama border

Counties: Chattooga

Suitable For: Cruising

Appropriate For: Families, beginners, intermediates, advanced

Months Runnable: All

Interest Highlights: Scenery

Scenery: Pleasant

Difficulty: International Scale I
Numerical Points 3

Average Width: 20-40 ft.
Velocity: Slack
Gradient: 3.5 ft./mi.

Runnable Water Level Minimum 2.0 ft.
(US 27 gauge) Maximum 5.0 ft.

Hazards: Strainers, deadfalls

Coppermine Rapid, Chestatee River.

Scouting: None required

Portages: None required

Rescue Index: Accessible to accessible but difficult

Mean Water Temperature (°F)

Jan 47	Feb 49	Mar 52	Apr 58	May 65	Jun 70
Jul 73	Aug 72	Sep 68	Oct 60	Nov 53	Dec 50

Access Point	Access Code	Access Key
A	1357	1 Paved Road
B	1357	2 Unpaved Road
C	1357	3 Short Carry
D	1357	4 Long Carry
E	1357	5 Easy Grade
F	1357	6 Steep Incline
G	1357	7 Clear Trail
H	1357	8 Brush and Trees
I	1357	9 Launching Fee Charged
J	1357	10 Private Property, Need Permission
		11 No Access, Reference Only

Chapter 5

Streams of the Eastern Piedmont

North Fork Broad River

The North Fork Broad River is a Broad River tributary with its headwaters in Stephens County near Toccoa. It flows out of Stephens County and traverses most of Franklin County. Three miles west of Franklin Springs it merges with the Middle Fork Broad River and is therafter known as the Broad River.

Although it is navigable in the hilly areas of southern Stephens County, the consistently mild gradient produces few rapids or shoals. A great deal of the river's course in Franklin County is slow flowing and marshy. From GA 154 (access point E) to GA 327 (access point J), the gradient is less than four feet per mile. Most paddlers prefer to begin at GA 327 (access point J) or GA 51 (access point K). Here the progress of the boater is aided by an increase in flow volume and a gradient of over thirteen feet per mile. Streamside environment is mostly miles of secluded paddling and potential wildlife encounters. It is inadvisable, however, to attempt the sections above GA 327 unless there has been average or above-average rainfall.

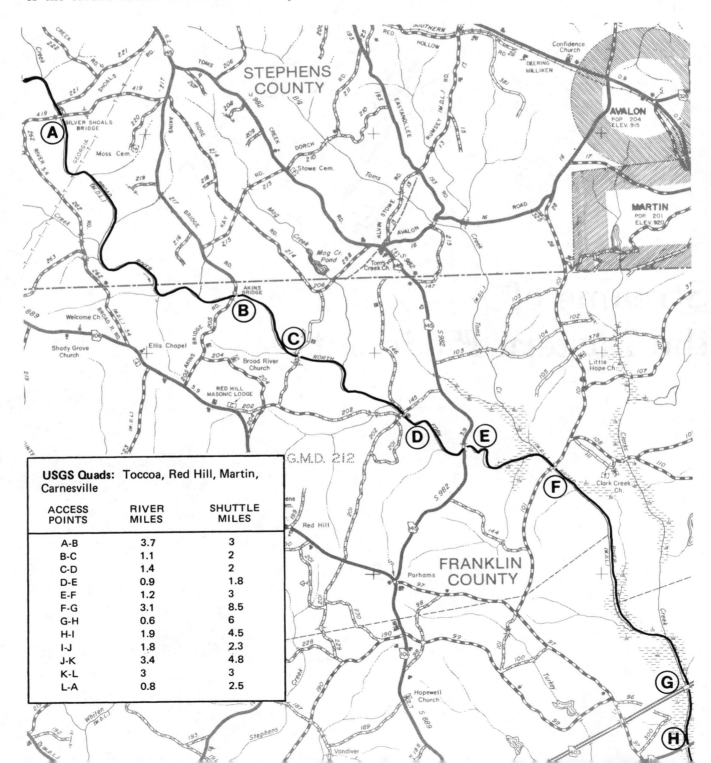

USGS Quads: Toccoa, Red Hill, Martin, Carnesville		
ACCESS POINTS	RIVER MILES	SHUTTLE MILES
A-B	3.7	3
B-C	1.1	2
C-D	1.4	2
D-E	0.9	1.8
E-F	1.2	3
F-G	3.1	8.5
G-H	0.6	6
H-I	1.9	4.5
I-J	1.8	2.3
J-K	3.4	4.8
K-L	3	3
L-A	0.8	2.5

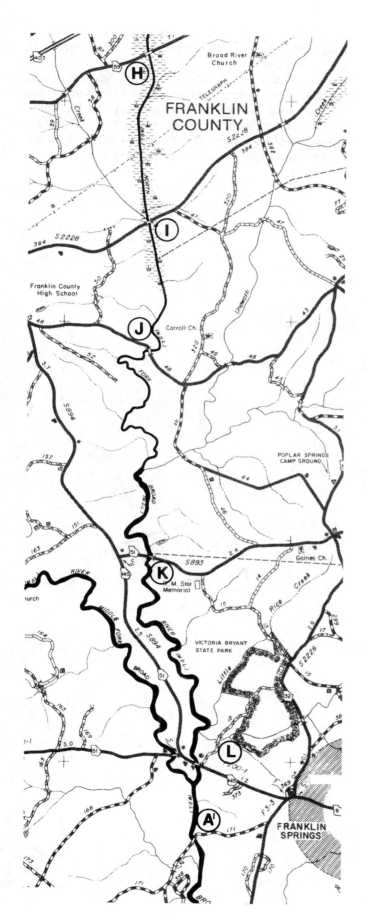

Section: Silver Shoals Bridge to Middle Fork Broad River

Counties: Stephens, Franklin

Suitable For: Cruising, camping

Appropriate For: Families, beginners, intermediates, advanced

Months Runnable: Upper sections, January through July; lower sections, all months

Interest Highlights: Scenery

Scenery: Fair to pretty

Difficulty: International Scale I-II
Numerical Points 1-8

Average Width: 15-45 ft.
Gradient: 7.8 ft./mi.
Velocity: Slack to moderate

Runnable Water Level: Minimum No gauge
Maximum Up to flood stage

Hazards: Strainers, deadfalls

Scouting: None required

Portages: None required

Rescue Index: Accessible to accessible but difficult

Mean Water Temperature (°F)

| Jan 43 | Feb 44 | Mar 49 | Apr 58 | May 66 | Jun 74 |
| Jul 77 | Aug 75 | Sep 69 | Oct 60 | Nov 52 | Dec 46 |

Source of Additional Information: Franklin County Sheriff Dept. (706) 384-7111

Access Point	Access Code	Access Key
A	1357	1 Paved Road
B	1357	2 Unpaved Road
C	2357	3 Short Carry
D	2357	4 Long Carry
E	1357	5 Easy Grade
F	1357	6 Steep Incline
G	1358(11)	7 Clear Trail
H	1358	8 Brush and Trees
I	1358	9 Launching Fee Charged
J	1357	10 Private Property, Need Permission
K	1357	11 No Access, Reference Only
L	1357	
A¹	1357	

¹On the main Broad River

Middle Fork Broad River

The Middle Fork Broad River is born in Habersham County in the outflow of Lake Russell and flows across Banks County into Franklin County. In periods of favorable rainfall it becomes suitable for canoeing in the northwestern corner of Franklin County.

The proximate terrain is usually rolling forested hills but occasional intrusions of farm land make man's influence easily felt. The drop in elevation averages less than five feet per mile. Some sections are so slack that no drop is discernible. Bridges are frequent, usually less than two miles apart, so access is good.

Some Class I-II shoals are found, with the most notable ones being between the Atkinson bridge (access point K) and GA 51 (access point L). There are twenty miles of cruisable water between access point A and the junction with the North Fork Broad River where the Broad River is created.

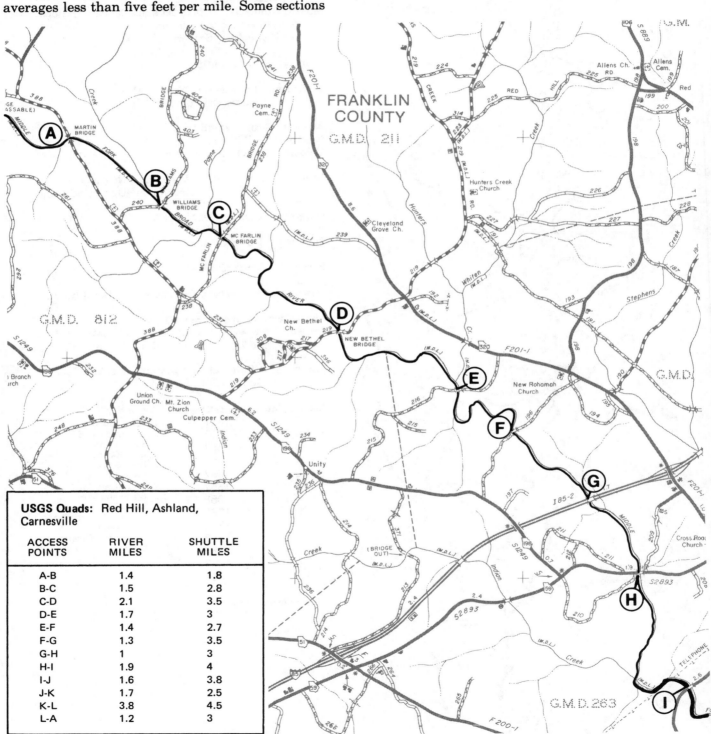

USGS Quads: Red Hill, Ashland, Carnesville		
ACCESS POINTS	RIVER MILES	SHUTTLE MILES
A-B	1.4	1.8
B-C	1.5	2.8
C-D	2.1	3.5
D-E	1.7	3
E-F	1.4	2.7
F-G	1.3	3.5
G-H	1	3
H-I	1.9	4
I-J	1.6	3.8
J-K	1.7	2.5
K-L	3.8	4.5
L-A	1.2	3

Section: Martins Bridge to North Fork Broad River

Counties: Franklin

Suitable For: Cruising

Appropriate For: Families, beginners, intermediates, advanced

Months Runnable: January through July except for lower sections

Interest Highlights: Scenery

Scenery: Pretty

Difficulty: International Scale I (II)
Numerical Points   5-7

Average Width: 20-40 ft.
Velocity: Slack to slow
Gradient: 4.8 ft./mi.

Runnable Water Level: Minimum   No gauge
Maximum   Up to flood stage

Hazards: Strainers, deadfalls

Scouting: None required

Portages: None required

Rescue Index: Accessible to accessible but difficult

Mean Water Temperature (°F)

| Jan 43 | Feb 45 | Mar 49 | Apr 57 | May 67 | Jun 74 |
| Jul 77 | Aug 76 | Sep 68 | Oct 61 | Nov 52 | Dec 45 |

Source of Additional Information: Franklin County Sheriff Dept. (706) 384-7111

Access Point	Access Code	Access Key
A	1357	1 Paved Road
B	2357	2 Unpaved Road
C	2357	3 Short Carry
D	1357	4 Long Carry
E	2357	5 Easy Grade
F	2357	6 Steep Incline
G	1357 (11)	7 Clear Trail
H	1357	8 Brush and Trees
I	1357	9 Launching Fee Charged
J	1357	10 Private Property, Need Permission
K	2357	11 No Access, Reference Only
L	1357	
A¹	1357	

¹On the main Broad River

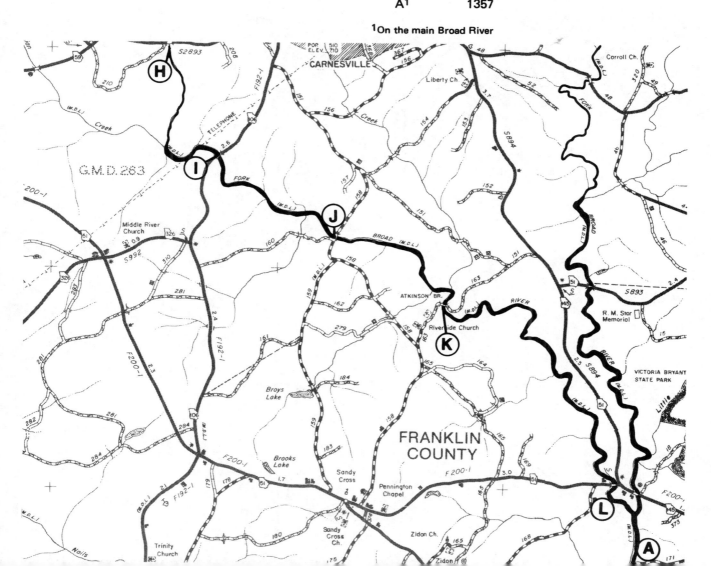

Hudson River

The Hudson river is a Broad River tributary. It is born in western Banks County and flows across that county and becomes the boundary marker between Franklin and Madison County. It enters the Broad River four miles south of Franklin Springs.

For those who desire an extremely athletic experience portaging over, under, around, and through many deadfalls, there are many possible launch points in Banks County. Cruising does not become sensible, however, until the Hudson crosses GA 59 to the east of Homer and I-85. Here the stream is still quite narrow and shallow, and deadfalls blocking the stream are still frequent.

Below GA 326 (access point D) the Hudson changes its character and becomes more lively. Many rippling shoals keep the boater entertained, but none of the shoals is a problem to navigate. The best section is from GA 106 (access point E) to the Broad River junction.

USGS Quads: Homer, Ashland, Ila, Danielsville North

ACCESS POINTS	RIVER MILES	SHUTTLE MILES
A-B	2.5	3.3
B-C	1.5	3
C-D	3	5.5
D-E	6.1	6.5
E-F	3.7	7.5
F-C	6	7.3

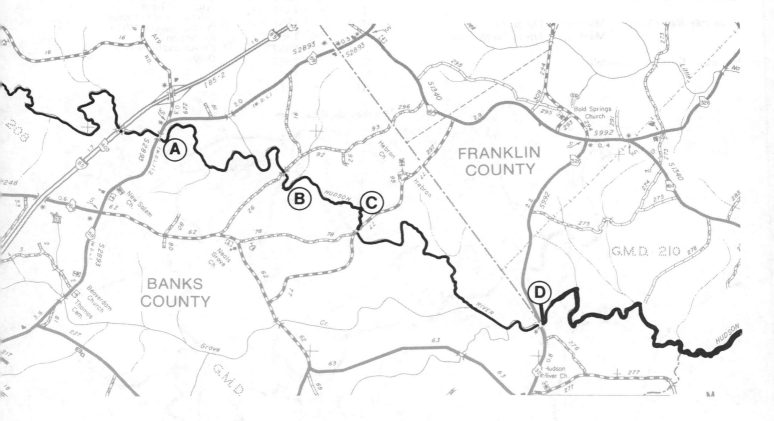

Section: GA 59 to US 29 (near Broad River)

Counties: Banks, Franklin, Madison

Suitable For: Cruising, camping

Appropriate For: Families, beginners, intermediates, advanced

Months Runnable: All except during dry spells

Interest Highlights: Scenery

Scenery: Beautiful, especially in spring and fall

Difficulty: International Scale I-II
Numerical Points 9

Average Width: 15-33 ft.
Velocity: Slack to fast
Gradient: 5.4 to 8.9 ft./mi.

Runnable Water Level: Minimum 1.5 ft.
(GA 15 gauge)[1] Maximum 5 ft.

Hazards: Strainers, deadfalls

Scouting: None required

Portages: Around deadfalls

Rescue Index: Accessible to accessible but difficult

Mean Water Temperature (°F)

Jan 42	Feb 43	Mar 47	Apr 55	May 62	Jun 69
Jul 71	Aug 68	Sep 66	Oct 58	Nov 51	Dec 45

Source of Additional Information:
High Country (404) 391-9657

Access Point	Access Code	Access Key
A	1357	1 Paved Road
B	2357	2 Unpaved Road
C	1357	3 Short Carry
D	1357	4 Long Carry
E	1357	5 Easy Grade
F	1357	6 Steep Incline
C[2]	1357	7 Clear Trail
		8 Brush and Trees
		9 Launching Fee Charged
		10 Private Property, Need Permission
		11 No Access, Reference Only

[1] In Homer
[2] On the Broad River

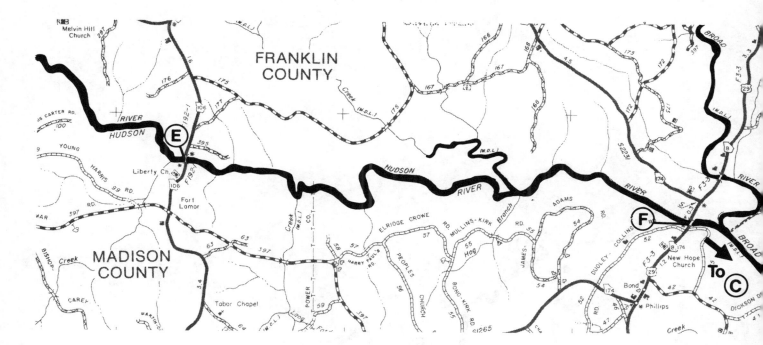

South Fork Broad River

The South Fork Broad River is a short but sweet Broad River tributary. Rising in northwestern Madison County, it flows southeastward through predominantly agricultural land and forms the border between Madison and Oglethorpe counties for its final fourteen miles before entering the Broad River.

At most water levels the uppermost access for boating would be at GA 22 just south of the city of Comer. The South Fork takes a lazy winding course with no measurable rapids down to Watson Mill State Park. There is an old covered bridge at the park that is interesting to investigate. It is the longest covered bridge in the state. The park also contains permanent picnic facilities.

Just below the covered bridge is a small dam that must be portaged. There are rapids below the dam that may be run if water conditions are favorable. These rapids may reach Class III difficulty in high water.

The river continues its sinuous meandering to its junction with the main Broad River. The only other shoals of appreciable difficulty appear below access point D. A three-foot dam creates a slack backwater just below the bridge. The dam should be portaged and rapids scouted. Usually the rapids will not exceed Class II. One final series of shoals is approximately two miles farther down, just above the Broad River junction. The next access point is eight miles down the Broad River at GA 77 (Broad River access point F).

USGS Quads: Danielsville South, Carlton, Elberton West			
ACCESS POINTS	RIVER MILES	SHUTTLE MILES
A-B	3	4.8
B-C	2.3	6.5
C-D	5.1	5
D-F	11.2	10

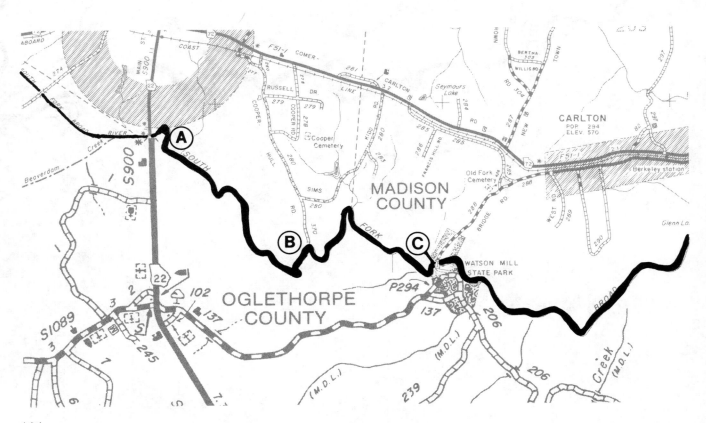

Section: GA 22 (near Comer) to Broad River

Counties: Madison, Oglethorpe

Suitable For: Cruising

Appropriate For: Families, beginners, intermediates, advanced

Months Runnable: All

Interest Highlights: Scenery, history

Scenery: Pretty

Difficulty: International Scale I-II
Numerical Points 8

Average Width: 20-50 ft.
Velocity: Slack to slow
Gradient: 3 to 10+ ft./mi.

Runnable Water Level: Minimum 2.0 ft.
(GA 72 gauge) Maximum 12 ft.

Hazards: Strainers, deadfalls, dams

Scouting: Rapids below Watson Mill dam

Portages: Dam at Watson Mill and small dam before Broad River

Rescue Index: Accessible to accessible but difficult

Mean Water Temperature (°F)

| Jan 43 | Feb 44 | Mar 48 | Apr 56 | May 65 | Jun 73 |
| Jul 76 | Aug 75 | Sep 68 | Oct 61 | Nov 53 | Dec 46 |

Source of Additional Information: Broad River Outpost (706) 795-3242

Access Point	Access Code
A	1357
B	2357
C	1357
D	1357
F1	1357

[1] On the Broad River

Access Key
1 Paved Road
2 Unpaved Road
3 Short Carry
4 Long Carry
5 Easy Grade
6 Steep Incline
7 Clear Trail
8 Brush and Trees
9 Launching Fee Charged
10 Private Property, Need Permission
11 No Access, Reference Only

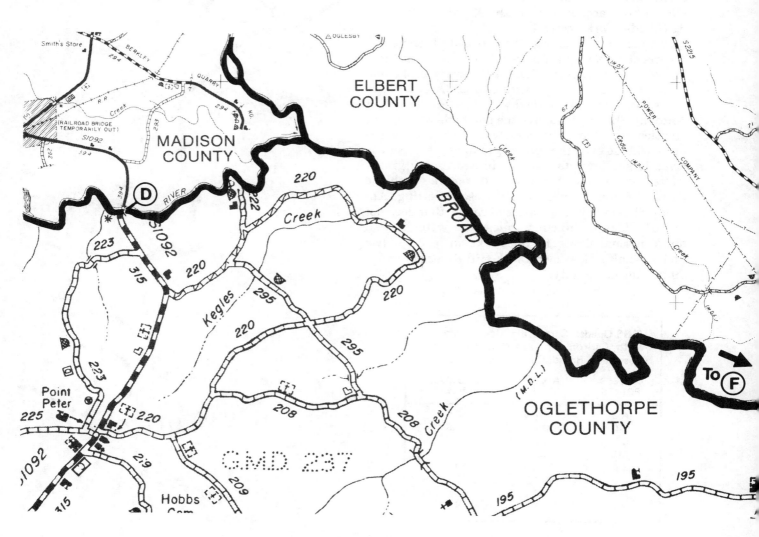

Broad River

The Broad River is created by the confluence of the North Fork Broad River and the Middle Fork Broad River in Franklin County about two miles west of Franklin Springs. It flows out of Franklin County into Madison County and becomes the boundary between Elbert County and Madison and Oglethorpe counties. It is a tributary of the Savannah River system.

Because of the volume of its feeder streams, the Broad is suitable for canoeing year round except in periods of extreme drought. There are over fifty miles of good canoeing between Franklin Springs and Clark Hill Reservoir.

For most of its course the Broad is a pastoral stream, eminently suited for beginning canoeists and those desiring a relaxed canoe-camping experience. The Broad passes near many towns but goes through none of them, so much of the scenery remains unspoiled woodland or minimally developed agricultural land. Wildlife is abundant, particularly birds, small mammals, and turtles.

To float the entire length of the Broad River, access may be found on the North Fork on GA 145 (North Fork access L) or on the Middle Fork on GA 51 (Middle Fork access L).

The moderate gradient of the Broad River creates a current that is quite powerful at times, but there are very few rapids. Class I-II rapids are found between GA 281 (access point C) and GA 172 (access point D). Other noteworthy rapids are found at Anthony Shoals just above the point where the river empties into Clark Hill Reservoir. Here the river is quite wide so even though the gradient is steeper the river is shallow, its force is diluted. Many grassy islets and the rocky stream bed combine with the rushing water to make a picturesque setting. Anthony Shoals is a long series of rapids that does not exceed Class II difficulty unless the water is well above normal flow. The final take-out point is two and one-half miles down Clark Hill Reservoir at GA 79 in Lincoln County.

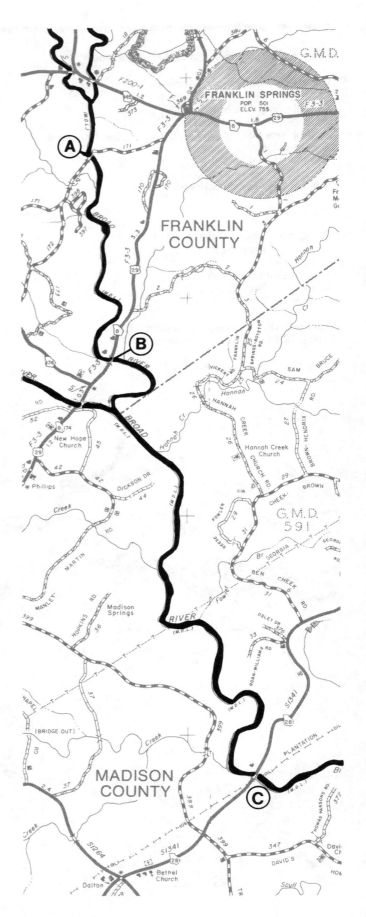

USGS Quads: Carnesville, Danielsville North, Carlton, Elberton West, Jacksons Crossroads, Broad, Chennault

ACCESS POINTS	RIVER MILES	SHUTTLE MILES
A-B	2.7	3.5
B-C	6.7	8.5
C-D	5.5	5.5
D-E	9.2	12.5
E-F	11.6	10
F-G	8.4	13
G-H	6.8	13
H-I	2.4	8

Section: GA 145 to Clark Hill Reservoir

Counties: Franklin, Elbert, Madison, Oglethorpe, Wilkes, Lincoln

Suitable For: Cruising, camping

Appropriate For: Families, beginners, intermediates, advanced

Months Runnable: All

Interest Highlights: Scenery, wildlife

Scenery: Pretty

Difficulty: International Scale I-II
Numerical Points 4-8

Average Width: 30-100 ft.
Velocity: Slack to moderate
Gradient: 4.8 ft./mi.. (8+ ft./mi. in places)

Runnable Water Level: Minimum 1.5 ft.
(GA 72 gauge)　　Maximum 12 ft.

Hazards: Strainers, deadfalls; powerboats on Clark Hill Reservoir

Scouting: None required

Portages: None required

Rescue Index: Accessible to accessible but difficult

Mean Water Temperature (°F)

| Jan 43 | Feb 46 | Mar 50 | Apr 60 | May 69 | Jun 75 |
| Jul 77 | Aug 75 | Sep 71 | Oct 61 | Nov 52 | Dec 45 |

Source of Additional Information: Broad River Outpost (706) 795-3242

Access Point	Access Code	Access Key
A	1357	1 Paved Road
B	1357	2 Unpaved Road
C	1357	3 Short Carry
D	1357	4 Long Carry
E	1357	5 Easy Grade
F	1357	6 Steep Incline
G[1]	1357	7 Clear Trail
H	2357	8 Brush and Trees
I	1367	9 Launching Fee Charged
		10 Private Property, Need Permission
		11 No Access, Reference Only

[1] Boat ramp

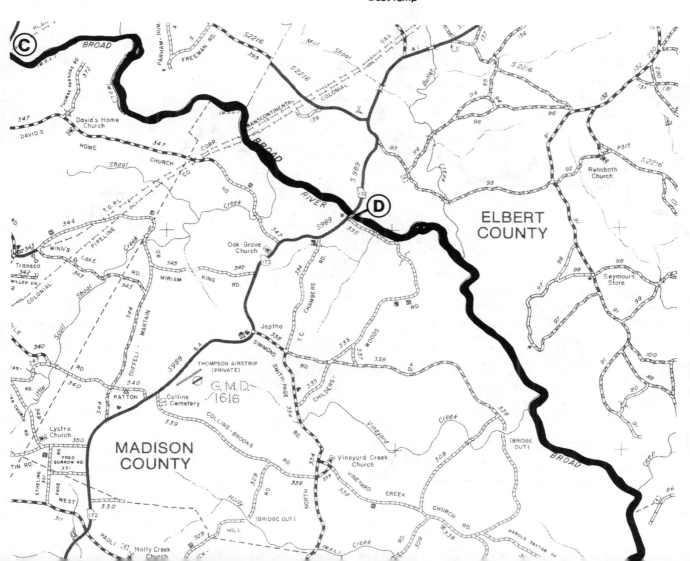

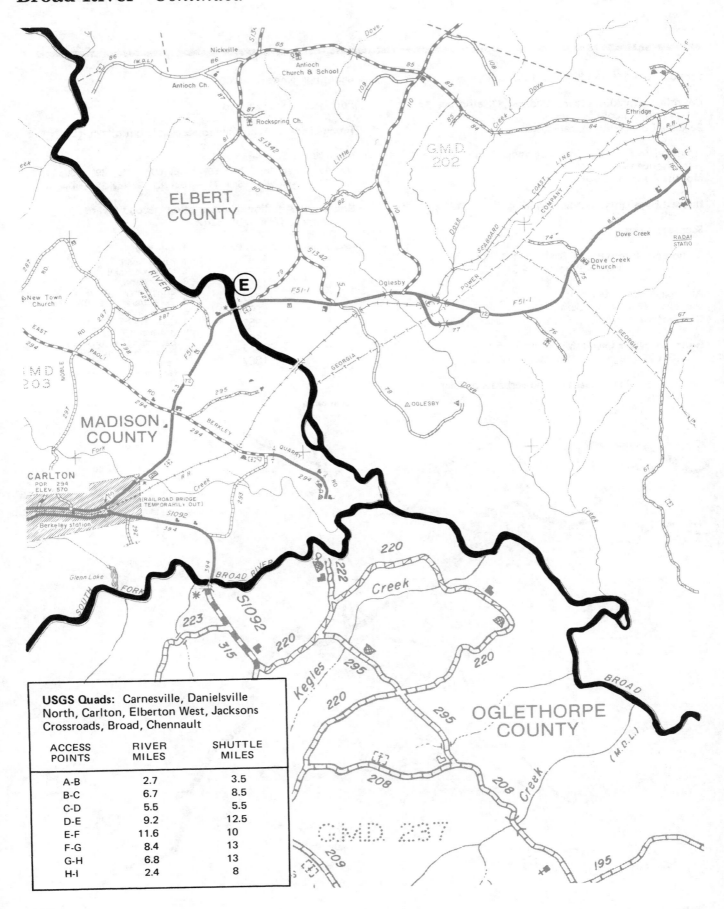

USGS Quads: Carnesville, Danielsville North, Carlton, Elberton West, Jacksons Crossroads, Broad, Chennault

ACCESS POINTS	RIVER MILES	SHUTTLE MILES
A-B	2.7	3.5
B-C	6.7	8.5
C-D	5.5	5.5
D-E	9.2	12.5
E-F	11.6	10
F-G	8.4	13
G-H	6.8	13
H-I	2.4	8

Section: GA 145 to Clark Hill Reservoir

Counties: Franklin, Elbert, Madison, Oglethorpe, Wilkes, Lincoln

Suitable For: Cruising, camping

Appropriate For: Families, beginners, intermediates, advanced

Months Runnable: All

Interest Highlights: Scenery, wildlife

Scenery: Pretty

Difficulty: International Scale   I-II
Numerical Points   4-8

Average Width: 30-100 ft.
Velocity: Slack to moderate
Gradient: 4.8 ft./mi.. (8+ ft./mi. in places)

Runnable Water Level: Minimum   1.5 ft.
(GA 72 gauge)   Maximum   12 ft.

Hazards: Strainers, deadfalls; powerboats on Clark Hill Reservoir

Scouting: None required

Portages: None required

Rescue Index: Accessible to accessible but difficult

Mean Water Temperature (°F)

| Jan 43 | Feb 46 | Mar 50 | Apr 60 | May 69 | Jun 75 |
| Jul 77 | Aug 75 | Sep 71 | Oct 61 | Nov 52 | Dec 45 |

Source of Additional Information: Broad River Outpost (706) 795-3242

Access Point	Access Code	Access Key
A	1357	1 Paved Road
B	1357	2 Unpaved Road
C	1357	3 Short Carry
D	1357	4 Long Carry
E	1357	5 Easy Grade
F	1357	6 Steep Incline
G[1]	1357	7 Clear Trail
H	2357	8 Brush and Trees
I	1367	9 Launching Fee Charged
		10 Private Property, Need Permission
		11 No Access, Reference Only

[1] Boat ramp

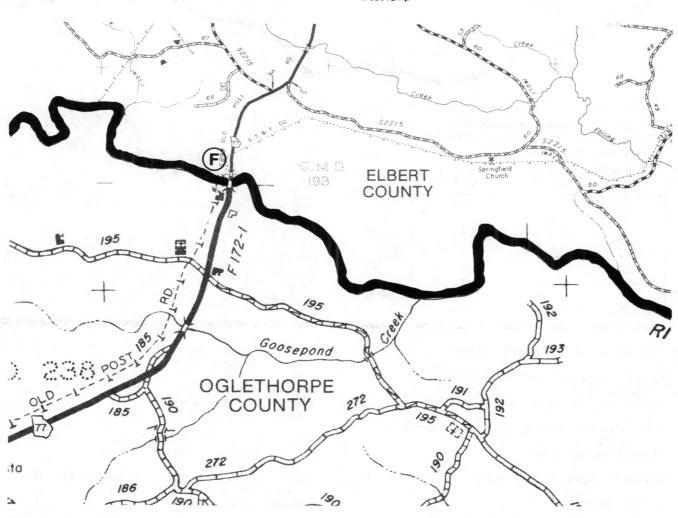

Broad River—*Continued*

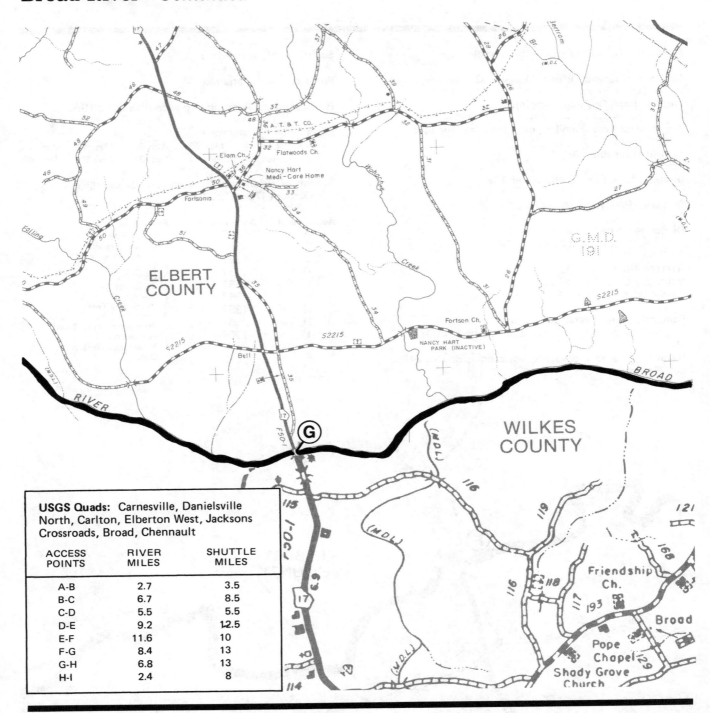

USGS Quads: Carnesville, Danielsville North, Carlton, Elberton West, Jacksons Crossroads, Broad, Chennault

ACCESS POINTS	RIVER MILES	SHUTTLE MILES
A-B	2.7	3.5
B-C	6.7	8.5
C-D	5.5	5.5
D-E	9.2	12.5
E-F	11.6	10
F-G	8.4	13
G-H	6.8	13
H-I	2.4	8

Section: GA 145 to Clark Hill Reservoir

Counties: Franklin, Elbert, Madison, Oglethorpe, Wilkes, Lincoln

Suitable For: Cruising, camping

Appropriate For: Families, beginners, intermediates, advanced

Months Runnable: All

Interest Highlights: Scenery, wildlife

Scenery: Pretty

Difficulty: International Scale I-II
Numerical Points 4-8

Average Width: 30-100 ft.
Velocity: Slack to moderate
Gradient: 4.8 ft./mi.. (8+ ft./mi. in places)

Runnable Water Level: Minimum 1.5 ft.
(GA 72 gauge) Maximum 12 ft.

Hazards: Strainers, deadfalls; powerboats on Clark Hill Reservoir
Scouting: None required

120

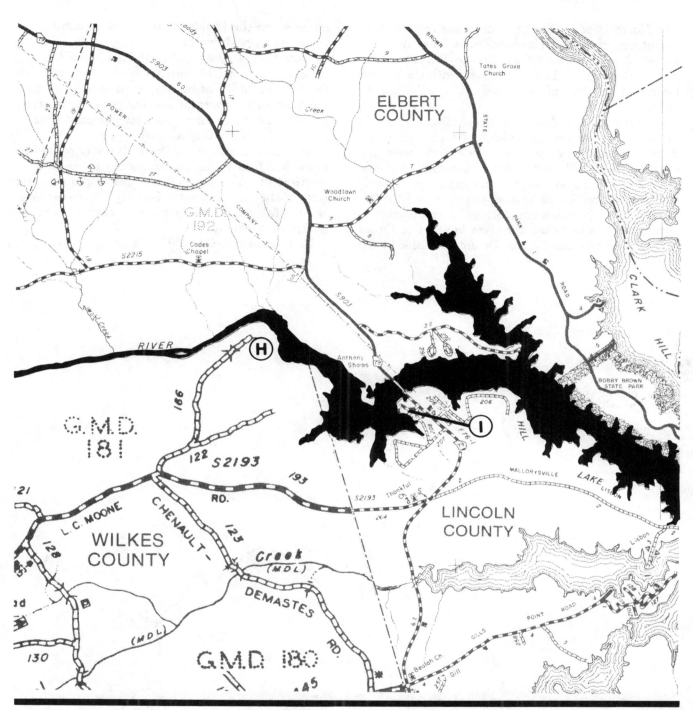

Portages: None required

Rescue Index: Accessible to accessible but difficult

Mean Water Temperature (°F)

Jan 43	Feb 46	Mar 50	Apr 60	May 69	Jun 75
Jul 77	Aug 75	Sep 71	Oct 61	Nov 52	Dec 45

Source of Additional Information: Broad River
    Outpost (706) 795-3242

Access Point	Access Code
A	1357
B	1357
C	1357
D	1357
E	1357
F	1357
G[1]	1357
H	2357
I	1367

Access Key
1 Paved Road
2 Unpaved Road
3 Short Carry
4 Long Carry
5 Easy Grade
6 Steep Incline
7 Clear Trail
8 Brush and Trees
9 Launching Fee Charged
10 Private Property, Need Permission
11 No Access, Reference Only

[1]Boat ramp

North Oconee River

The North Oconee River has its headwaters in Hall County northeast of Gainesville. It flows into and across Jackson County to Clarke County. After passing through Athens, it merges with the Middle Oconee and thereafter is known simply as the Oconee River.

Because of its size, the North Oconee is not attractive to boaters until it enters Jackson County. Access is possible at several points to the west and south of Maysville. The flow is through woodland and farm land and contains no rapids or hazards until below the GA 82 bridge (access point E). A few hundred yards below the bridge a small dam is encountered and below the dam is a set of rapids known as Hurricane Shoals. Do not be misled by the

name since the rapids would barely reach Class II intensity in high water.

From I-85 (access point D) to the edge of Athens at access point L, the North Oconee traverses over twenty-two miles of bucolic environment. A gradient average of less than five feet per mile creates no rapids. There are many possible camping sites and good roads for boating access.

Athens is the home of the University of Georgia. Some will find a side trip to this city interesting and worthwhile. The river flows through the eastern part of the city and some heavily populated areas. Be careful where you park your car or leave your boating equipment.

Just below the GA 10/US 78 bridge (access point

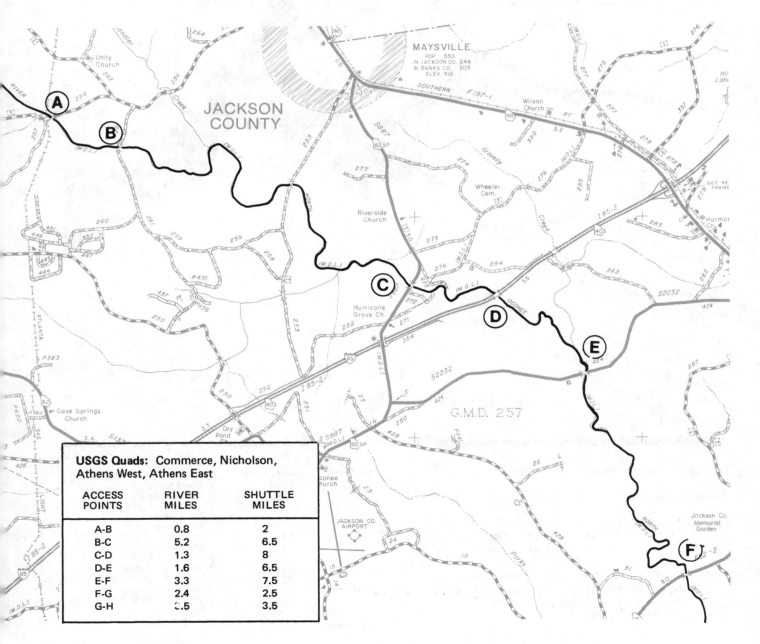

USGS Quads: Commerce, Nicholson, Athens West, Athens East		
ACCESS POINTS	RIVER MILES	SHUTTLE MILES
A-B	0.8	2
B-C	5.2	6.5
C-D	1.3	8
D-E	1.6	6.5
E-F	3.3	7.5
F-G	2.4	2.5
G-H	C.5	3.5

O) the remains of an old dam create a rapid. Scout this one before running it. Its difficulty ranges from Class II to Class III, depending on the water level.

Below access point P the river begins to slow down and soon becomes the backwater for the small dam, Oconee Dam, approximately 2.8 miles below P. Portage on either side. Just below the dam is a series of Class II rapids extending almost to the Whitehall bridge (access point Q). From Whitehall to the junction with the Middle Oconee River are three miles of wooded shorelines and rippling shoals. After the North Oconee and the Middle Oconee join, the river becomes known as the Oconee. An additional three miles of paddling brings one to the next access at County Line Road bridge (access A on main Oconee).

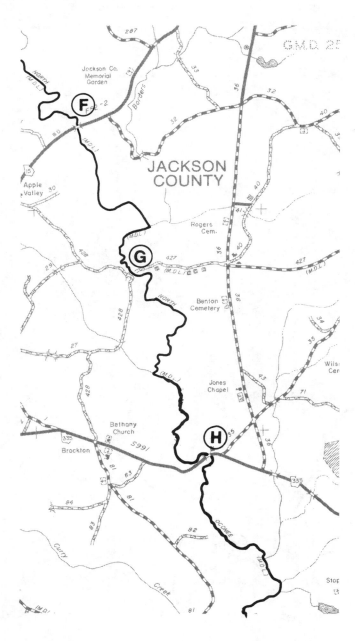

Section: Maysville to GA 335 (near Nicholson)

Counties: Jackson

Suitable For: Cruising, camping

Appropriate For: Families, beginners, intermediates, advanced

Months Runnable: Upper sections, January through July; lower sections, all year

Interest Highlights: Scenery, local culture

Scenery: Unattractive to pretty

Difficulty: International Scale I-III
Numerical Points 8

Average Width: 15-35 ft.
Velocity: Moderate
Gradient: 4.5 ft./mi.

Runnable Water Level: Minimum 1.2 ft.
(US 29 gauge)[1] Maximum 10.0 ft., open; up to flood stage, decked

Hazards: Strainers, deadfalls

Scouting: Old dam below GA 10/US 78 bridge

Portages: Oconee Dam

Rescue Index: Accessible to accessible but difficult

Mean Water Temperature (°F)

| Jan 42 | Feb 44 | Mar 50 | Apr 58 | May 67 | Jun 73 |
| Jul 75 | Aug 73 | Sep 69 | Oct 59 | Nov 52 | Dec 45 |

Access Point	Access Code	Access Key
A	1357	1 Paved Road
B	2357	2 Unpaved Road
C	1357	3 Short Carry
D	1357	4 Long Carry
E	1357	5 Easy Grade
F	1357	6 Steep Incline
G	2367	7 Clear Trail
H	1357	8 Brush and Trees
		9 Launching Fee Charged
		10 Private Property, Need Permission
		11 No Access, Reference Only

[1]On the Middle Oconee River

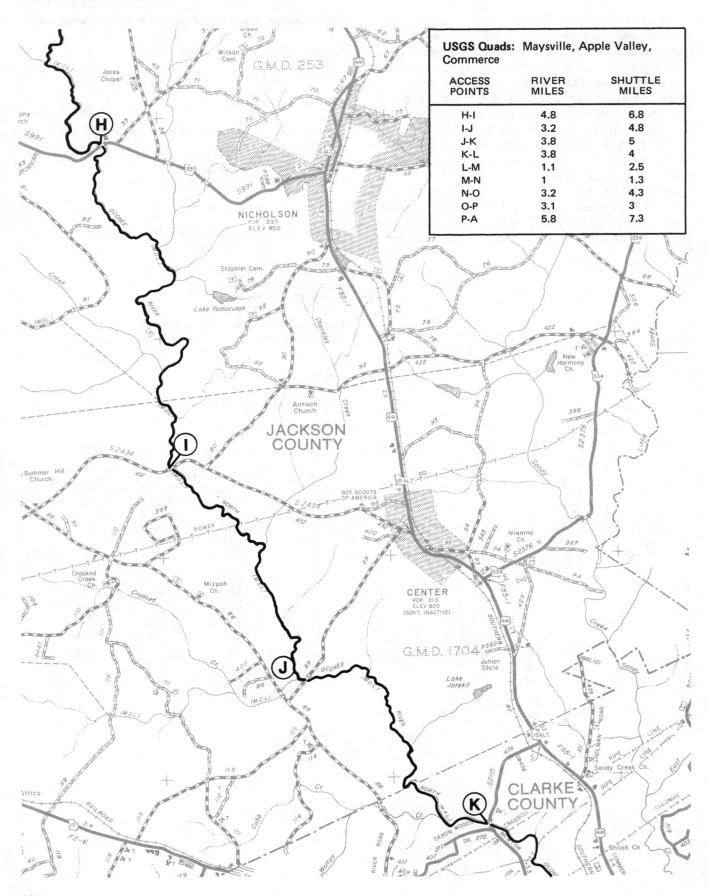

ACCESS POINTS	RIVER MILES	SHUTTLE MILES
H-I	4.8	6.8
I-J	3.2	4.8
J-K	3.8	5
K-L	3.8	4
L-M	1.1	2.5
M-N	1	1.3
N-O	3.2	4.3
O-P	3.1	3
P-A	5.8	7.3

USGS Quads: Maysville, Apple Valley, Commerce

Section: GA 335 (near Nicholson) to Athens

Counties: Jackson, Clarke

Suitable For: Cruising, camping

Appropriate For: Families, beginners, intermediates, advanced

Months Runnable: All

Interest Highlights: Scenery

Scenery: Unattractive to pretty

Difficulty: International Scale I-II
Numerical Points 8

Average Width: 15-35 ft.
Velocity: Moderate
Gradient: 4.5 ft./mi.

Runnable Water Level: Minimum 1.2 ft.
(US 29 gauge)[1] Maximum 10.0 ft., open;
up to flood stage, decked

Hazards: Dams, strainers, deadfalls

Scouting: None required

Portages: Dam below access point P

Rescue Index: Accessible to accessible but difficult

Mean Water Temperature (°F)

Jan 42	Feb 44	Mar 50	Apr 58	May 67	Jun 73
Jul 75	Aug 73	Sep 59	Oct 59	Nov 52	Dec 45

Access Point	Access Code	Access Key
H	1357	1 Paved Road
I	1357	2 Unpaved Road
J	1357	3 Short Carry
K	1357	4 Long Carry
L	1357	5 Easy Grade
M	1357	6 Steep Incline
N	1357	7 Clear Trail
O	1357	8 Brush and Trees
P	1357	9 Launching Fee Charged
A[2]	1357	10 Private Property, Need Permission
		11 No Access, Reference Only

[1]On the Middle Oconee River
[2]On the Oconee River

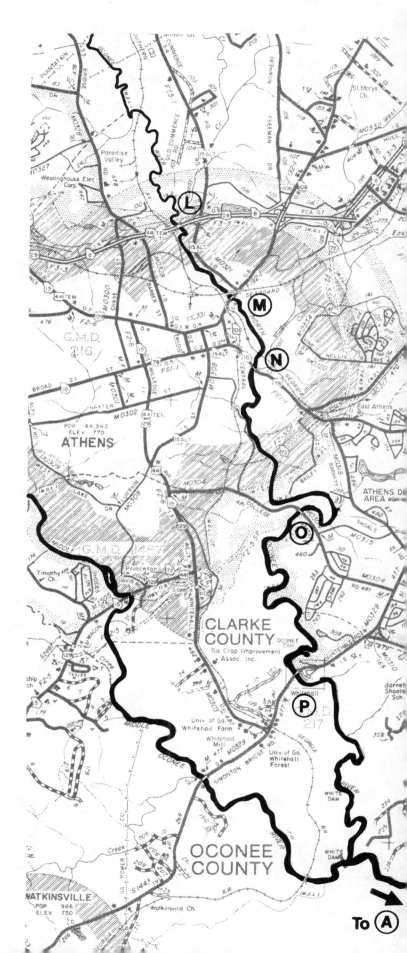

Middle Oconee River

The Middle Oconee River is one of the major headwater feeders of the Oconee River system. If favorable water conditions exist, boaters may begin at US 129 south of Pendergrass. The river flows across Jackson County and into Clarke County where it merges with the North Oconee River to create the Oconee.

Navigation in the upper regions may not be desirable for many boaters. Near US 129 a large poultry processing plant contributes some refuse to the stream. The river moves slowly through a swampy area until access point E, 5.5 miles downstream. Sections of the stream have been artificially channeled. However, this segment of the river has proven to be good for duck hunting.

The river's flow is increased by the entrance of the Mulberry River below GA 319 (access point F), but no rapids or hazards are encountered until you pass beyond GA 330 (access point H) northwest of Athens. Below the bridge a small dam blocks the stream and forms a lake. Two large islands bisect the lake. Portage the dam on the right to run the rapids (Class II) below.

After drifting slowly below the railroad bridge approximately five miles below GA 330, the river again becomes the backwater for a small lake. Beyond this dam the river becomes very wide and rocky but no formidable rapids are created. More small dams are encountered three miles below US 78 (access point K) and there's another dam two miles below access point M, Simonton Bridge Road. This dam is less than one mile above the junction with the North Oconee. Take out on County Line Road (Oconee River access A). The sections of the river below US 78 provide a feeling of woodland seclusion in spite of the proximity of the city of Athens. The blight on this section is the dumping from the sewage treatment plant below US 441 (access point L).

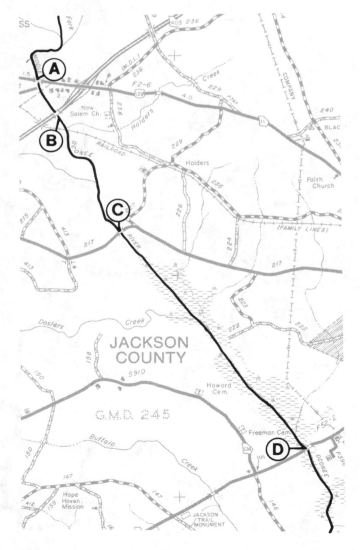

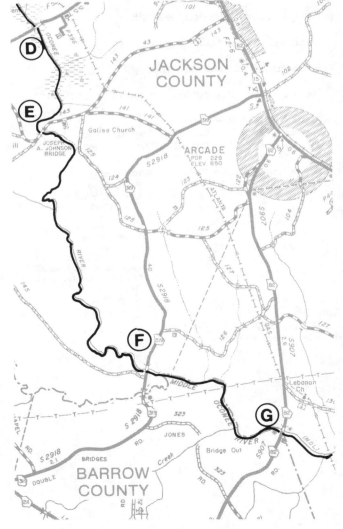

Section: GA 129 to Athens

Counties: Jackson, Clarke

Suitable For: Cruising

Appropriate For: All

Months Runnable: (A-F) January through July; (F-M) all year
Interest Highlights: Scenery

Scenery: Unattractive to pretty

Difficulty: International Scale I-II
Numerical Points 1-8

Average Width: 15-35 ft.
Velocity: Slow
Gradient: 5.1 ft./mi.

Runnable Water Level: Minimum 1.6 ft.
(US 29 gauge)* Maximum Up to flood stage

Hazards: Strainers, deadfalls

Scouting: None

Portages: Dams below GA 330, US 78, and Simonton Bridge Rd.
Rescue Index: Accessible to accessible but difficult

Mean Water Temperature (°F)

Jan 43	Feb 44	Mar 50	Apr 59	May 67	Jun 74
Jul 75	Aug 73	Sep 68	Oct 60	Nov 52	Dec 46

Access Point	Access Code	Access Key
A	1357	1 Paved Road
B[1]	1357	2 Unpaved Road
C	1357	3 Short Carry
D	1357	4 Long Carry
E	1357	5 Easy Grade
F	1357	6 Steep Incline
G	1357	7 Clear Trail
H	1367	8 Brush and Trees
I	1357	9 Launching Fee Charged
J	1357	10 Private Property, Need Permission
K	1357	11 No Access, Reference Only
L	1357	
M	1357	
A[2]	1357	

[1] Not recommended
[2] On the Oconee River

*2 mi. west of Athens; ½ mi. upstream from US 29

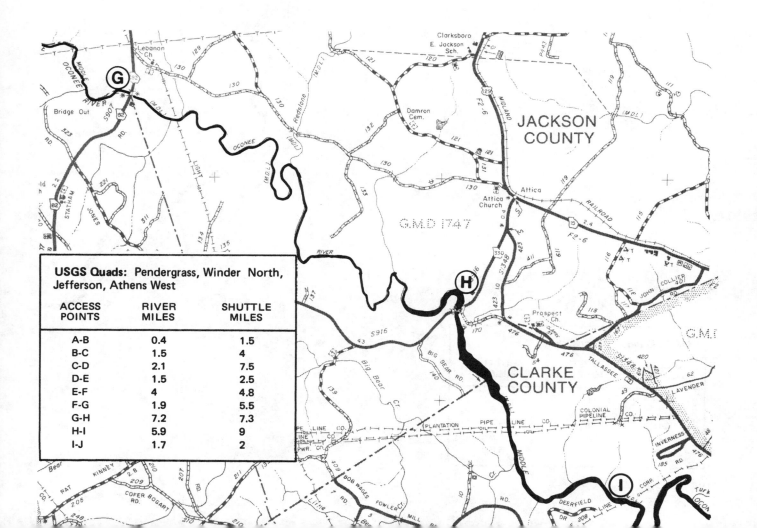

USGS Quads: Pendergrass, Winder North, Jefferson, Athens West

ACCESS POINTS	RIVER MILES	SHUTTLE MILES
A-B	0.4	1.5
B-C	1.5	4
C-D	2.1	7.5
D-E	1.5	2.5
E-F	4	4.8
F-G	1.9	5.5
G-H	7.2	7.3
H-I	5.9	9
I-J	1.7	2

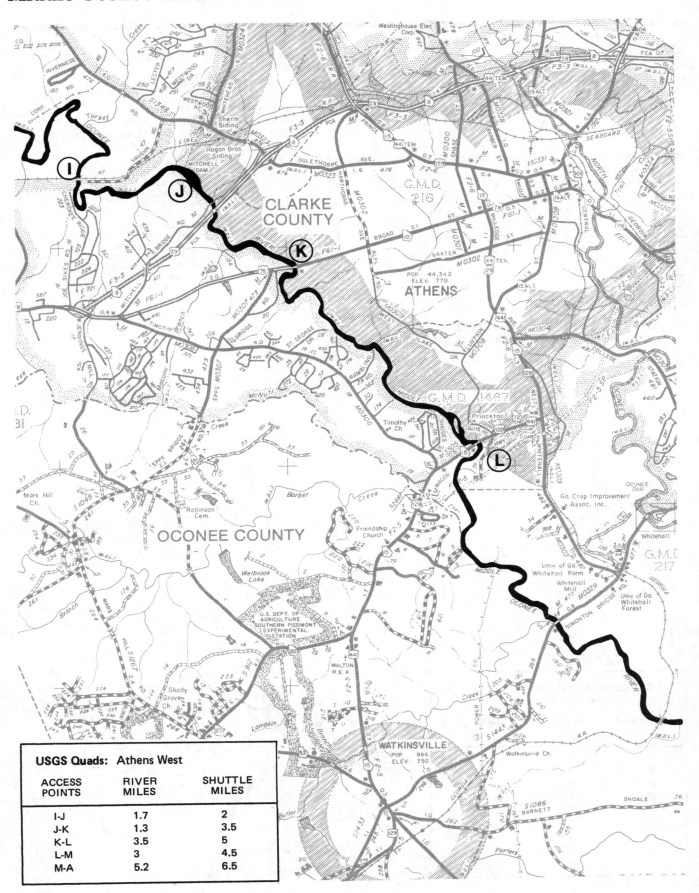

USGS Quads: Athens West		
ACCESS POINTS	RIVER MILES	SHUTTLE MILES
I-J	1.7	2
J-K	1.3	3.5
K-L	3.5	5
L-M	3	4.5
M-A	5.2	6.5

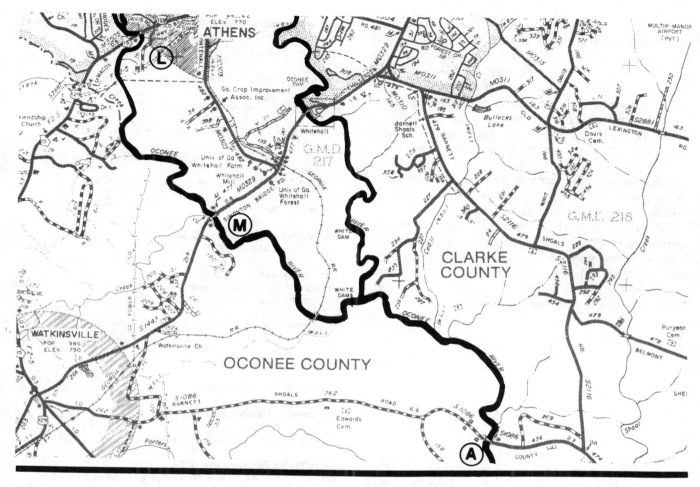

Section: GA 129 to Athens

Counties: Jackson, Clarke

Suitable For: Cruising

Appropriate For: All

Months Runnable: (A-F) January through July;
(F-M) all year

Interest Highlights: Scenery

Scenery: Unattractive to pretty

Difficulty: International Scale I-II
Numerical Points 1-8

Average Width: 15-35 ft.
Velocity: Slow
Gradient: 5.1 ft./mi.

Runnable Water Level: Minimum 1.6 ft.
(US 29 gauge)* Maximum Up to flood stage

Hazards: Strainers, deadfalls

Scouting: None

Portages: Dams below GA 330, US 78, and Simonton
Bridge Rd.

Rescue Index: Accessible to accessible but difficult

Mean Water Temperature (°F)

| Jan 43 | Feb 44 | Mar 50 | Apr 59 | May 67 | Jun 74 |
| Jul 75 | Aug 73 | Sep 68 | Oct 60 | Nov 52 | Dec 46 |

Access Point	Access Code	Access Key
I	1357	1 Paved Road
J	1357	2 Unpaved Road
K	1357	3 Short Carry
L	1357	4 Long Carry
M	1357	5 Easy Grade
A[1]	1357	6 Steep Incline
	1357	7 Clear Trail
	1367	8 Brush and Trees
	1357	9 Launching Fee Charged
	1357	10 Private Property, Need Permission
	1357	11 No Access, Reference Only
	1357	
	1357	
	1357	
	1357	

[1] On the Oconee River
*2 mi. west of Athens; ½ mi. upstream from US 29

Mulberry River

The Mulberry River is an Oconee River tributary. It originates in southeastern Hall County and flows southeastward forming the boundary between Jackson County and Barrow County. It unites with the Middle Oconee six miles south of Jefferson.

A small stream, the Mulberry must be caught at a favorable water level to make boating pleasant. Deadfalls are frequent and high water creates potentially hazardous strainers. On the other hand, the stream is sometimes too low to run at all. No gauges are on the stream, so wait for periods of moderate to heavy rainfall and be prepared for debris clogging the stream.

The best potential for canoeing is from GA 124 (access point C) on to the junction with the Middle Oconee. Scenery is not dramatic but it is pleasing to the eye. Most is hardwood forest periodically interrupted by farm land. There are no significant rapids. The gradient is approximately five feet per mile.

Section: GA 211 to GA 319 (Oconee River)

Counties: Hall, Jackson, Barrow

Suitable For: Cruising, camping

Appropriate For: Families, beginners, intermediates, advanced

Months Runnable: During wet weather and after heavy rains

Interest Highlights: Scenery

Scenery: Pretty

Difficulty: International Scale I
Numerical Points   6

Average Width: 15-35 ft.
Velocity: Slow to moderate
Gradient: 5.2 ft./mi.

Runnable Water Level: Minimum   Unknown
(no gauge)   Maximum   Unknown

Hazards: Strainers, deadfalls

Scouting: None required

Portages: Around deadfalls

Rescue Index: Accessible to accessible but difficult

Mean Water Temperature (°F)

| Jan 43 | Feb 44 | Mar 49 | Apr 57 | May 66 | Jun 74 |
| Jul 77 | Aug 75 | Sep 69 | Oct 60 | Nov 52 | Dec 46 |

Source of Additional Information:
High Country (404) 391-9657

Access Point	Access Code	Access Key
A	1357	1 Paved Road
B	1357	2 Unpaved Road
C	1357	3 Short Carry
D	1357	4 Long Carry
E	1357	5 Easy Grade
F	1357	6 Steep Incline
G	1357	7 Clear Trail
H	1357	8 Brush and Trees
		9 Launching Fee Charged
		10 Private Property, Need Permission
		11 No Access, Reference Only

USGS Quads: Chestnut Mtn., Auburn, Winder North, Jefferson

ACCESS POINTS	RIVER MILES	SHUTTLE MILES
A-B	2.4	3
B-C	1.7	3
C-D	2	4.5
D-E	5.8	5.5
E-F	6	7
F-G	2.4	3
G-H	4	6.25

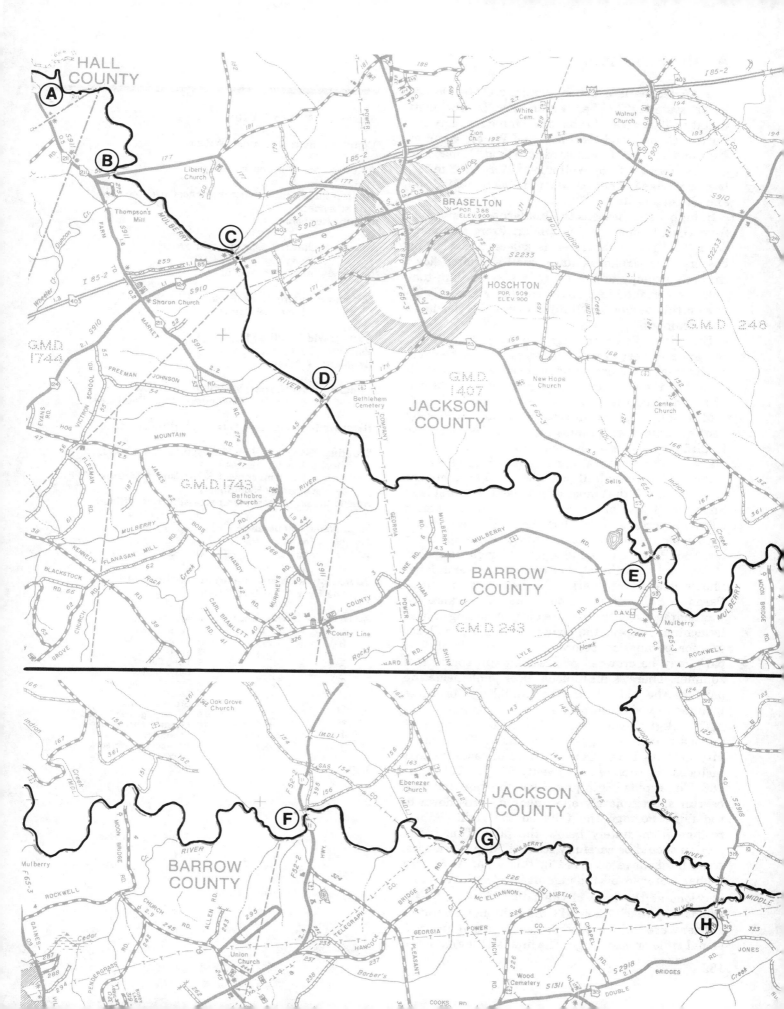

Apalachee River

The Apalachee is a major tributary of the Oconee River system. The headwaters are in Gwinnett County. The river forms the boundary between Barrow County and Gwinnett and Walton counties and continues southeastward to bound Oconee and Greene counties from Walton and Morgan counties. It enters Lake Oconee between the towns of Madison and Greshamville.

In high water seasons the Apalachee is navigable from GA 81 southeast of Winder. From this point down to US 78, the river is seldom traveled by boaters. The stream is quite small and often flows through swampy areas. There is a small dam that must be portaged just above US 78. Other difficulties on this section are limited to possible deadfalls and strainers.

The river flows through no large population centers and very few small towns. The streamside environment is mostly undeveloped woodland with some farm land. Many enticing camping spots can be found along the way.

Most of the Apalachee's course is characterized by gentle gradient with rapids that do not exceed Class II difficulty. A few obstacles to navigation both man-made and natural must be noted, however.

Below Caruthers Mill (just above US 78) there are two more dams that must be portaged. The first is at Snows Mill just above county road S1049 (access point L); portage on the left shore. The second and higher dam is in the community of High Shoals at GA 186. Portage either side but the right is easier.

The land immediately bordering the river at High Shoals is a private park/recreation area known as Paradise Falls Park. At one time an entrance fee was charged to enter this area for swimming or boat launching. Respect the owner's rights and at least ask for permission before crossing this land. The park may be crowded on weekends in spring and summer. There is an unusual beer joint inside the park in the old power plant building, for those inclined to visit such places.

The High Shoals area also contains the first serious natural navigational obstacle. The community gets its name from a series of cascades that includes one drop of over twenty feet just below GA 186. The rapids begin just below the dam and may be run approximately one hundred yards down to the falls. Portage the falls on the right. Rapids resume immediately below the falls. This entire section should be carefully scouted. Many accidents, some fatal, have occurred in this area. At certain higher water levels a dangerous hydraulic reversal develops at the base of the falls. Avoid it. These rapids may reach Class III+ difficulty in high water.

There are only two other rapids above an occasional riffle or easy ledge. The first is at the old Price

Section: GA 81 to GA 10

Counties: Barrow, Oconee, Walton

Suitable For: Cruising, camping

Appropriate For: Families, beginners, intermediates, advanced
Months Runnable: All

Interest Highlights: Scenery, whitewater

Scenery: Pretty to beautiful

Difficulty: International Scale   I-III (IV)
      Numerical Points   12

Average Width: 20-50 ft.
Velocity: Slack to fast
Gradient: 9 ft./mi.

Runnable Water Level: Minimum   Unknown
      Maximum   Up to flood stage

Hazards: Strainers, deadfalls, dams, difficult rapids

Scouting: Rapids at High Shoals, Price Mill Shoals, shoal below US 129/441
Portages: Small dam above US 78; dam at Caruthers Mill; dam at town of High Shoals
Rescue Index: Accessible to accessible but difficult

Mean Water Temperature (°F)

| Jan 45 | Feb 46 | Mar 51 | Apr 60 | May 68 | Jun 74 |
| Jul 77 | Aug 75 | Sep 69 | Oct 62 | Nov 54 | Dec 47 |

Source of Additional Information: Go With The Flow (404) 992-3200

Access Point	Access Code	Access Key
A	1357	1 Paved Road
B	2357	2 Unpaved Road
C	2357	3 Short Carry
D	1357	4 Long Carry
E	1357	5 Easy Grade
F	2357	6 Steep Incline
G	1357	7 Clear Trail
H	1357	8 Brush and Trees
I	2357	9 Launching Fee Charged
J	1357	10 Private Property, Need Permission
		11 No Access, Reference Only

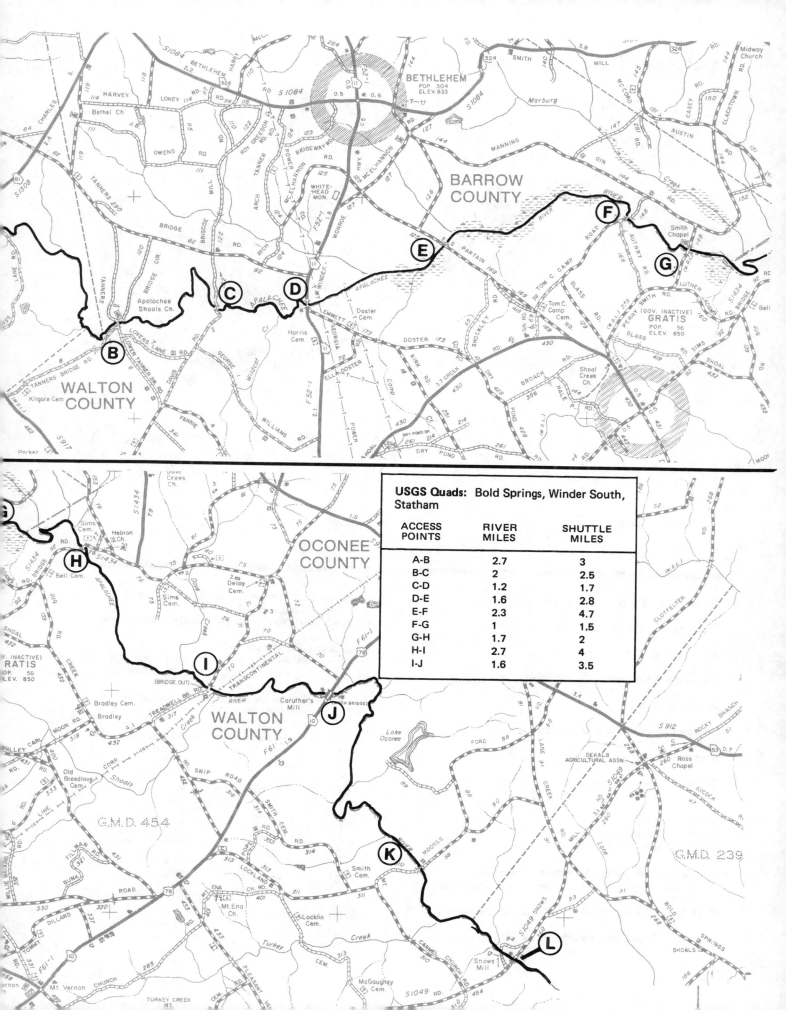

ACCESS POINTS	RIVER MILES	SHUTTLE MILES
A-B	2.7	3
B-C	2	2.5
C-D	1.2	1.7
D-E	1.6	2.8
E-F	2.3	4.7
F-G	1	1.5
G-H	1.7	2
H-I	2.7	4
I-J	1.6	3.5

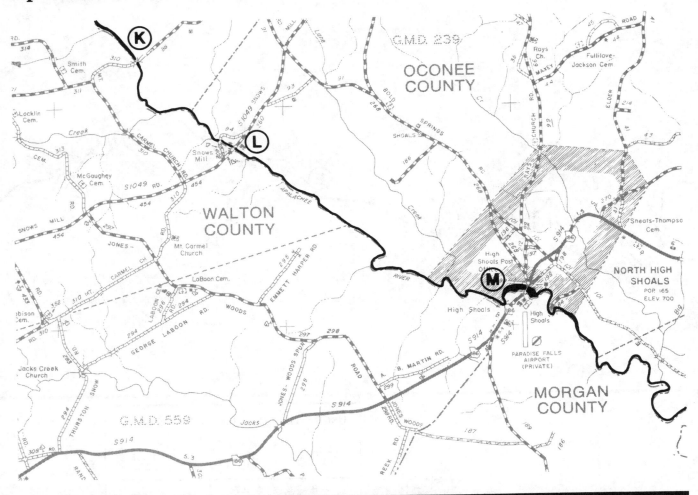

Section: GA 10 to Oconee River

Counties: Walton, Oconee, Morgan, Greene

Suitable For: Cruising, camping

Appropriate For: Families, beginners, intermediates, advanced

Months Runnable: All

Interest Highlights: Scenery, whitewater

Scenery: Pretty to beautiful

Difficulty: International Scale   I-III (IV)
Numerical Points   18

Average Width: 20-50 ft.
Velocity: Slack to fast
Gradient: 9 ft./mi. (20+ ft./mi.)

Runnable Water Level: Minimum   Unknown
Maximum   Up to flood stage

Hazards: Strainers, deadfalls, difficult rapids, dams

Scouting: Rapids below High Shoals Falls and GA 441

Portages: Dams above and at High Shoals and High Shoals Falls (Paradise Falls)
Rescue Index: Accessible to accessible but difficult

Mean Water Temperature (°F)

Jan 45	Feb 46	Mar 51	Apr 60	May 68	Jun 74
Jul 77	Aug 75	Sep 69	Oct 62	Nov 54	Dec 47

Source of Additional Information: Go With The Flow (404) 992-3200

Access Point	Access Code	Access Key
J	1357	1 Paved Road
K	2357	2 Unpaved Road
L	1357	3 Short Carry
M	1357	4 Long Carry
N	1357	5 Easy Grade
O	1357	6 Steep Incline
P	2357	7 Clear Trail
Q	2357	8 Brush and Trees
R	2357	9 Launching Fee Charged
S	2357	10 Private Property, Need Permission
D[1]	(11)	11 No Access, Reference Only
E	1357	

[1]On the Oconee River

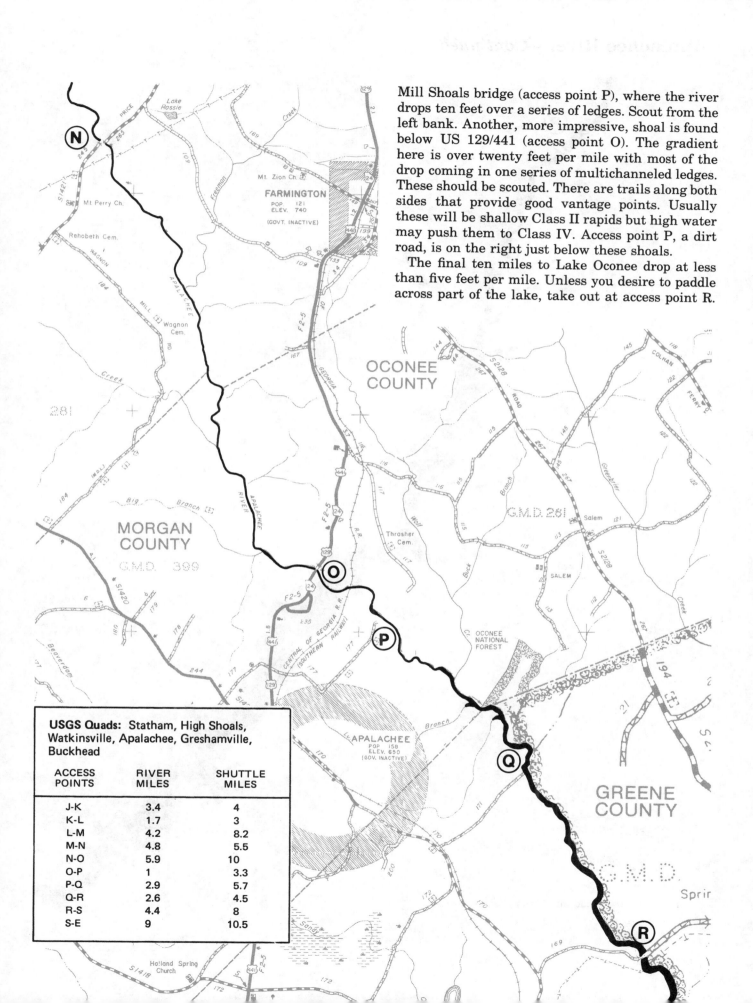

Mill Shoals bridge (access point P), where the river drops ten feet over a series of ledges. Scout from the left bank. Another, more impressive, shoal is found below US 129/441 (access point O). The gradient here is over twenty feet per mile with most of the drop coming in one series of multichanneled ledges. These should be scouted. There are trails along both sides that provide good vantage points. Usually these will be shallow Class II rapids but high water may push them to Class IV. Access point P, a dirt road, is on the right just below these shoals.

The final ten miles to Lake Oconee drop at less than five feet per mile. Unless you desire to paddle across part of the lake, take out at access point R.

USGS Quads: Statham, High Shoals, Watkinsville, Apalachee, Greshamville, Buckhead

ACCESS POINTS	RIVER MILES	SHUTTLE MILES
J-K	3.4	4
K-L	1.7	3
L-M	4.2	8.2
M-N	4.8	5.5
N-O	5.9	10
O-P	1	3.3
P-Q	2.9	5.7
Q-R	2.6	4.5
R-S	4.4	8
S-E	9	10.5

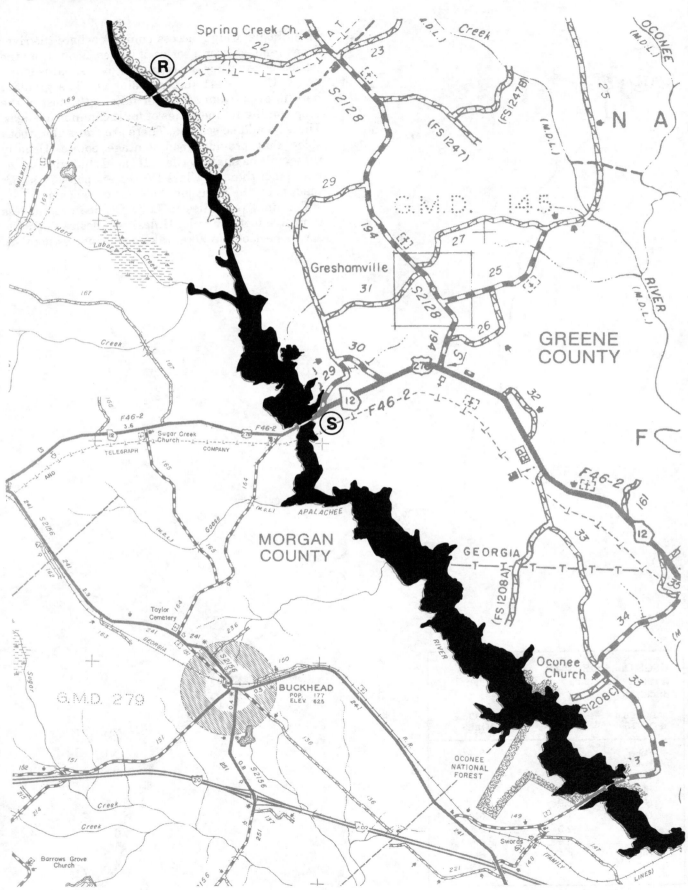

Section: GA 10 to Oconee River

Counties: Walton, Oconee, Morgan, Greene

Suitable For: Cruising, camping

Appropriate For: Families, beginners, intermediates, advanced

Months Runnable: All

Interest Highlights: Scenery, whitewater

Scenery: Pretty to beautiful

Difficulty: International Scale I-III (IV)
            Numerical Points   18

Average Width: 20-50 ft.
Velocity: Slack to fast
Gradient: 9 ft./mi. (20+ ft./mi.)

Runnable Water Level: Minimum   Unknown
                        Maximum   Up to flood stage

Hazards: Strainers, deadfalls, difficult rapids, dams

Scouting: Rapids below High Shoals Falls and GA 441

Portages: Dams above and at High Shoals and High Shoals Falls (Paradise Falls)
Rescue Index: Accessible to accessible but difficult

Mean Water Temperature (°F)

Jan 45	Feb 46	Mar 51	Apr 60	May 68	Jun 74
Jul 77	Aug 75	Sep 69	Oct 62	Nov 54	Dec 47

Source of Additional Information: Go With The Flow (404) 992-3200

Access Point	Access Code	Access Key
J	1357	1 Paved Road
K	2357	2 Unpaved Road
L	1357	3 Short Carry
M	1357	4 Long Carry
N	1357	5 Easy Grade
O	1357	6 Steep Incline
P	2357	7 Clear Trail
Q	2357	8 Brush and Trees
R	2357	9 Launching Fee Charged
S	2357	10 Private Property, Need Permission
D[1]	(11)	11 No Access, Reference Only
E	1357	

[1]On the Oconee River

USGS Quads: Statham, High Shoals, Watkinsville, Apalachee, Greshamville, Buckhead

ACCESS POINTS	RIVER MILES	SHUTTLE MILES
J-K	3.4	4
K-L	1.7	3
L-M	4.2	8.2
M-N	4.8	5.5
N-O	5.9	10
O-P	1	3.3
P-Q	2.9	5.7
Q-R	2.6	4.5
R-S	4.4	8
S-E	9	10.5

Little River of Putnam County

The Little River is a major tributary of the Oconee and drains portions of Morgan, Putnam, and Jasper counties. Originating in southern Morgan County, the Little runs southeast over a rock and clay bed between thickly wooded banks of three to six feet with an average slope of 40 to 65 degrees. Runnable downstream of GA 300 northwest of Eaton in periods of wet weather, the Little sports intermittent Class II rapids and shoals almost all the way to the GA 44 bridge. Below GA 44 the Little flows peacefully until it encounters the backwaters of Lake Sinclair. A wild stream, the Little is pristine and secluded almost all the way to the lake, with the entire canoeable section either being in or on the boundary of the Oconee National Forest. Averaging 40 to 55 feet in width, the river is winding and convoluted throughout its length. Deadfalls are common in the section just below GA 300 to where an unimproved road crosses the stream below the mouth of Pearson creek. Below this crossing down to the GA 16 bridge is the most continuous whitewater section. Unfortunately, the Little is high in transported sediment thus making "whitewater" somewhat a misnomer since the actual color of the water (at runnable periods) is mustard brown.

Farther downstream, past an unnumbered highway bridge (access point D), is a dam that must be portaged, followed by the last significant section of shoals. Level of difficulty is Class I–II with deadfalls, mild rapids, and the dam mentioned being the primary hazards to navigation. Access is excellent and surrounding terrain consists mainly of low, forested hills.

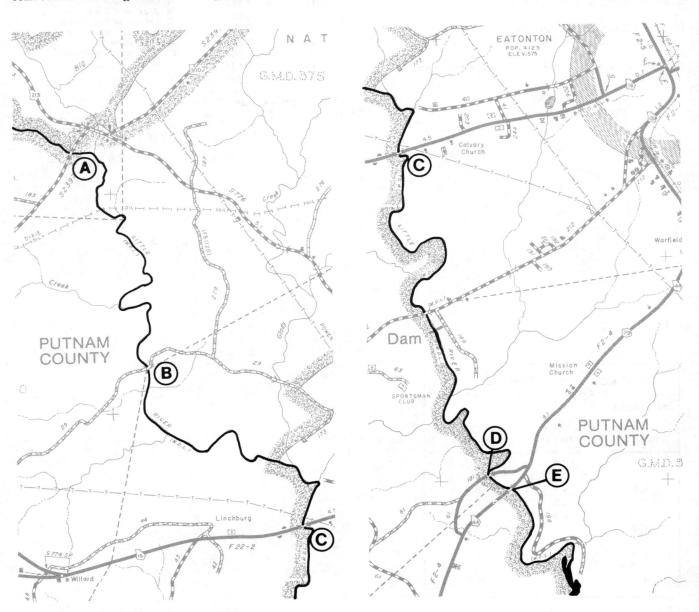

Section: GA 213 bridge to Lake Sinclair

Counties: Putnam

Suitable For: Cruising

Appropriate For: Practiced beginners, intermediates, advanced paddlers

Months Runnable: Late December to early May and during wet weather

Interest Highlights: Scenery, wildlife, whitewater

Scenery: Beautiful in spots

Difficulty: International Scale   I-II
                 Numerical Points   9

Average Width: 40-55 ft.
Velocity: Moderate
Gradient: 4.06 ft./mi.

Runnable Water Level: Minimum Unknown
                            Maximum Up to flood stage

Hazards: Deadfalls, dams, mild rapids

Scouting: At rapids and shoals

Portages: Dam below Stanfordville Rd.

Rescue Index: Accessible but difficult

Mean Water Temperature (°F)

Jan 45	Feb 47	Mar 52	Apr 60	May 68	Jun 74
Jul 77	Aug 75	Sep 70	Oct 60	Nov 53	Dec 49

Access Point	Access Code	Access Key
A	1368	1 Paved Road
B	2368	2 Unpaved Road
C	1357	3 Short Carry
D	1358	4 Long Carry
E	1357	5 Easy Grade
F	1357	6 Steep Incline
		7 Clear Trail
		8 Brush and Trees
		9 Launching Fee Charged
		10 Private Property, Need Permission
		11 No Access, Reference Only

USGS Quads: Eatonton, Lake Sinclair West

ACCESS POINTS	RIVER MILES	SHUTTLE MILES
A-B	4	4
B-C	3.4	6.5
C-D	5.6	8.5
D-E	0.2	0.7
E-F	6.6	7.5

Oconee River

The Oconee River is born in Hall County south of Lake Lanier where several small feeder streams supply the North and Middle forks of the Oconee. Flowing southeastward and draining Jackson County, the forks join to form the Oconee River south of Athens. Continuing southeastward the Oconee is the major drainage for Clark, Oconee, Greene, Morgan, Putman, Hancock, and Baldwin counties as it moves through the Piedmont. This section, essentially from Athens to Lake Sinclair, has been smoothed by a series of dams and now contains very little in the way of whitewater save for an occasional riffle. Its banks are of clay, four to seven feet in height, 30 to 60 degrees in slope, and treelined and well vegetated. The current is lively between dam pools.

As with most streams draining the Piedmont, the Oconee carries a large amount of sediment, which adversely affects the aesthetic appearance of the water, causing it to vary in color from a greenish brown to a pale mustard yellow. Between Athens and Lake Sinclair signs of habitation are rare and the river setting is generally secluded since the Oconee National Forest borders the stream on the east from the confluence of Big Creek downstream to the vicinity of the GA 15 bridge in Greene County. Surrounding terrain rises quickly from Oconee's narrow floodplain to a gently dipping plateau and valley topography. Wildlife is plentiful and stream flora diverse with river birch, sycamore, sugarberry, and green ash interspersed with several varieties of bottomland oak and stands of sweetgum and box elder.

Moving current in the Piedmont section of the Oconee terminates just below the GA 12 bridge where the river encounters the backwaters of Lake Oconee. Below Wallace Dam the waters of the Oconee are simply transferred from Lake Oconee to Lake Sinclair.

The level of difficulty for the Oconee from Athens to Lake Sinclair is Class I with dams (as mentioned) and occasional deadfalls being the primary hazards to navigation. The river's width where moving current exists averages 70–110 feet; channel configuration usually tends toward a moderate to long, straight or gently turning section followed by a sharp bend. The upper Oconee is runnable all year providing the Barnett Shoals Dam and Powerhouse are releasing. (The Oconee River below Lake Sinclair is described in a companion book, *Southern Georgia Canoeing: A Canoeing and Kayaking Guide to the Streams of the Western Piedmont, Coastal Plain, Georgia Coast and Okefenokee Swamp*.)

USGS Quads: Barnett Shoals, Greshamville, Buckhead, Harmony, Liberty, Rockville, Lake Sinclair West		
ACCESS POINTS	RIVER MILES	SHUTTLE MILES
A-B	12.2	17
B-C	12.2	17.5
C-D	4.3	12
D-E	7.6	12.5
E-F	16	15

Section: Forks of Oconee to Lake Sinclair

Counties: Clark, Oconee, Oglethorpe, Greene, Putnam

Suitable For: Cruising, camping

Appropriate For: Beginners, intermediates, advanced

Months Runnable: All

Interest Highlights: Scenery, wildlife

Scenery: Pretty

Difficulty: International Scale I+
            Numerical Points   5

Average Width: 70-110 ft.
Velocity: Moderate
Gradient: 3.33 ft./mi.

Runnable Water Level: Minimum 580 cfs
  (Greensboro gauge)   Maximum Up to flood stage

Hazards: Deadfalls, dams

Scouting: None

Portages: Wallace Dam

Rescue Index: Accessible to accessible but difficult

Mean Water Temperature (°F)

Jan 44	Feb 46	Mar 51	Apr 60	May 68	Jun 75
Jul 78	Aug 75	Sep 70	Oct 60	Nov 52	Dec 46

Source of Additional Information: Game and Fish
Division, Fishery Management section, East Central
Regional Office (706) 557-2591

Access Point	Access Code	Access Key
A	1357	1 Paved Road
B	1357	2 Unpaved Road
C	1357	3 Short Carry
D	(11)	4 Long Carry
E	1357	5 Easy Grade
F	1357	6 Steep Incline
		7 Clear Trail
		8 Brush and Trees
		9 Launching Fee Charged
		10 Private Property, Need Permission
		11 No Access, Reference Only

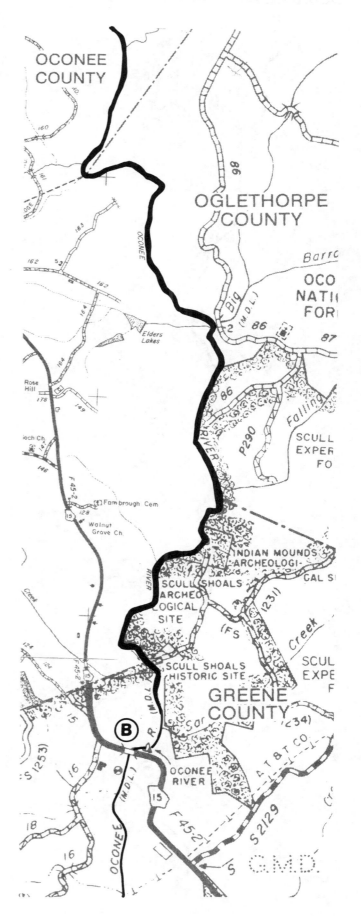

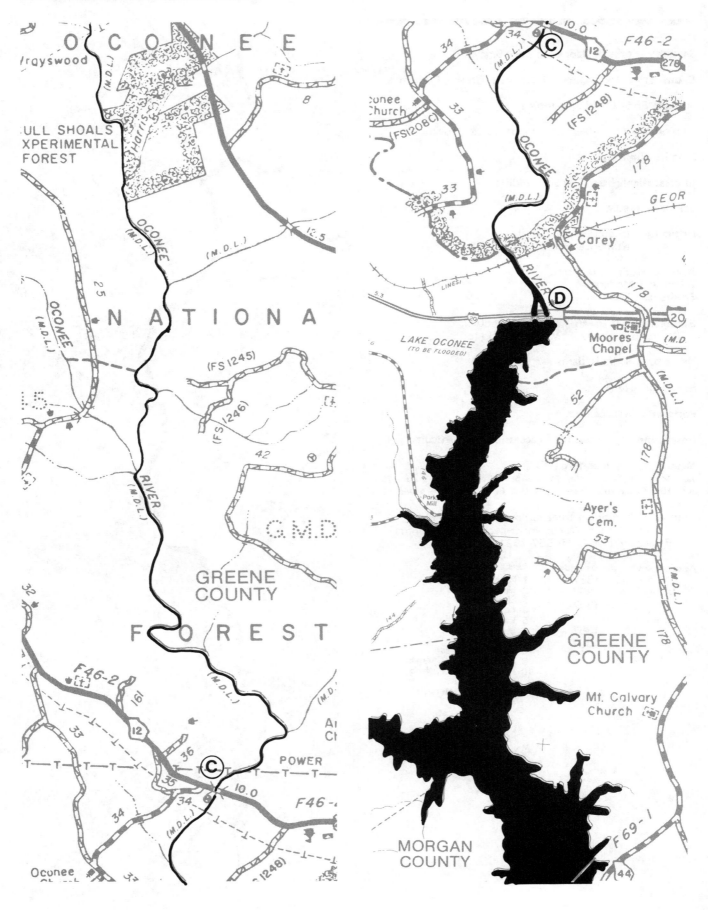

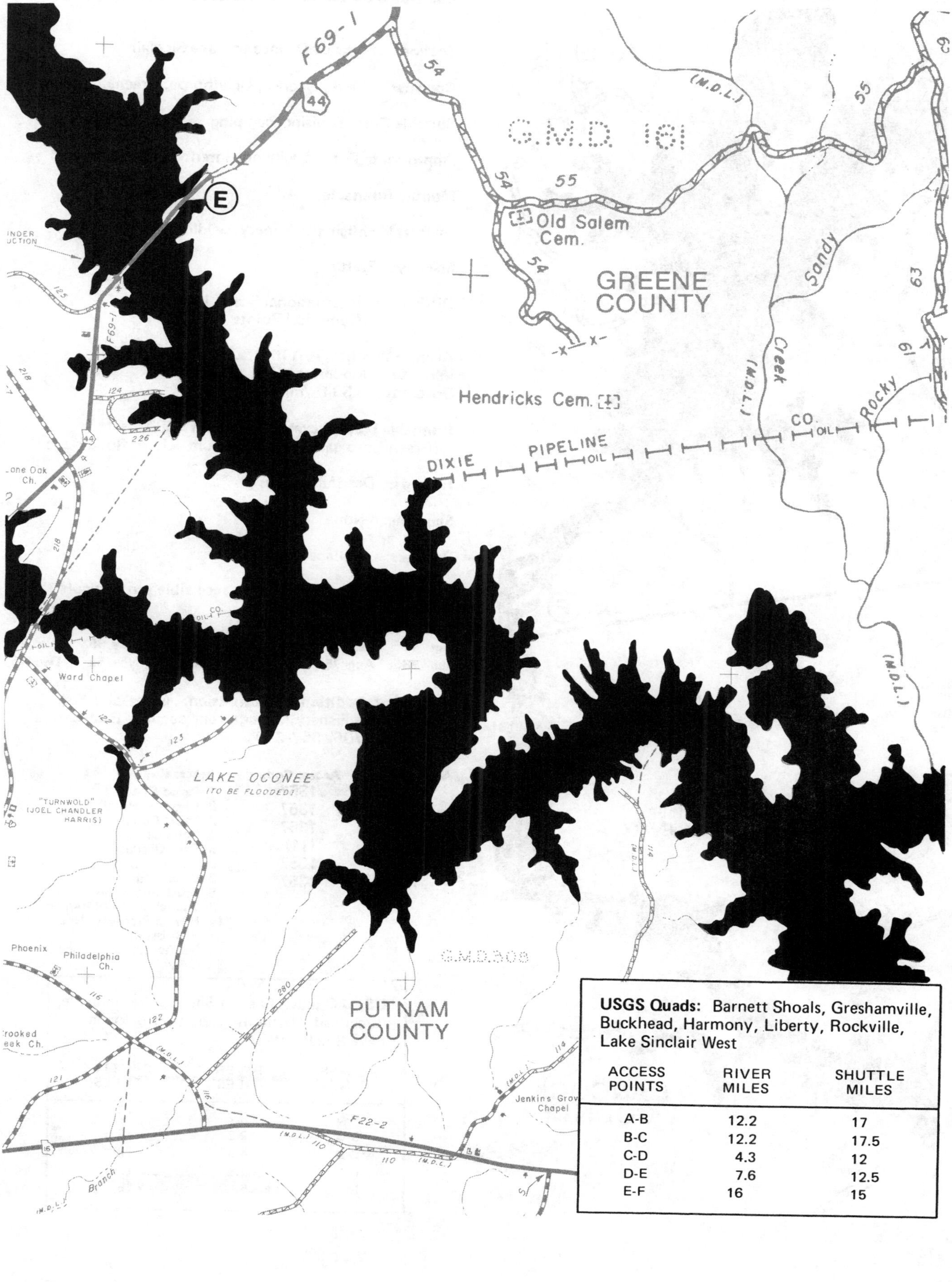

F69-1

44

54

(M.D.L.)

55

C9

G.M.D. 181

54   55

☐ Old Salem
Cem.

54

GREENE
COUNTY

E

INDER
JCTION

125

F69-1

218
7

124

44

226

Lone Oak
Ch.

218

Sandy

Creek

Rocky

(M.D.L.)

63

61

CO.   OIL   ☐ ⊢

Hendricks Cem. ☐

DIXIE   PIPELINE   ⊢⊢⊢⊢⊢⊢ OIL ⊢⊢⊢⊢⊢⊢⊢⊢⊢⊢⊢⊢⊢⊢

CO.
OIL

(M.D.L.)

Ward Chapel

122

125

OIL

LAKE OCONEE
(TO BE FLOODED)

"TURNWOLD"
(JOEL CHANDLER
HARRIS)

116

(M.D.L.)

G.M.D. 308

Phoenix   Philadelphia
Ch.

116

280

PUTNAM
COUNTY

Jenkins Grove
Chapel

116

122

(M.D.L.)

911

Crooked
eek Ch.

121

(M.D.L.)

116

F22-2

110   (M.D.L.)

110   (M.D.L.)

Branch

(M.D.L.)

USGS Quads:	Barnett Shoals, Greshamville,	
Buckhead, Harmony, Liberty, Rockville,		
Lake Sinclair West		
ACCESS POINTS	RIVER MILES	SHUTTLE MILES
A-B	12.2	17
B-C	12.2	17.5
C-D	4.3	12
D-E	7.6	12.5
E-F	16	15

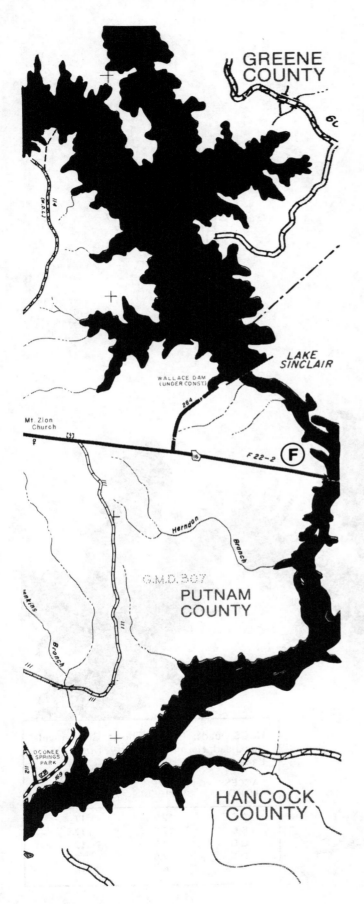

Section: Forks of Oconee to Lake Sinclair

Counties: Clark, Oconee, Oglethorpe, Greene, Putnam

Suitable For: Cruising, camping

Appropriate For: Beginners, intermediates, advanced

Months Runnable: All

Interest Highlights: Scenery, wildlife

Scenery: Pretty

Difficulty: International Scale I+
Numerical Points 5

Average Width: 70-110 ft.
Velocity: Moderate
Gradient: 3.33 ft./mi.

Runnable Water Level: Minimum 580 cfs
(Greensboro gauge) Maximum Up to flood stage

Hazards: Deadfalls, dams

Scouting: None

Portages: Wallace Dam

Rescue Index: Accessible to accessible but difficult

Mean Water Temperature (°F)

Jan 44	Feb 46	Mar 51	Apr 60	May 68	Jun 75
Jul 78	Aug 75	Sep 70	Oct 60	Nov 52	Dec 46

Source of Additional Information: Game and Fish Division, Fishery Management section, East Central Office (706) 557-2591

Access Point	Access Code	Access Key
A	1357	1 Paved Road
B	1357	2 Unpaved Road
C	1357	3 Short Carry
D	(11)	4 Long Carry
E	1357	5 Easy Grade
F	1357	6 Steep Incline
		7 Clear Trail
		8 Brush and Trees
		9 Launching Fee Charged
		10 Private Property, Need Permission
		11 No Access, Reference Only

USGS Quads: Barnett Shoals, Greshamville, Buckhead, Harmony, Liberty, Rockville, Lake Sinclair West

ACCESS POINTS	RIVER MILES	SHUTTLE MILES
A-B	12.2	17
B-C	12.2	17.5
C-D	4.3	12
D-E	7.6	12.5
E-F	16	15

Ocoee River.

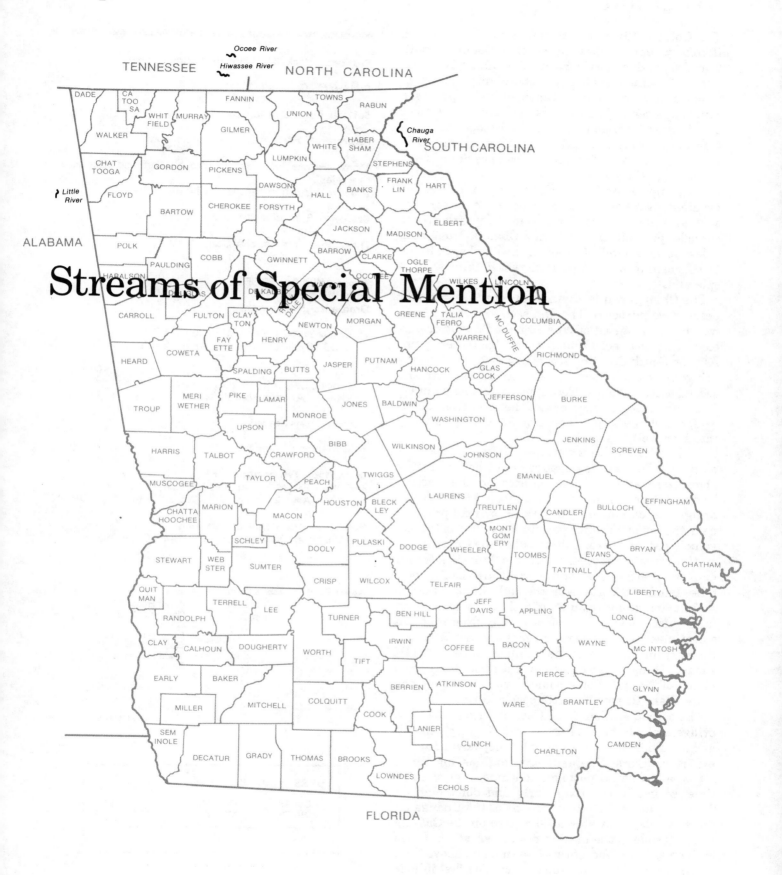

Chapter 6

Streams of Special Mention

Chauga River

The Chauga River is a tributary of the Savannah River system. It lies in Oconee County, South Carolina, and is mostly within the Sumter National Forest. It is included here because of its proximity to Georgia paddlers and because of its merit as a canoeing stream. The Chauga has been described as a miniature version of the Chattooga or as a Chattooga alternative. These descriptions fail to do it justice, however. The Chauga can speak for itself.

Although there are slack areas on the Chauga, the lasting impression is one of plunging in frenzy. The gradient averages 60 to 80 feet per mile through several small gorges. Numerous tributary creeks cascade periodically into the Chauga from both sides. It is a land of steep rocky banks, hanging ferns, rushing water. The scenery is nothing short of splendid.

The Chauga can be divided into three sections for descriptive purposes. The first section is from Blackwell bridge just east of Whetstone to Cassidy bridge, east of Long Creek. Blackwell bridge (access point A) is on South Carolina secondary road 193. Cassidy bridge is on Stumphorse Road, (access point B). The second section ends at Cobbs bridge (access point C). The third section encompasses the river from Cobbs bridge to US 123 just north of the Chauga's entry into Hartwell Reservoir.

With favorable high water conditions (at least 1.7 on the US 76 Chattooga gauge or at least two inches above zero at the gauge painted on the Cassidy bridge pillar), boaters may launch at Blackwell bridge. Be careful not to park on private property near the bridge; ask for permission if you do leave a vehicle parked there. A dirt road on the western side of the stream provides alternate launch sites. A 45-foot waterfall is encountered within the first half mile. Land and portage on the right bank. There is an unusual 20-foot column of rock at the base of the falls. Just below is a 10-foot sliding drop that can sometimes be run. The river drops another 70 feet in the next mile and has some technical Class II and III shoals. Things then quiet down a little, but expect plenty of Class II rapids, some downed trees, and one more Class III rapid a little past mid-run.

The second section, from Cassidy bridge to Cobbs bridge, called the Chauga Gorge, is very difficult and should be attempted only by very advanced and expert paddlers. Frequent scouting, setting throw ropes, and several portages consume a lot of extra time, so get to the river early and don't plan on running one of the other sections of the Chauga on the same day. A water level of zero on the Cassidy bridge gauge is the minimum necessary; six inches is the maximum for a first-time run, and above that, expect heavy and dangerous water. The first mile is within a little valley with only gentle rapids. Recent

Section: Blackwell bridge to Cassidy bridge

Counties: Oconee (SC)

Suitable For: Cruising, camping

Appropriate For: Advanced paddlers only

Months Runnable: January through April and after heavy rains

Interest Highlights: Scenery, wildlife, whitewater

Scenery: Exceptionally beautiful

Difficulty: International Scale II-IV
Numerical Points 27

Average Width: 20-35 ft.
Velocity: Fast
Gradient: 51.8 ft./mi.

Runnable Water Level: Minimum 1.7 ft.
(US 76 gauge) Maximum 2.8 ft.

Hazards: Strainers, deadfalls, difficult rapids, undercut rocks, keeper hydraulics
Scouting: At all major rapids

Portages: As needed

Rescue Index: Remote

Mean Water Temperature (°F)

| Jan 39 | Feb 41 | Mar 45 | Apr 54 | May 62 | Jun 70 |
| Jul 73 | Aug 72 | Sep 66 | Oct 58 | Nov 47 | Dec 42 |

Source of Additional Information:
Chattooga Whitewater Shop (803) 647-9083

Access Point	Access Code	Access Key
A	1367(10)	1 Paved Road
B	1367	2 Unpaved Road
		3 Short Carry
		4 Long Carry
		5 Easy Grade
		6 Steep Incline
		7 Clear Trail
		8 Brush and Trees
		9 Launching Fee Charged
		10 Private Property, Need Permission
		11 No Access, Reference Only

USGS Quads: Whetstone		
ACCESS POINTS	RIVER MILES	SHUTTLE MILES
A-B	4.2	8

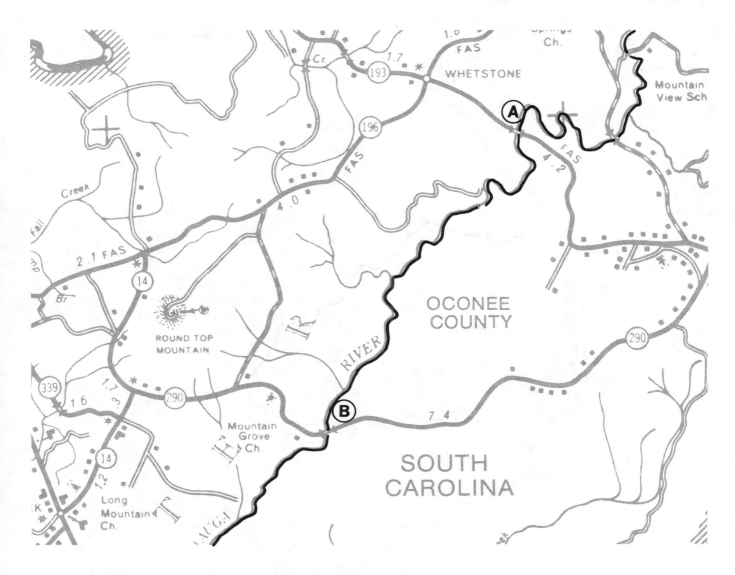

logging in this area has put a great deal of debris in the stream, watch for possible strainers during and after high water flows. The valley ends abruptly with a waterfall that must be portaged on the left.

Within the next mile another waterfall is encountered that has a strong Class II rapid just above. Get to the left bank promptly to scout or portage. This drop can be run with favorable conditions. At Spider Valley Creek junction the river turns east and starts dropping in earnest, with the gradient initially exceeding 180 feet per mile. A slanting waterfall that most will choose to portage is followed by almost continuous Class III and IV rapids for the next two miles. Most drops are quite technical and recovery pools are short. Careful scouting and the use of safety boats and ropes is especially important because yours may be the only party on the river and evacuation from the gorge is very difficult. After a couple of miles, the gradient decreases, but several more Class III rapids remain, and about two miles

above Cobbs bridge is a sheer falls that must be portaged on the right. The flow is relatively placid from the falls to Cobbs bridge.

The most popular run on the lower Chauga is from Cobbs bridge to Horseshoe Bend bridge. This section is really a Piedmont rather than mountain river, with long stretches of flatwater interrupted occasionally by granite shoals. The high sandy banks and loblolly pines are also characteristic of the Piedmont. Though there are only seven significant rapids, they have great interest and variety, and portaging back upstream for reruns is unusually easy. This makes the lower Chauga an excellent training ground for intermediates. The most convenient gauge is on the Chattooga at US 76, which is right on the way for most Georgia paddlers. A reading of 1.8 is the minimum for a decent run, 2.5 is optimum, and, above that, some of the rapids get mean and dangerous. There are private homes at the put-in and take-out, so be extra considerate.

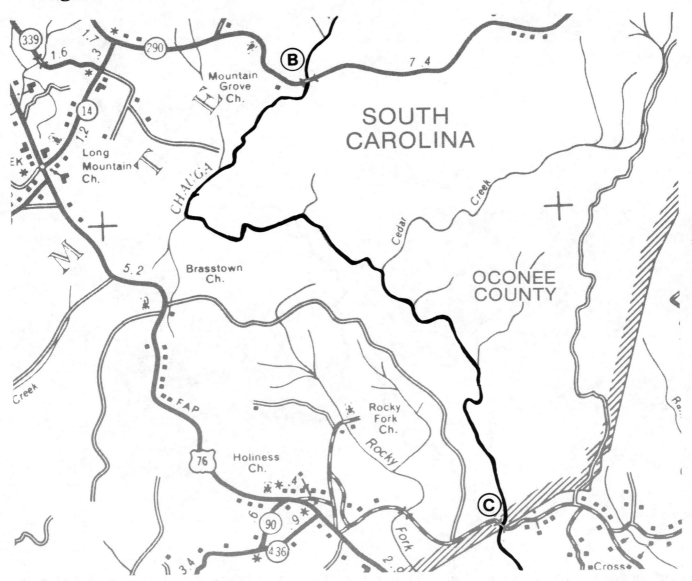

USGS Quads:	Whetstone, Holly Springs	
ACCESS POINTS	RIVER MILES	SHUTTLE MILES
B-C	8	11

The Class II rapid below Cobbs bridge is run down the right side. Just downriver is a big, slanting ledge that can be scouted from the left bank. At about three and a half miles, cables across the river precede a really interesting Class II rapid that can be scouted from a center landing. The right eddy turn after the left side chute will nearly dislocate your shoulder. This is a good spot for lunch.

Soon after the US 76 bridge is a complex shoal that can be scouted from the left bank. A short pool leads to Pumphouse, a Class III rapid named for the water-pumping facility just below. Land carefully on the rocks just left of center to scout. Chau-Ram County Park is just below on the left, where you can stop to see the falls on Ramsey Creek. This is a convenient take-out if you don't mind missing the last two rapids. Just downstream, get to the right bank and scout the slanting, five-foot ledge with the waterspout. The hole there gets dangerous in higher water. The last rapid is just around the bend and can be scouted from the left. The water pours over a V-shaped slot and past an undercut rock to some smaller drops. The two remaining miles are mostly flat, with deadfalls the only hazard. Past Horseshoe Bend bridge, there is little gradient, and the river soon reaches the backwaters of Hartwell Reservoir.

Section: Cassidy bridge to Cobbs bridge

Counties: Oconee (SC)

Suitable For: Cruising, camping

Appropriate For: Advanced paddlers only

Months Runnable: January through April and after heavy rains

Interest Highlights: Scenery, wildlife, whitewater

Scenery: Spectacular

Difficulty: International Scale III-V
Numerical Points 29

Average Width: 20-35 ft.
Velocity: Fast
Gradient: 51.8 ft./mi.

Runnable Water Level: Minimum 1.7 ft.
(US 76 gauge) Maximum 2.8 ft.

Hazards: Strainers, deadfalls, difficult rapids, undercut rocks, keeper hydraulics
Scouting: At all major rapids

Portages: Falls below Cassidy bridge and falls 2 mi. above Cobbs bridge; elsewhere as needed
Rescue Index: Accessible but difficult to remote

Mean Water Temperature (°F)

Jan 39	Feb 41	Mar 45	Apr 54	May 62	Jun 70
Jul 73	Aug 72	Sep 66	Oct 58	Nov 67	Dec 42

Source of Additional Information:
Chattooga Whitewater Shop (803) 647-9083

Access Point	Access Code	Access Key
B	1367	1 Paved Road
C	1357	2 Unpaved Road
		3 Short Carry
		4 Long Carry
		5 Easy Grade
		6 Steep Incline
		7 Clear Trail
		8 Brush and Trees
		9 Launching Fee Charged
		10 Private Property, Need Permission
		11 No Access, Reference Only

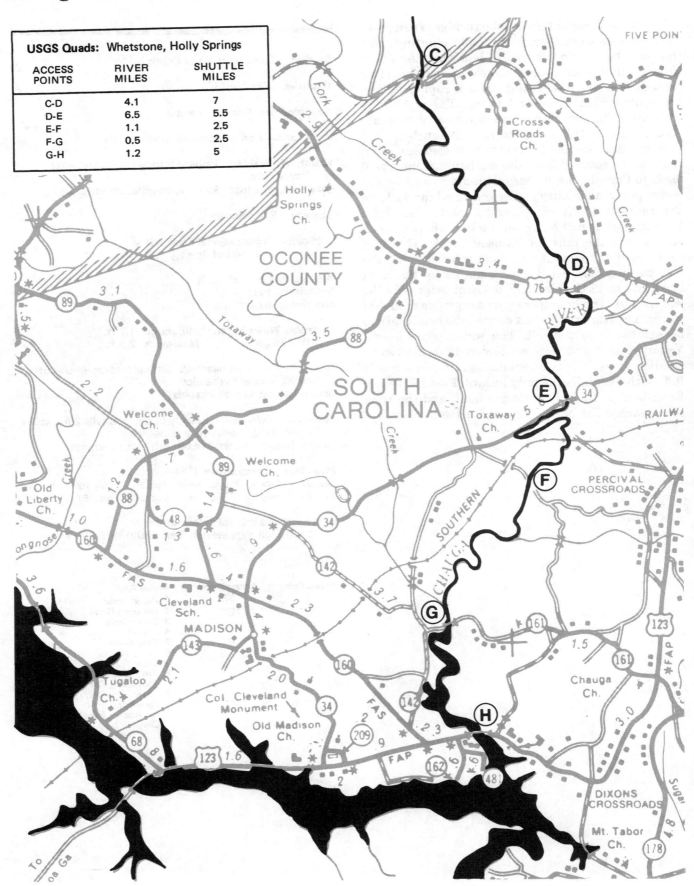

USGS Quads: Whetstone, Holly Springs

ACCESS POINTS	RIVER MILES	SHUTTLE MILES
C-D	4.1	7
D-E	6.5	5.5
E-F	1.1	2.5
F-G	0.5	2.5
G-H	1.2	5

Section: Cobbs bridge to US 123

Counties: Oconee (SC)

Suitable For: Cruising, camping

Appropriate For: Intermediate and advanced paddlers

Months Runnable: January through April and after heavy rains

Interest Highlights: Scenery, wildlife, whitewater

Scenery: Exceptional

Difficulty: International Scale I-III
Numerical Points 18

Average Width: 40-50 ft.
Velocity: Moderate to fast
Gradient: 14.2 ft./mi.

Runnable Water Level: Minimum 1.7 ft.
(US 76 gauge) Maximum 2.8 ft.

Hazards: Strainers, deadfalls, difficult rapids, undercut rocks

Scouting: At major rapids

Portages: As needed

Rescue Index: Accessible but difficult

Mean Water Temperature (°F)

| Jan 39 | Feb 41 | Mar 45 | Apr 54 | May 62 | Jun 70 |
| Jul 73 | Aug 72 | Sep 66 | Oct 58 | Nov 47 | Dec 42 |

Source of Additional Information:
High Country (404) 391-9657

Access Point	Access Code	Access Key
C	1357	1 Paved Road
D	1357	2 Unpaved Road
E	1357	3 Short Carry
F	2357	4 Long Carry
G	2357	5 Easy Grade
H	1357	6 Steep Incline
		7 Clear Trail
		8 Brush and Trees
		9 Launching Fee Charged
		10 Private Property, Need Permission
		11 No Access, Reference Only

Ocoee River (Whitewater Section)

For years, paddlers traveling the Old Copper Road (US 64) in southeastern Polk County (TN) would marvel at the dry, rocky Ocoee riverbed beside the highway. They couldn't help but conjecture about potential souse holes, rapids, and falls. But high on the mountainside, also beside that stretch of roadway, a leaky 65-year-old wooden flume carried the river's entire flow to a powerhouse seven miles downstream. One day, only a few years past, that old wooden boxway could carry the liquid load no more; seventeen megawatts of generated power was transformed back into 1000 cfs of river flow. The paddlers would conjecture no more. Double Trouble, Diamond Splitter, Table Saw, and Hell's Hole were exciting manifestations of the newly found, 57-foot-drop-per-mile water. Instant notoriety came as river runners tried to learn how various flow levels might affect their craft on this new whitewater. Commer-cial raft outfitters sprang up. National decked-boat championship races appeared. Government river-carrying-capacity studies were initiated, and TVA has proposed repairing the flume.

For the time being, one of the most taxing whitewater streams in the southeast exists along seven miles of the Old Copper Road from Ocoee No. 2 Dam to Ocoee No. 2 Powerhouse. This run is marginal for open boats. Only whitewater canoes rigged with extra flotation should attempt the run; and the paddler should be a *confident* expert. Damage reports from the Ocoee are legendary. Know what you are doing or stay off. And know advanced paddling techniques. The Ocoee white-water is not general recreational canoeing. It is solid Class III and IV. (However, the road is nearby along the entire run, so you *can* walk out.)

The Ocoee is Tennessee's portion of Georgia's

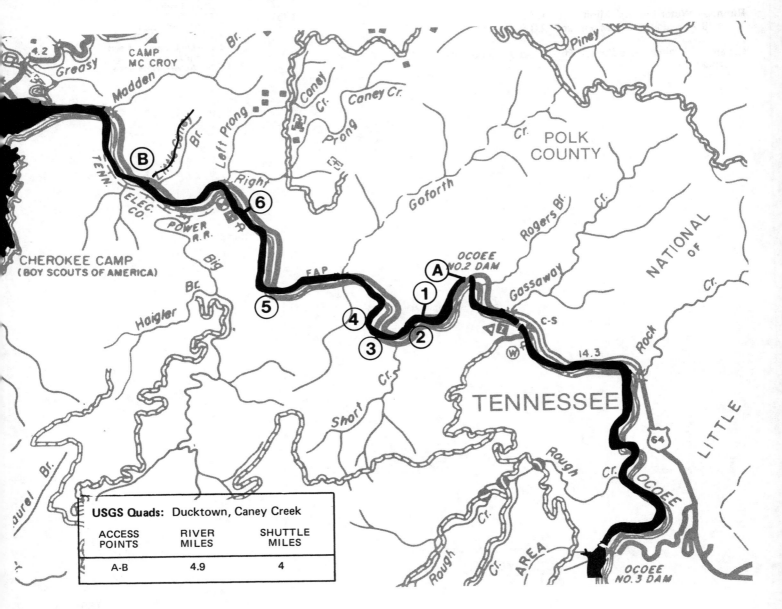

USGS Quads: Ducktown, Caney Creek

ACCESS POINTS	RIVER MILES	SHUTTLE MILES
A–B	4.9	4

Section: Ocoee No. 3 dam to Ocoee No. 2 powerhouse

Counties: Polk (TN)

Suitable For: Cruising

Appropriate For: Advanced paddlers

Months Runnable: All

Interest Highlights: Scenery, whitewater, history

Scenery: Beautiful

Difficulty: International Scale III, IV
Numerical Points 26

Average Width: 40-60 ft.
Velocity: Fast
Gradient: 57 ft./mi.

Runnable Water Level: Minimum 700 cfs
Maximum 3500 cfs, open;
4000 cfs, decked

Hazards: Keeper hydraulics, difficult rapids

Scouting: At major rapids

Portages: None required

Rescue Index: Accessible

Mean Water Temperature (°F)

Jan 43	Feb 45	Mar 52	Apr 61	May 63	Jun 67
Jul 70	Aug 71	Sep 69	Oct 63	Nov 55	Dec 48

Source of Additional Information:
Tennessee Valley Authority, (615) 745-1783

Access Point	Access Code	Access Key
A	1357	1 Paved Road
B	1357	2 Unpaved Road
		3 Short Carry
		4 Long Carry
		5 Easy Grade
		6 Steep Incline
		7 Clear Trail
		8 Brush and Trees
		9 Launching Fee Charged
		10 Private Property, Need Permission
		11 No Access, Reference Only

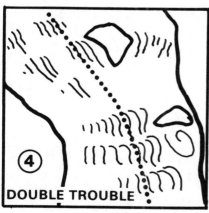

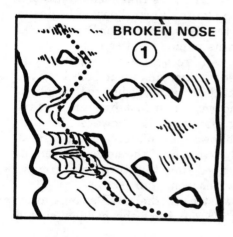

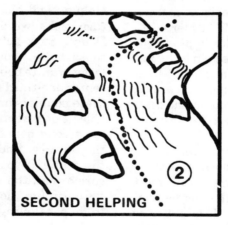

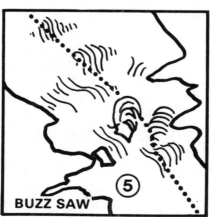

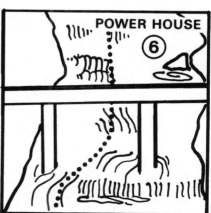

Ocoee River—*Continued*

Toccoa River (see Chapter 4) an attractive mountain stream skirting the southern reaches of the Smokies. Unfortunately, at the Georgia—Tennessee border the Copperhill mining basin fouls the water quality. Sulphuric acid leached from forty years of mining and smelting has completely sterilized the Ocoee tributaries coming out of the great copper basin. Years of airborne acid have also denuded the forested hillsides in the basin. (This little red dot amid the sea of Smoky green, along with the Great Wall of China, is one of the few man-made earth modifications visible to the orbiting astronauts.) The bare hillsides of the basin also choke the same dead Ocoee tributaries with fine-grained red silt. Water quality coming down this premier white-water run is somewhere between repulsive and lethal. Keep you mouth closed!

Hazards on this run begin before you even get your boat in the water. The only safe loading and parking area is somewhat inconveniently situated a quarter-mile upstream of the put-in on the lake side of the Ocoee No. 2 dam. This spacious parking area is generally forsaken, however, for the challenge of unloading amid the dizzying fumes of speeding diesels and the careening autos of rubbernecking tourists on US 64. Here, with nothing at risk but your life, you can park on a constricted ribbon of road shoulder right next to the put-in and attempt feverishly to unload your gear, a little at a time, when breaks in the traffic allow. TVA, alerted to this danger, has widened the shoulder to provide a twenty-minute unloading zone. On weekends during the summer, a TVA official is posted at the put-in to assist with traffic control. At other times you are on your own, though TVA prefers that you unload first, and then park in the lot as opposed to trying to carry boats down the highway.

When the Ocoee "reopened" several years ago, most paddlers groped precariously down the steep banks just below the dam to put in. Now most boaters use a put-in developed by the commercial rafters a little farther downstream. This put-in is infinitely easier on body and equipment but has the disadvantage of eliminating much of the first rapid.

Once in the water, the paddler will find the Ocoee to be synonomous with continuous action. The pace is intense and the eddies are not always where you would like them to be. Below the put-in, Class II and III rapids follow one upon the other and consist primarily of big waves and some respectable holes. These rapids are agreeably straightforward for the most part and have recognizable routes. Following this stretch of warm-up rapids, however, the river broadens and runs shallow over a long series of wide, shallow ledges known as Gonzo Shoals. Route selection is anything but obvious, and the going (particularly at minimal flow) is extremely technical.

Below the wide, shallow stretch, the river begins to narrow slightly and bend to the right. This is the approach to Broken Nose (formerly known as Veg-O-Matic), a potentially lethal series of three drops in rapid succession. The drops are near the right bank. Powerful crosscurrents surge between each of the drops and a keeper hydraulic lurks at the base of the final drop. There is a cheat route along the far left for those who perfer not to encounter the main activity in Broken Nose Rapid.

Action continues and bears back to the left on through a Class II–III series that includes Second Helping and Moon Chute. When the river begins to turn back toward the right, prepare for Double Suck. Double Suck gets its name from two closely spaced souse holes. You will recognize the rapid by the large granite boulders thrusting up and blocking the center one-third of the stream. Go just to the right of these boulders and over a four-foot drop into the first hole. Don't relax after this one, however, because the second hole follows immediately, and it will eat the unwary. Eddy out behind the large boulders in the center if you need time to recover your composure or bail the water from your boat.

Continuing downstream, the river swings away from paralleling US 64. Here the paddler should move to the far right for Double Trouble, a double set of holes and waves. Below Double Trouble, a number of smaller rapids lead into a long pool known as the Doldrums. This, the longest pool on the river, signals the presence of Class IV Table Saw about three-fourths miles ahead. At the end of the Doldrums the stream broadens conspicuously and laps playfully over the shallows with little riffles and waves. Protruding from the right bank, a large rock shelf or boulder beach funnels the water to the left.

The river narrows and the current deepens and picks up speed as it enters the most formidable rapid on the Ocoee. Table Saw is named for a large rock situated in the middle of a chute that splits the current and sends up an impressive rooster tail. Below the rock is a violent diagonal hole that fortunately is not a keeper. Table Saw can be scouted from the boulder beach on the right or from eddies on the left. In either event, key on the rooster tail and run just to its left, bracing hard as you hit the hole at the bottom. Rescue can be set on river right just below the hole where there is a nice, if not overly spacious eddy. Speedy rescue of people and equipment is important here due to the proximity of Diamond Splitter just downstream.

Consisting of yet another river-dividing boulder, Diamond Splitter rises ponderously out of the water presenting a potential for broaching or entrapment. The generally preferred route is to the right of the boulder. From here Class II and III rapids rampage more or less continuously with only one significant intervening pool as the Ocoee approaches the powerhouse. A quarter of a mile upstream of the powerhouse is Torpedo, a long, confusing, technical rapid with several powerful holes. Frequently omitted in descriptions of the Ocoee, this rapid can be very rough on a boater who chooses the wrong route. Most easily scouted from the road while running the shuttle, Torpedo should be of particular interest to first-timers.

Torpedo is separated from Hell's Hole, an enormous, deep, aerated, river-dominating hole by a pool just upstream of the powerhouse and bridge. Situated toward the right bank of the river about 45 feet upstream of the bridge, Hell's Hole can be played, surfed, or punched with the happy prospect of being flushed out in case of an upset. While Hell's Hole monopolizes the channel, a technical run skirting the hole on the left is possible (and generally advisable for open boats). It is hard to consider Hell's Hole, however, without indicating that it is only the first part of a double rapid with an obstacle course insinuated neatly in the middle. Not twenty yards beyond the fearsome hole itself is the drop known as Powerhouse Rapid. Powerhouse consists of a four-foot vertical ledge and nasty hydraulic spanning the left two-thirds of the stream, with more manageable tongue spilling down on the right. Between Hell's Hole and Powerhouse is a TVA plant bridge. Arriving safely at the bottom of all this requires making it through or around Hell's Hole, fighting the current at the bottom of the hole, which tries to carry you left, and working hard to the right to clear the bridge piling and to line up for the tongue through Powerhouse. Have a good roll if you try to play Hell's Hole, and anticipate the current kicking you left as you wash out. When the water is high (1800+ cfs) Hell's Hole washes out while the Powerhouse hydraulic becomes lethal. In this situation, run close to the right bank to avoid being carried too far left as you approach the bridge. Scout this complex stretch either while running the shuttle or from the TVA plant bridge.

If you make it this far you can drift the rest of the way (a quarter mile) to the take-out at the TVA parking lot shortly downstream.

Hiwassee River

Georgia's *Hiwassee* River (described in Chapter 4) leaves Georgia, cuts across the forested foot of a couple of North Carolina peaks, and plunges into Tennessee via the Appalachia powerhouse release as the *Hiwassee* River. It's a big watershed and an equally large riverbed for this Tennessee portion of the river.

For a non-paddling experience on the Hiwassee, take a look at the interesting and scenic 15-mile section of the river between the dam and the powerhouse. This bed is now mostly dry and carries water only during periods of extremely high natural flow from heavy rainfall. Hiking access is via the railroad tracks (still in regular use) for the entire distance. The scenery is beautiful, with mountains on both sides and unusual rock formations. There are high trestles crossing over brooks and at one point the track crosses over itself, which is famous in railroad circles. The railroad makes more than a complete circle, known as the Hiwassee Loop, to gain altitude. Nearer the powerhouse is the abandoned townsite of McFarland and the Narrows, where the river is constricted between the tracks and high rocks of unusual formation.

Downstream from the powerhouse, where the river is again, canoeable, the water is COLD. Releases come from deep in the impoundment. It is rather unusual to find such cold water in a wide, shallow stream. Trout thrive; dunked canoeists shiver.

After all its mountain meandering, this river still has one ridge left to clear in its surge towards the Tennessee River. And it is a beautiful, scenic setting as the clear-water, bouncing river makes a dramatic horseshoe bend at the foot of Tennessee's Hood Mountain. It is truly a worthy member of the state's scenic river system.

Fishermen and canoeists have almost learned to coexist on this stretch of rockbound water. When there's no dam release, the waders line the rocky outcroppings in the riverbed hunting the pooled-up fish. When the 1500-cfs dam release comes along,

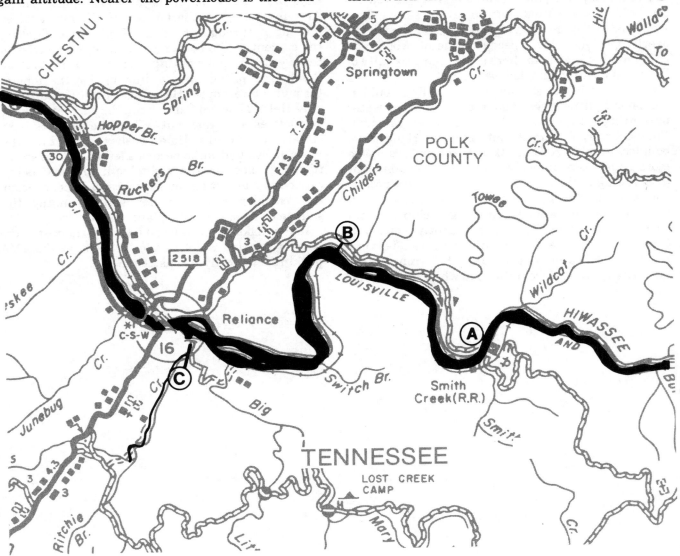

tubers, rafters, and paddlers of all types come with it, plunging over those same rock ledges and recovering in those same fished-out pools.

The first five miles of the Hiwassee below the powerhouse is Class I and II with a couple of rapids rating a strong Class II. It's a fun ride, the Hiwassee is a forgiving stream, but one that accelerates a desire to hone your skills. Swift current and the wide reach across the river can often make recovery a difficult, chilly experience. The put-in is at the powerhouse access ramp (about a quarter mile below the powerhouse). Two miles downstream is the Big Bend parking lot hidden in the trees at the foot of a series of ledges. If rain, cold, or mishap creates a need to take out early, you should know how to find that access—there isn't another one until the ramp at Reliance. Between the powerhouse and Reliance, you'll encounter a mixed bag of paddling possibilities: swift current and bouncy waves at Cabin Bend; big, unstable drops at No. 2 Rapids and Oblique Falls; tricky crosscurrents at Bigneys Rock and follow-the-flow, water-reading exercises at the Ledges and the Stairsteps; peel-off and eddy-turn practice at the Needles; and big swamper waves at Devils Shoals. Below Reliance, the river flattens out as it makes it's final run out of the mountains. Six miles downstream you'll find the U.S. Forest Service Quinn Springs fee campground across TN 30 from the fishing access on river left and the Tennessee State Park's Gee Creek campground along river just below. The Gee Creek ramp is up the creek a few yards and its entrance is marked by an old Indian-built fishtrap of V-shaped shallow rock shoals just below the mouth of the creek in the Hiwassee.

Section: Powerhouse to Reliance

Counties: Polk (TN)

Suitable For: Cruising, training

Appropriate For: Families, beginners, intermediates, advanced

Months Runnable: All

Interest Highlights: Scenery, whitewater

Scenery: Beautiful

Difficulty: International Scale   II
Numerical Points   12

Average Width: 200-400 ft.
Velocity: Fast
Gradient: 14.54 ft./mi.

Runnable Water Level: Minimum 1,500 cfs
Maximum 5,000 cfs, open;
10,000 cfs, decked

Hazards: Undercut rocks

Scouting: None required

Portages: None required

Rescue Index: Accessible

Mean Water Temperature (°F)

| Jan 44 | Feb 46 | Mar 52 | Apr 53 | May 57 | Jun 59 |
| Jul 61 | Aug 62 | Sep 61 | Oct 58 | Nov 55 | Dec 49 |

Source of Additional Information:
Webb Brothers General Store (615) 338-2373

Access Point	Access Code	Access Key
A	2357	1 Paved Road
B	2357	2 Unpaved Road
C	2357	3 Short Carry
		4 Long Carry
		5 Easy Grade
		6 Steep Incline
		7 Clear Trail
		8 Brush and Trees
		9 Launching Fee Charged
		10 Private Property, Need Permission
		11 No Access, Reference Only

USGS Quads: McFarland, Oswald Dome		
ACCESS POINTS	RIVER MILES	SHUTTLE MILES
A-B	2.4	2
B-C	3.1	3.5

Little River Canyon of Alabama

To one unfamiliar with the infinite variety of landscapes in the southeastern United States, the term "Alabama whitewater" may seem to present a ludicrous contradiction. Laughter may begin in earnest when Alabama canyons are mentioned. Laugh no more, for it is all there in the Little River Canyon in northeastern Alabama.

Located approximately 40 miles west of Rome, Georgia, just across the state line in Alabama, the Little River Canyon is an impressive cleft in the sandstone–granite countryside with a sparkling clear stream running through it. The Little River has deep mirror-surfaced pools, gentle ripples, and boulder-smashing, highly technical whitewater.

Because of the extreme seasonal fluctuations of the water level, the difficulty of an emergency exit from the bottom of the canyon, and the boating skills required to successfully complete the run, the first stop before any trip begins in the river gauge on the AL 35 bridge. The gauge is hand painted on one of the bridge pilings. Acceptable levels are a minimum of 0.5 and a maximum of 1.5. It is possible to run it at higher levels, but the mutilated carcasses of canoes, kayaks, and rafts scattered throughout the canyon offer mute testimony for those who tried and failed. Boaters should have intermediate to advanced skill levels before attempting the Little River Canyon.

The put-in is one of the more memorable parts of the trip. One descends approximately six hundred feet straight down from the rim of the canyon to its floor. Begin at the site of the old chairlift at Eberharts Point on the Canyon Rim Parkway (AL 275). It is an arduous carry to the river, but do not succumb to the urge to weep and toss your boat into the abyss. The river is well worth the struggle.

Scenery ranges from delightful to magnificent. The water is usually clear, with the deep, shimmering, turquoise pools. Cedars, pines, hardwoods, and, in spring, a profusion of wild flowers adorn the cliffs on either side of the river. Small tributaries plummet to merge with the primary flow, creating many intimate coves with excellent photographic potential.

Do not become too enthralled with the scenic vistas, for the river demands your full attention at times. Rapids are numerous and good boat control is essential. If dependable eddy turns, ferrying skills, and good judgment are not part of your paddling program, then do not venture here.

Most rapids are not described in detail here. Scout anything that is not clearly visible. Often there is more than one possible route and at least one impossible one. Huge boulders will often obscure the downstream view. The heaviest rapids (Class III–IV) are more concentrated in the first third of the run.

Section: Eberharts Point (old chairlift) to AL 273

Counties: De Kalb (AL), Cherokee (AL)

Suitable For: Cruising

Appropriate For: Intermediate and advanced paddlers

Months Runnable: November through May

Interest Highlights: Scenery, wildlife, whitewater, geology
Scenery: Spectacular

Difficulty: International Scale III-IV, V
Numerical Points 28

Average Width: 30-50 ft.
Velocity: Fast
Gradient: 31.25 ft./mi.

Runnable Water Level: Minimum 0.5 ft.
(AL 35 bridge gauge) Maximum 1.5 ft.
Hazards: Strainers, undercut rocks, flashflooding

Scouting: At rapids and blind curves

Portages: As needed according to water level and skill level

Rescue Index: Remote to extremely remote

Mean Water Temperature (°F) Data not available

Jan	Feb	Mar	Apr	May	Jun
Jul	Aug	Sep	Oct	Nov	Dec

Source of Additional Information: Desoto State Park (205) 845-0051

Access Point	Access Code	Access Key
A	1468	1 Paved Road
B	1357	2 Unpaved Road
C	1357	3 Short Carry
		4 Long Carry
		5 Easy Grade
		6 Steep Incline
		7 Clear Trail
		8 Brush and Trees
		9 Launching Fee Charged
		10 Private Property, Need Permission
		11 No Access, Reference Only

One rapid of special merit, Bottleneck (Class IV), can be deadly. It is recognizable by a Class II–III series of waves surging toward the left bank and disappearing into a jumble of boulders. Run these and scout the next section from the left bank. Go back toward the right, eddy out, and scout the final drop from the right side. Take your time or you may end up in a blind alley. The final drop is reminiscent of Corkscrew on Section IV of the Chattooga. The large curler at the bottom can eat decked as well as open boats.

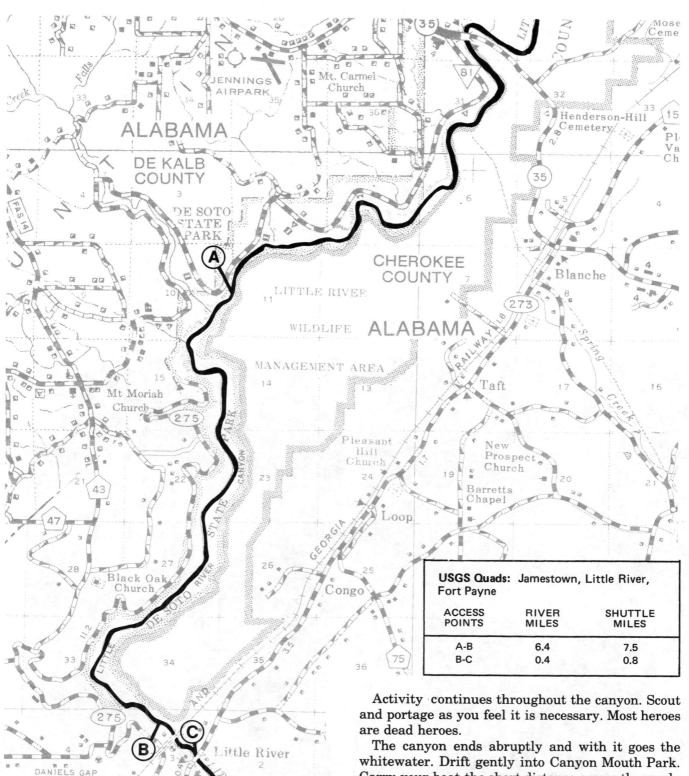

USGS Quads:	Jamestown, Little River, Fort Payne		
ACCESS POINTS	RIVER MILES	SHUTTLE MILES	
A-B	6.4	7.5	
B-C	0.4	0.8	

Activity continues throughout the canyon. Scout and portage as you feel it is necessary. Most heroes are dead heroes.

The canyon ends abruptly and with it goes the whitewater. Drift gently into Canyon Mouth Park. Carry your boat the short distance across the sandy beach to the parking area, take a hot shower in the conveniently located bathhouse, and congratulate yourself and your companions on another good day on the river.

If the Canyon Mouth Park is closed, an alternate take-out is approximately one mile farther downstream at the AL 273 bridge.

161

Nantahala River, North Carolina.

Appendixes

Appendix A

Commercial Raft Trips and Expeditions

Several commercial raft outfitters operate in the state of Georgia. All operate on whitewater streams of varying difficulty and are reputable, safety conscious, and professional. There are, however, several companies that will rent rafts or other inflatables for use on rated whitewater to individuals who are totally ignorant and naïve about the dangers involved. These companies normally do not run guided trips but rather send unsuspecting clients down the river on their own to cope with whatever problems or hazards materialize. It is our position that safe enjoyment of whitewater requires education and experience, and that attempting to paddle whitewater in any type of craft, privately owned or rented, without the prerequisite skills or without on-river professional guidance is dangerous in the extreme. That various companies will rent boats or rafts to the unknowing only proves that some people are unscrupulous, not that whitewater paddling is safe for the unaccompanied beginner.

All the reputable raft companies in Georgia operate guided excursions only, where professional whitewater guides accompany and assist their clients throughout the run. This type of experience has an unparalleled safety record in the United States and represents an enjoyable and educational way of exposing the newcomer to this whitewater sport. Through professional outfitters, thousands of people every year are turned on to the exhilaration of paddling. Spouses and friends of paddlers, who are normally relegated to enjoying our beautiful rivers vicariously through the stories of their companions, are made welcome and provided the thrill of experiencing the tumbling cascades firsthand.

Choosing a commercial outfitter is made somewhat easier by the Eastern Professional River Outfitters' Association (EPRO), the professional organization for commercial river runners in the eastern United States and Canada. Through its devotion to safety and its strict membership admission requirements, EPRO ensures that its members companies epitomize the highest standards in professional river outfitting. EPRO members operating guided raft trips in Georgia include:

Nantahala Outdoor Center, 13077 Highway 19 W, Bryson City, NC 28713-9114. Phone: (704) 488-2175.
Guided raft trips on the Ocoee and Chattooga rivers.

Southeastern Expeditions, 2936 N. Druid Hills Road, Atlanta, GA 30329. Phone: (404) 329-0433 (Atlanta) or (706) 782-4331 (Clayton).
Guided raft trips on the Chattooga River.

Wildwater, Ltd., P.O. Box 101 Long Creek, SC 29658. Phone: (803) 647-5336.
Guided raft trips on the Chattooga and Ocoee rivers.

Educational Field Trips

Wilderness Southeast, 711 Sandtown Road, Savannah, GA 31410. Phone: (912) 897-5108.
Nonprofit outdoor school in southern Georgia.

Wolfcreek Wilderness, Inc., 2158 W. Wolfcreek Rd., Blairsville, GA 30512. Phone: (706) 745-5553.
Nonprofit outdoor school.

Commercial River Outfitters (Canoe Liveries)

Blue Ridge Mountain Sports
Lenox Square
3393 Peachtree Rd. NE
Atlanta, GA 30326
(404) 266-8372

Chattooga Whitewater Shop
US Hwy 76
Long Creek, SC 29658
(803) 647-9083

High Country Outfitters, Inc.
4400 Ashford-Dunwoody Road
1412 Perimeter Mall
Atlanta, GA 30346
(404) 391-9657

Wildewood Shop
Box 999
Helen, GA 30545
(706) 878-4451

Appalachian Outfitters
P.O. Box 793
Highway 60 S.
Dahlonega, GA 30533
(706) 864-7117

Go With The Flow
4 Elizabeth Way
Roswell, GA 30075
(404) 992-3200

Mountaintown Outfitters

(706) 635-2524

Broad River Outpost
Rt. 3, Box 3449
Danielsville, GA 30633
(706) 795-3242

Some state parks rent canoes for use at their locations only. See the state park information in another part of this Appendix.

Upper Chattahoochee River.

Photo by Don Otey.

Appendix B

Canoeing Organizations

Georgia

Local canoe clubs render an invaluable service to paddlers of all skill levels. Georgia clubs provide well-rounded programs including competition, whitewater and flatwater scheduled cruises, clinics, conservation programs, social outings, winter pool sessions, and regular meetings. In addition most clubs publish monthly or bimonthly newsletters. Dues vary as do services to members but the general range is $5.00 to $12.00 a year.

Atlanta Whitewater Club
P.O. Box 33
Clarkston, GA 30021

Georgia Canoeing Association
Box 7023
Atlanta, GA 30309

Neighboring States

Tennessee Scenic Rivers Association
P.O. Box 3104
Nashville, TN 37219

East Tennessee Whitewater Club
P.O. Box 3074
Oak Ridge, TN 37830

Tennessee Valley Canoe Club
P.O. Box 11125
Chattanooga, TN 37401

Sewanee Canoe and Outing Club
The University of the South
Sewanee, TN 37375

Chota Canoe Club
P.O. Box 8270, University Station
Knoxville, TN 37916

Jackson Rapids Transit
P.O. Box 3034
Jackson, TN 38301

Bluff City Canoe Club
P.O. Box 4523
Memphis, TN 38104

Birmingham Canoe Club
P.O. Box 951
Birmingham, AL 35201

Tennessee Eastman Recreation Club
Gordon Newland Building, 150-B
P.O. Box 511
Kingsport, TN 37662

Carolina Canoe Club
Box 9011
Greensboro, NC 27408

National

American Canoe Association
P.O. Box 248
Lorton, VA 22079

American Whitewater Affiliation
P.O. Box 321
Concord, NH 03301

U.S. Canoe Association
P.O. Box 9
Winamac, IN 46996

Appendix C

Where to Buy Maps

As indicated in the introductory material, maps included in this book are intended to supplement rather than replace U.S. Geological Survey topographic quadrangles and county road maps. Maps can be purchased from the following locations.

United States Geological Survey (USGS)

Topographic Quadrangles

Eastern U.S.

Distribution section
U.S. Geological Survey
1200 South Eads Street
Arlington, VA 22202

Georgia

Department of Natural Resources Map Sales
Fourth Floor, Agriculture Building
19 Martin Luther King Jr. Drive SW
Atlanta, GA 30334
Phone (404) 656-3214

Albany

Albany Metropolitan Planning Commission
225 Pine Ave.
Zip 31703

Atlanta

Lowe Engineers, Inc.
1920 Monroe Dr. NE
Zip 31703

Atlanta General Microfilm Map Co.
3060 Pharr Court North, C
Zip 31702

Mayes, Sudderth & Etheredge, Inc.
1775 The Exchange
Zip 31705

John J. Harte Associates, Inc.
3290 Cumberland Club Drive
Zip 31703

Augusta

Augusta Blueprint & Microfilm, Inc.
No. 6 Eighth St.
Zip 30904

Besson & Pope Consulting Engineers
1005 Emmett St., Suite B
Zip 30903

Brunswick

Coastal Area Planning & Development Commission
Zip 31520

Columbus

White's Book Store
Cross Country Plaza
Zip 31906

Wickham's Outdoor World
Cross Country Plaza
Zip 31906

Dalton

North Georgia Area Planning & Development
Commission
212 North Pentz St.
Zip 30720

Decatur

Reeder & McGaughey, Inc.
2024 Lawrenceville Hwy.
Zip 30033

Jonesboro

Hoffman, Butler & Associates, Inc.
Arrowhead Professional Park
409 Arrowhead, Building A
Zip 30236

Marietta

Aerial Surveys
107 Church St. NW
Zip 30062

Morrow

Reeder & McGaughey, Inc.
1221 Southlake Mall
Zip 30260

Savannah

Savannah Blue Print Company
11 East York St.
Zip 31404

Stockbridge

Lewis Hurd Engineers
May's Corner, US 23N
Zip 30281

Toccoa

Harris Sporting Goods
Grant Plaza
Zip 30577

County Road Maps

County road maps are also usually available at individual county office buildings and local highway department and Department of Transportation offices.

Georgia

Department of Transportation
Map Room, Room 10
Number 2, Capital Square
Atlanta, GA 30334

Tennessee

Department of Transporation
Research and Planning
Room 400 Doctors Building
706 Church Street
Nashville, TN 37203
ATTN: Map Sales

North Carolina

Department of Transportation
Division of Highways
Raleigh, NC 27611
ATTN: Map Sales

Virginia

Department of Highways and Transportation
1221 East Broad Street
Richmond, VA 23219
ATTN: Map Sales

Lake Maps

U.S. Army Corps of Engineers
Public Affairs Office
30 Pryor Street, S.W.
Atlanta, GA 30303

South Carolina

Department of Highways and Public Transportation
ATTN: Map Sales
P.O. Box 191
Columbia, SC 29202

Alabama

State of Alabama Highway Department
Bureau of State Planning
ATTN: Map Room
Montgomery, AL 36130

Florida

Department of Transportation
ATTN: Maps and Publications
Mail Station 13
Haydon Burns Building
Tallahassee, FL 32301

Appendix D

Suggested Reading

Paddling Guides of Surrounding States

Appalachian Whitewater, Volume I, The Southern Mountains, by Bob Sehlinger, Don Otey, Bob Benner, William Nealy, and Bob Lantz, 1986.

A Canoeing and Kayaking Guide to the Streams of Tennessee, Volumes I and II, by Bob Sehlinger and Bob Lantz, 1979.

Carolina Whitewater, by Bob Benner, revised edition, 1979.

Southern Georgia Canoeing: A Canoeing and Kayaking Guide to the Streams of the Western Piedmont, Coastal Plain, Georgia Coast and Okefenokee Swamp, by Bob Sehlinger and Don Otey, 1980.

All books published by Menasha Ridge Press, Post Office Box 59257, Birmingham, AL 35259-9257.

Appendix E

Georgia Fish and Wildlife

The following compilations of fish and animal life have been adapted from *The Natural Environments of Georgia,* by Charles H. Wharton, published jointly by the Geologic and Water Resources Division and Resource Planning Section of the Office of Planning and Research, Georgia Department of Natural Resources, Atlanta, Georgia, in 1978.

Georgia Department of Natural Resources Game and Fish Offices

Calhoun Game & Fish Office
P.O. Box 786
Calhoun, GA 30703-0786
(706) 629-8674

Gainesville Game & Fish Office
Route 13, Box 322A
Gainesville, GA 30501
(404) 532-5302

Thomson Game & Fish Office
142 Bob Kirk Road
Thomson, GA 30824
(706) 595-4211

Walton Game & Fish Office
Route 2 2109 U.S. 278 SE
Social Circle, GA 30279
(706) 557-2227

Manchester Game & Fish Office
601 3rd Avenue
Manchester, GA 31816
(706) 846-8448

Metter Game & Fish Office
Rt. 2, Box 4B
Metter, GA 30439
(912) 685-2145

Waycross Game & Fish Office
P.O. Box 2089
Waycross, GA 31502
(912) 285-6093

Brunswick Game & Fish Office
1 Conservation Way
Brunswick, GA 31523
(912) 264-7237

Demeries Creek Game & Fish Office
Rt. 2, Box 219R
Richmond Hill, GA 31324
(912) 727-2111

Albany Game & Fish Office
2024 Newton Rd.
Albany, GA 31708
(912) 430-4252

Game Fish

Chattahoochee River

brown trout
rainbow trout
brook trout
redfin or grass pickerel
chain pickerel
muskellunge
channel catfish
white bass
striped bass
striped-white bass hybrid
rock bass
flier
redbreast sunfish
warmouth
bluegill
dollar sunfish
longear sunfish
redear sunfish
spotted sunfish (stumpknocker)
redeye bass
smallmouth bass
largemouth bass
spotted bass
white crappie
black crappie
sauger
walleye

Oconee River

American shad
redfin or grass pickerel
chain pickerel
muskellunge
channel catfish
white bass
striped bass
striped-white bass hybrid
redbreast sunfish
warmouth
bluegill
dollar sunfish
redear sunfish
spotted sunfish (stumpknocker)
redeye bass
spotted bass
largemouth bass
white crappie
black crappie
walleye

Savannah River

hickory shad
American shad
brown trout
rainbow trout
brook trout
redfin or grass pickerel
chain pickerel
muskellunge
channel catfish
flathead catfish
white bass
striped bass
striped-white bass hybrid
flier
redbreast sunfish
warmouth
bluegill
dollar sunfish
redear sunfish
spotted sunfish (stumpknocker)
redeye bass
smallmouth bass
largemouth bass
white crappie
black crappie
sauger
walleye

Vertebrate Fauna of Northern Georgia
(Blue Ridge Mountains, Ridge & Valley, Cumberland Plateau Regions)

A. Salamanders

Hellbender*
Common mudpuppy*
Cherokee salamander*
Black-bellied salamander*
Shovel-nosed salamander*
Blue Ridge two-lined salamander*
Carolina Mountain spring
  salamander*
Long-tailed salamander*
Mountain dusky salamander*
Green salamander
Appalachian woodland salamander
Northern dusky salamander*
Spotted dusky salamander*
Slimy salamander*
Cave salamander
Zig zag salamander*
Northeast purples*

B. Frogs and Toads

Mountain chorus frog
Northern leopard frog
Wood frog
Northern cricket frog
Northern spring peeper
Northern green frog
American Toad
Bullfrog*
Gray tree frog
Fowler's toad
Eastern spadefoot toad
Eastern narrow-mouthed toad

C. Turtles

Eastern painted turtle*
Cumberland turtle*
Snapper*
Florida snapper*

Gulf coast smooth softshell turtle
Map turtle*
Midland painted turtle*

D. Snakes

Northern banded water snake*
Northern ringneck snake
Black rat snake
Eastern milk snake
Dekay's brown snake
Green snake*
Eastern worm snake
Northern black racer
Black king snake
Northern pine snake
Northern copperhead
Timber rattlesnake
Southern ground snake
King snake
Eastern ribbon snake
Southern ribbon snake
Red-bellied snake
Southern hognose snake
Rough green snake
Corn snake
Coachwhip snake
Northern scarlet snake

E. Mammals

Masked shrew
Pigmy shrew
Red squirrel
Deer mouse
Smoky shrew
Wood rabbit
Woodland jumping mouse
Harvest mouse
Meadow jumping mouse
Ground hog

Eastern chipmunk
White-footed mouse
Big-eared bat
Eastern wood rat
Mountain lion (cougar, puma)
Big brown bat
Red bat
Cotton rat
Rice rat*
Muskrat*
Mink*
Black bear
Opossum
Swamp rabbit*
Raccoon*
Short-tailed shrew
Eastern mole
Gray squirrel
Southern flying squirrel
Long-tailed weasel
Bobcat
White-tailed deer
Red fox
Gray fox
Fox squirrel
East spotted skunk
Stripped skunk
Cottontail rabbit

F. Lizards

Northern coal skink
Southern coal skink
Northern fence lizard
Green anole
Five-lined skink
Ground skink
Six-lined race runner

*Likely to be encountered on or
around streams

Vertebrate Fauna of the Piedmont

A. Salamanders

Small-mouthed salamander
Eastern four-toed salamander
Georgia red-backed salamander
Eastern mud salamander*
Southern two-lined salamander*
Three-lined salamander*
Northern red salamander*
Red-backed salamander
Red-spotted newt
Mole salamander
Marbled salamander*
Slimy salamander
Spotted salamander
Spotted dusky salamander*

B. Frogs and Toads

Eastern chorus frog
Northern spring peeper

Northern green frog
Pickerel frog
American toad*
Green tree frog*
Bird-voiced tree frog
Eastern bird-voiced tree frog*
Bronze frog*
Southern leopard frog*
Upland chorus frog
Eastern narrow-mouthed toad
Bullfrog*
Gray tree frog
Fowler's toad

C. Turtles

Three-toed box turtle
Eastern painted turtle*
Barbour's map turtle*
River cooter*

Yellow-bellied turtle*
Gulf coast spiny softshell turtle
Snapper*
Loggerhead musk turtle*
Florida snapper*
Gulf coast smooth softshell turtle*

D. Lizards

Northern fence lizard
Slender glass lizard
Green anole lizard
Five-lined skink
Ground skink
Southeastern five-lined skink
Six-lined race runner

E. Snakes

Yellow-bellied water snake*
Midland banded water snake*

Midwest worm snake
Eastern worm snake
Northern black racer
Black king snake
Northern pine snake
Northern copperhead
Red-bellied water snake*
Brown water*
Southern ringneck snake
Gray rat snake*
Scarlet king snake
Eastern cottonmouth*
Timber rattlesnake
Southern ground snake
King snake
Eastern ribbon snake
Southern ribbon snake
Red-bellied snake
Eastern hognose snake
Rough green snake
Mole snake
Corn snake
Coachwhip snake
Northern scarlet snake

Winter camping.

Garter snake
Crowned snake

F. Mammals

Silver-haired bat
Harvest mouse
Meadow vole
Meadow jumping mouse
Groundhog
Eastern chipmunk
White-footed mouse
Seminole bat
Beaver*
River otter*
Southeast shrew
Hoary bat
Cotton mouse
Least shrew
Eastern pipistrelle
Big brown bat
Evening bat
Red bat
Cotton rat

Muskrat*
Mink*
Golden mouse
Black bear
Opossum
Swamp rabbit*
Raccoon*
Short-tailed shrew
Gray squirrel
Eastern mole
Southern flying squirrel
Pine vole
Long-tailed weasel
Bobcat
White-tailed deer
Old-field mouse
Fox squirrel
Red fox
Gray fox
Spotted skunk
Striped skunk
Cottontail rabbit

*Likely to be encountered on or
around streams

171

Appendix A

Camping Sites

The following camp sites have been selected from listings of the Georgia
State Bureau of Industry and Trade and the U.S. Forest Service

NEAREST TOWN	CAMP NAME	DIRECTIONS & ADDRESS	FACILITIES	SEASON
Calhoun A-1	Hidden Creek (Chattahoochee Nat. Forest)	7 1/2 mi. SW on GA 156; 2 mi NW on FS Rd. 231; 3 mi. SW on FS Rd. 228; 1 mi. N on FS Rd. 955. Armuchee Ranger Dist. (706) 638-1085	16 sites; no hookups; pit toilets; picnic tables; fire area.	May 1 to Oct. 31 Maximum: 14 days
Chatsworth	Fort Mountain State Park	8 mi. E on GA 52 from jct. of 52/76. (706) 695-2621	74 sites; 70 water & electric; flush toilets; hot showers; picnic tables; fire area.	Year Round Maximum: 14 days
	Lake Conasauga	14 mi. E on US 76; 3 mi. NW on FS Rd. 18; 10 mi. N on FS Rd. 68. Cohutta Ranger Dist. 401 Old Ellijay Rd., Chatsworth, Ga. 30705. (706) 695-6736	35 sites; 32' max. RV length; 35 no hookup; flush toilets; picnic tables; fire area.	Apr. 15 to Oct. 31 Maximum: 14 days
Rossville	Holiday Inn Travel-Park	US 41 & I-75 (Southbound exit 1/ North-bound exit 1B); 1/2 mi. W on US 41N; 1/2 mi. S on Mack Smith Rd. (706) 891-9766	171 sites; 101 full hookups; 52 water & electric (20, 30 & 50 amp receptacles); 18 no hookups; flush toilets; hot showers: dump stations; laundry; public phone; full service store/RV supplies; LP gas refill; ice; picnic tables.	Year Round; full facility Memorial Day thru Labor Day
Summerville	James H. Floyd State Park	US 27 & GA 100; 3 mi. E on Marble Springs Rd. (706) 857-0826	26 sites; 26 water & electric; no motorcycles; flush toilets; picnic tables; fire area; showers.	Year Round Maximum: 14 days
Blairsville A-2	Canal-Lake Campground	US 129 & US 76; 2 mi. N on US 129/US 19; follow signs. (706) 745-1501	15 sites; 10 water & electric; 3 pull-thrus; flush toilets; hot showers; dump facility; laundry; public phone; grocery; gas; ice; picnic tables; fire rings; wood.	Year Round
	Lake Winfield Scott (Chattahoochee Nat. Forest)	10 1/4 mi. S on W 19; 6 1/2 mi. W on GA 180. Brasstown Ranger Dist. (706) 896-2556	36 sites; 32' max. RV length; 35 no hookups; flush toilets; hot showers; picnic tables; fire area.	May 1 to Nov. 1 Maximum: 14 days
	Trackrock Campground	US 129 & US 76; 2 3/4 mi. S on US 129; 4 mi. E on county road. (706) 745-2420	90 sites; 38 full hookups; 52 water & electric (15 amp receptacles) 10 pull-thrus; flush toilets; hot showers; dump facility; laundry; public phone; LP gas refill; ice; 77 picnic tables; grills; wood.	Year Round; full facility Memorial Day thru Labor Day
	Vogel State Park	US 76 & US 129/19; 11 mi. S on US 129/19. (706) 745-2628	100 sites; 95 water & electric; flush toilets; hot showers; dump facility; picnic tables; fire area.	Year Round Maximum: 14 days
Blue Ridge	Lake Blue Ridge Campground	US 76 & GA 5; 2 mi. E on US 76; 2 mi. S on FS Rd. 605 Toccoa Ranger Dist. (706) 632-3031	56 sites; 22' max RV length; 56 no hookups; flush toilets; picnic tables; wood.	Apr. 19 to Oct 31 Maximum: 14 days
Dahlonega	Cooper Creek (Chattahoochee Nat. Forest)	25 1/2 mi. N on GA 60; 6 mi NE on FS Rd. 4. Toccoa Ranger Dist. (706) 632-3031	17 sites; 32' max RV length; 17 no hookups; flush toilets; picnic tables; fire area.	Apr. 1 to Oct 31 Maximum: 14 days
	Dockery Lake (Chattahoochee Nat. Forest)	11 1/2 mi. N on GA 60; 3/4 mi NE on FS Rd. 654 Chestatee Ranger Dist. (706) 864-6173	11 sites; 32' max RV length; 11 no hookups; flush toilets; picnic tables; fire area.	May 1 to Oct 31 Maximum: 14 days
	Frank Gross (Chattahoochee Nat. Forest)	27 mi. N on GA 60; 5 mi. SW on FS Rd. 69 Toccoa Ranger Dist. (706) 632-3031	9 sites; 9 no hookups; flush toilets; picnic tables; fire area.	Apr. 1 to Oct 31 Maximum: 14 days
	Mulky (Chatta-hoochee Nat. Forest)	25 1/2 mi. N on GA 60 4 3/4 mi NE on FS Rd. 4 Toccoa Ranger Dist. (706) 632-3031	11 sites; 11 no hookups; flush toilets; picnic tables; fire area.	Apr. 1 to Oct 31 Maximum: 14 days
	Waters Creek (Chattahoochee Nat. Forest)	12 1/4 mi. NE on US 19; 1 mi. NW on FS Rd. 34 Chestatee Ranger Dist. (706) 864-6173	8 sites; 8 no hookups; flush toilets; picnic tables; fire area.	May 1 to Oct 31 Maximum: 14 days
	Deep Hole (Chattahoochee Nat. Forest)	27 mi. N on GA 60. Toccoa Ranger Dist. (706) 632-3031	8 sites; 8 no hookups; flush toilets; picnic tables.	Apr. 1 to Oct 31 Maximum: 14 days
Ellijay	Doll Mountain Campground on Carters Lake (Corps of Engineers)	5 mi. S on GA 5; 5 mi. W on Flat Creek Rd.; 5 mi. N to Doll Mountain sign; 1 mi. E to park entrance. (706) 276-4413	55 sites; 25 no hookups; no motorcycles; flush toilets; hot showers; picnic tables; fire area; grills.	Apr. 1 thru Labor Day Maximum: 14 days

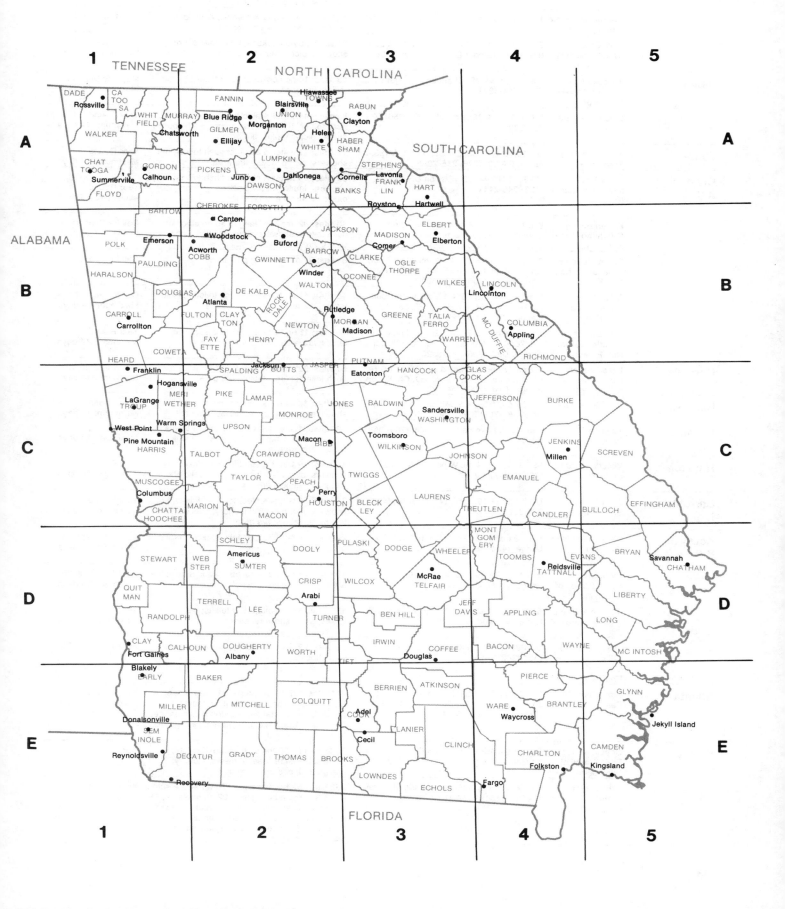

Hiawassee	Hickory Nut Cove Trout Farms & Campground	US 76 & GA 75 2 mi. N on GA 75; 3 mi. E on Upper Bell Rd. (706) 896-5341	115 sites; 50 water & electric (20 amp receptacles); 25 no hookups; 30 pull-thrus; flush toilets; hot showers; dump facility; phone available; ice; picnic tables; wood.	Year Round
	Georgia Mountain Campground	1 mi. W of town off US 76. (706) 896-4191	187 sites; 187 water & electric; flush toilets; hot showers; public phone; ice.	Apr. 1 to Nov. 1
	Lake Chatuge (Chattahoochee Nat. Forest)	2 1/2 mi. W on US 76; 1 mi. S on GA 288. Brasstown Ranger Dist. (706) 896-2556	30 sites; 30 no hookups; flush toilets; hot showers; picnic tables; fire area.	May 1 to Nov. 1 Maximum: 14 days
Helen	Andrews Cove (Chattahoochee Nat. Forest)	6 mi. N on GA 75; Chattooga Ranger Dist. (706) 754-6221	10 sites; 10 no hookups; flush toilets; picnic tables; fire area.	May 1 to Sep. 10 Maximum: 14 days
	Unicoi State Park	GA 356 & GA 75; 1 mi. N on GA 356. (706) 878-2201	82 sites; 49 water & electric; 33 no hookups; flush toilets; hot showers; dump facility; public phone; picnic tables; fire area.	Year Round Maximum: 14 days
Juno	Amicalola Falls State Park	GA 136 & GA 183; 5 mi. NW on GA 183; 3 mi. on GA 52. (706) 265-2885	17 sites; 17 water & electric; flush toilets; hot showers; picnic tables; fire area.	Year Round Maximum: 14 days
Clayton A-3	Black Rock Mountain State Park	US 76 & US 441; 3 mi. N on US 441-23. (706) 746-2141	59 sites; 48 water & electric; flush toilets; hot showers; laundry; public phone; grocery; ice; picnic tables; fire area; wood.	Year Round Maximum: 14 days
	Rabun Beach (Chattahoochee Nat. Forest)	6 1/2 mi. S on US 441; 1/4. mi. W on County Rd. 10; 1 1/2 mi S on GA 15. Tallulah Ranger Dist. (706)782-3320	80 sites; 32' max RV length; some electric; flush toilets; showers; dump facility; picnic tables; fire area; wood.	Call for Season Maximum: 14 days
	Sandy Bottoms (Chattahoochee Nat. Forest)	9 mi. NW on US 76; 4 1/2. mi. N on County Rd. 70; 4 mi. NW on FS Rd. 70. Tallulah Ranger Dist. (706) 782-3320	8 sites; 8 no hook-ups; pit toilets.	Call for Season
	Tallulah River (Chattahoochee Nat. Forest)	8 mi. SW on US 76; 4 1/2 mi. N on County Rd.70; 4 mi. NW on FS Rd. 70. Tallulah Ranger Dist. (706) 782-3320	16 sites; 16 no hookups; flush toilets; picnic tables; fire area.	Call for Season Maximum: 14 days
	Tate Branch (Chattahoochee Nat. Forest)	9 mi. NW on US 76; 4 1/2. mi. N on County Rd. 70; 4 mi. NW on FS Rd. 70. Tallulah Ranger Dist. (706) 782-3320	11 sites; 11 no hookups; pit toilets; picnic tables; fire area.	Year Round Maximum: 14 days
Cornelia	Lake Russell (Chattahoochee Nat. Forest)	1/2 mi. NE on US 123; 1 mi. SE on FS Rd. 63; 2 3/4 mi. SE on FS Rd. 59. Chattooga Ranger Dist. (706) 754-6221	51 sites; 32' max RV length; 51 no hookups; flush toilets; picnic tables; fire area.	May 1 to Sep. 10 Maximum: 14 days
Hartwell	Hart State Park	US 29 & GA 51; 4 mi. W on GA 51; 3 mi. N on GA 8. (706) 376-8756	60 sites; 60 water & electric; flush toilets; hot showers; laundry; picnic tables; fire area.	Year Round Maximum: 14 days
Lavonia	Tugaloo State Park	6 mi. N off Lavonia on GA 328. (706) 356-4362	120 sites; 120 water & electric; flush toilets; hot showers; dump facility; laundry; picnic tables; fire area.	Year Round Maximum: 14 days
Royston	Victoria Bryant State Park	I-29 & GA 17; 4 mi. W on I-29 & GA 327. (706) 245-6270	19 sites; 19 water & electric; flush toilets; hot showers; dump facility; laundry; public phone; ice; picnic tables; fire area; wood.	Year Round Maximum: 14 days
Carrollton B-1	John Tanner State Park	US 27 & GA 16; 6 mi. W on GA 16. (404) 830-2222	36 sites; 36 water & electric; flush toilets; hot showers; dump facility; laundry; public phone; ice; picnic tables; fire area.	Year Round Maximum: 14 days
Acworth B-2	Clark Creek North (Corps of Engineers)	Exit 121 off I-75; Glade Rd. to Clark Creek bridge. (404) 382-4700	24 sites; 14 hookups; pit toilets; picnic tables; grills; showers.	April 1 to Sept. 26 Maximum: 14 days
	Clark Creek South (Corps of Engineers)	Exit 121 off I-75; Glade Rd. to Clark Creek bridge. (404) 382-4700	40 sites; 25 hookups; toilets; picnic tables; fire area; grills; showers; beach.	April 1 to Sept. 26 Maximum: 14 days
	McKinney Campground (Corps of Engineers)	5 mi. N on Glade Rd; 3/4 mi. W on King's Camp Rd. (404) 382-4700	150 sites; 142 hookups; pit toilets; picnic tables; grills; showers; beach.	Year Round Maximum: 14 days
	Old Hwy 41 #3 (Allatoona Lake Corps of Engineers)	GA 293 N of Acworth about 4 mi. on right. (404) 382-4700	50 sites; 22 water & electric; beach; shower/wash house.	April 1 to Sept. 26
Atlanta	Stone Mountain Park	I-85 & I-285; 5 1/2 mi. S on I-285 (exit 30-B); 7 1/2mi. E on US 78 (Stone Mountain Freeway). (404) 498-5710	441 sites; 110 full hookups; 31 water & electric (20 & 30 amp receptacles); flush toilets; hot showers; dump station; laundry; public phone; Grocery/RV supplies; LP-gas refill; ice; picnic tables; grills; wood.	Year Round Maximum: 14 days
Buford	Chestnut Ridge Park (Corps of Engineers)	GA 13 & GA 20; 7 mi. N on GA 13; 2 1/2 mi. on Gaines Ferry Rd. (404) 967-6710	32 tent sites; 59 trailer sites; flush toilets; picnic tables; fire area; showers; laundry; playground; beach.	Apr. 2 to Sept. 10
	Lake Lanier Islands Campground	GA 365 (exit 2) & GA 347; 4 1/2 mi. W on GA 347. (404) 932-7270.	252 sites; 52 full hookups; 178 water & electric (20 & 30 amp receptacles); 22 no hookups; 55 pull-thrus; flush toilets; hot showers; dump facility; laundry; public phone; grocery/RV supplies; LP-gas refill; marine gas; ice; picnic tables; grills; wood.	Year Round

	Old Federal Road Park (Corps of Engineers)	US 23 & GA 20; 10 mi. N off US 23. (404) 967-6757	24 tent sites; 59 trailer sites; flush toilets; picnic tables; fire area; showers; laundry.	Maximum: 14 days Mar. 10 to Oct. 29
	Sawnee Campground (Corps of Engineers)	US 23 & GA 20; 6 mi. W off GA 20. (404) 887-0592	56 sites; 44 hookups; flush toilets; picnic tables; fire area; showers; laundry.	Apr. 7. to Sept. 10
	Shady Grove Park (Corps of Engineers)	GA 400 N to exit 17; 1 mi. N on GA 301; right onto GA 369 for 1 mi.; right on Shady Grove Rd. for 1 mi. (404) 887-2067	119 sites; 45 hookups; flush toilets; picnic tables; fire area; 2 group sites; shower; laundry.	Apr. 2 to Sept. 12
	Shoal Creek Camping Area (Corps of Engineers)	5 mi. NW of town. (404) 945-9541	125 sites; 65 hookups; flush toilets; 2 group sites; showers; laundry.	Mar. 5 to Oct 24
Canton	Sweetwater Campground (Corps of Engineers)	5 1/2 mi. W on GA 20; 2 mi. S on Fields Chapel Rd. (404) 382-4700	148 sites; 108 no hookups; 40 water & electric; flush/pit toilets; 70 picnic tables; grills; showers.	Apr. 1 to Sept. 26 Maximum: 14 days
Woodstock	Victoria Campground (Corps of Engineers)	S on GA 5; 6 mi. W on GA 92; 2 mi. N on GA 205; 2.2 mi. W. on Victoria Rd.(404) 382-4700	74 sites; 74 electric; pit toilets; 10 picnic tables; grills; showers; beach.	Mar 1 to Nov. 1 Maximum: 14 days
Comer B-3	Watson Mill Bridge State Park	3 mi. S on GA 22. (706) 783-5349	24 sites; 21 water & electric; 3 primitive; flush toilets; hot showers; picnic tables; grills.	Year Round
Elberton	Bobby Brown State Park	GA 72 & GA 77; 18 mi. SE off GA 72 on shore of Clark Hill Lake. (706) 213-2046	61 sites; 61 water & electric; no motorcycles; flush toilets; cold showers; dump facility; laundry; picnic tables; fire area; wood.	Year Round Maximum: 14 days
Madison	Talisman RV Resort	I-20 & US 441 (exit 51); 1 3/4 mi. S on US 441. (706) 342-1799	74 sites; 15 full hookups; 49 water & electric (30 amp receptacles); 14 no hookups; 27 pull-thrus; public phone; grocery/RV supplies; ice; 30 picnic tables; wood; 24-hr. security.	Year Round; full facility May 15 to Sept 15
Rutledge	Hard Labor Creek State Park	2 mi. N of town off US 278. (706) 557-3001	50 sites; 50 water & electric; flush toilets; hot showers; dump facility; public phone; grocery; ice; picnic tables; fire area; wood.	Year Round Maximum: 14 days
Appling B-4	Mistletoe State Park	I-20 (exit 60); 12 mi. N. (706) 541-0321	107 sites; 107 water & electric; flush toilets; hot showers; dump facility; laundry.	Year Round Maximum: 14 days
Lincolnton	Elijah Clark State Park	US 378 & GA 47; 7 mi. NE on US 378 to shore of Clark Hill Lake. (706) 359-3458	165 sites; 165 water & electric; 20 cabins; flush toilets; hot showers; dump facility; laundry; picnic tables; fire area.	Year Round Maximum: 14 days
Columbus C-1	Lake Pines Campground	I-185 & US 80; 8 1/2 mi. E on US 80; 1/4 mi. S on Garrett Rd. (706) 563-5909	60 sites; 60 water & electric; 48 full hookups; flush toilets; hot showers; dump facility; laundry; public phone; LP gas; refill; picnic tables; wood.	Year Round
LaGrange	Holiday Park (Corps of Engineers)	10 mi. W on GA 109; over Chattahoochee River and follow signs. (706) 645-2937	144 sites; 93 water & electric; 134 no hookups; flush/pit toilets; hot showers; dump facility; grills.	Mar 1 to Nov. 30 Maximum: 14 days
	State Line Park (Corps of Engineers)	14 mi. W on GA 109 to GA 109 spur; then New State Line Rd. Off and follow signs. (706) 645-2937	123 sites; 56 water & electric; 67 no hookups; flush/pit toilets; hot showers; dump facility; picnic tables; grills.	Apr. 2 to Sept 12 Maximum: 14 days
	Whitetail Ridge (West Point Lake Corps of Engineers)	14 mi. W on GA 109 to GA 109 spur; then New State Line Rd. Follow signs. (404) 882-5439	58 sites; 58 water & electric; flush/pit toilets; showers; dump station; grills.	Mar 19 to Sept 30
Pine Mountain	Franklin D. Roosevelt State Park	US 27 alt. & GA 85 W; 3 mi. S on GA 85 W; 9 mi. W on GA 190. (706) 663-4858	140 sites; 140 water & electric; 35 pull-thrus; flush toilets; hot showers; dump station; public phone; limited grocery; ice; 140 picnic tables; grills	Year Round Maximum: 14 days
West Point	Amity Park (Corps of Engineers)	7 mi. N on New State Line Rd. and follow signs. (706) 645-2937 West Point Lake Corps of Engineers	96 sites; 93 water & electric; 3 no hookups; flush/pit toilets; hot showers; picnic tables; grills.	Mar 19 to Sept. 30 Maximum: 14 days
	R. Scheater Heard (Corps of Engineers)	3 mi. N on GA 29 and follow signs. (706) 645-2937	105 sites; 105 water & electric; flush/pit toilets; hot showers; dump facility; picnic tables; grills.	Year Round Maximum: 14 days
Jackson C-2	Indian Springs State Park	US 23 & GA 42; 4 mi. SE on GA 42. (404) 504-2277	90 sites; 90 water & electric; flush toilets; hot showers; dump facility; public phone; picnic tables; fire area.	Year Round
	I-75 South Travel Trailer Park	I-75 & GA 16 (exit 67); 1/10 mi. W on GA 16. (404) 228-3399	47 sites; 47 full hookups; (20 & 30 amp receptacles); 47 pull-thrus; flush toilets; hot showers; laundry; public phone; full service store/RV supplies; LP Gas & refill; gas; ice; 12 picnic tables.	Year Round

Macon	Tobesofkee Recreation Area	GA 74 & I-75; 8 mi. W on GA 74; 2 mi. S. on Mosley-Dickson Rd. (912) 474-8770	110 sites; 30' maximum RV length; 110 water & electric; no motorcycles; flush toilets; hot showers; dump facility; laundry; public phone; picnic tables; fire area; wood.	Year Round
Sandersville	Hamburg State Park	GA 24 & GA 15; 16 mi. N on GA 15 & GA 248 (Mitchell). (912) 552-2393	30 sites; 30 water & electric; flush toilets; hot showers; picnic tables; fire area	Year Round Maximum: 14 days
Fort Gaines D-1	Cotton Hill Park (Corps of Engineers)	6 mi. N on GA 39. (912) 768-2516	102 sites; 102 water & electric; picnic tables; grills.	Year Round
Arabi D-2	Arabi Campsites	I-75 (exit 30-Arabi); follow signs. (912) 273-6464	62 sites; 28 full hookups; 34 water & electric (20 amp receptacles); 28 pull-thrus; flush toilets; hot showers; dump facility; laundry; public phone; limited grocery; LP-gas Refill; ice picnic tables; wood.	Year Round
Douglas D-3	General Coffee State Park	US 441 & GA 32; 5 mi. E on GA 32. (912) 384-7082	51 sites; 51 water & electric; flush toilets; hot showers; laundry; picnic tables; fire area.	Year Round Maximum: 14 days
McRae	Little Ocmulgee State Park	US 441 & US 280; 1 mi. N on US 441-319 (912) 868-2832	52 sites; 52 water & electric; flush toilets; hot showers; dump facility; public phone; ice; picnic tables; fire area; wood.	Year Round Maximum: 14 days
Reidsville D-4	Gordonia Alatamaha State Park	City limits on US 280. (912) 557-6444	23 sites; 23 water & electric; flush toilets; hot showers; dump facility; laundry; public phone; picnic tables; fire area; wood.	Year Round Maximum: 14 days
Savannah D-5	Fort McAllister State Park	I-16 & US 17; 25 mi. S on US 17; exit at terminus of GA 144. (912) 727-2339	65 sites; 65 water & electric; flush toilets; hot showers; dump facility; picnic tables; fire area.	Year Round Maximum: 14 days
	Skidway Island State Park	I-16 to Lynes Pkwy. to Derenne Ave.; 5 lights to right on Waters Ave, then to the Island. (912) 598-2300	100 sites; 100 water & electric; hot showers; flush toilets; picnic tables; fire area.	Year Round
	Bellaire Woods Campground	I-95 exit 16, Old River Road, 4 mi. W on left. (912) 748-4000	Shaded pull-through sites; swimming pool; playground; hot showers; dump station; laundry; store.	Year Round
Blakely E-1	Kolomoki Mounts State Park	US 27 & GA 62. 6 mi. N on US 27. (912) 723-5296	24 sites; 24 water & electric; no motorcycles; flush toilets; hot showers; laundry; public phone; ice; picnic tables; fire area; pool.	Year Round Maximum: 14 days
Donalsonville	Seminole State Park	Hwy 253 & GA 39; 16 mi. S on GA 39. (912) 861-3137	50 sites; 50 water & electric; flush toilets; hot showers; dump facility; laundry; ice; picnic tables; fire area.	Year Round Maximum: 14 days
Adel E-3	Reed Bingham State Park	I-75 & GA 37; 6 mi. W on GA 37. (912) 896-3551	85 sites; 85 water & electric; flush toilets; hot showers; dump facility; laundry; public phone; picnic tables; fire area.	Year Round Maximum: 14 days
Fargo E-4	Stephan C. Foster State Park	GA 177 & GA 94; Left 1/2 mi. on Hwy 253. (912) 637-5274	66 sites; 66 water & electric; no motorcycles; flush toilets; hot showers; dump facility; ice; laundry; picnic tables; fire area.	Year Round Maximum: 14 days
Waycross	Laura S. Walker State Park	US 82 & US 84; 10 mi. SE on US 84 off GA 177. (912) 283-0410	44 sites; 44 water & electric; flush toilets; hot showers; dump facility; laundry; public phone; ice; picnic tables; fire area.	Year Round Maximum: 14 days
Jekyll Island E-5	Jekyll Island Campground	4 mi. N on Beachview Drive. (912) 635-3021	225 sites; 100 full hookups; 100 water & electric (20 & 30 amp receptacles); 50 no hookups; 24 pull-thrus; flush toilets; hot showers; dump facility; laundry; public phone; grocery/RV supplies; LP-gas refill; gas; ice; 225 picnic tables.	Year Round
Kingsland	Crooked River State Park	US 17 & GA 40; 12 mi. E on GA 40. (912) 882-5256	60 sites; 60 water & electric; flush toilets; hot showers; dump facility; ice; picnic tables; fire area.	Year Round Maximum: 14 days

Glossary of Paddling Terms

Blackwater stream. A river with waters dyed a reddish color by tannic acid from tree roots and rotting vegetation.

Bottom. The stream bottoms described in this book allude to what the paddler sees as opposed to the geological composition of the river bed. From a geologist's perspective, for example, a river may flow over a limestone bed. The paddler, however, because of the overlying silt and sediment, perceives the bottom as being mud.

Bow. The front of a boat.

Broaching. A boat that is sideways to the current and usually out of control or pinned to an obstacle in the stream.

By-pass. A channel cut across a meander that creates an island or oxbow lake.

cfs. Cubic feet per second; an accurate method of expressing river flow in terms of function of flow and volume.

C-1. One-person, decked canoe equipped with a spray skirt; frequently mistaken for a kayak. The canoeist kneels in the boat and uses a single-bladed paddle.

C-2. A two-person, decked canoe; frequently mistaken for a two-person kayak.

Chute. A clear channel between obstructions that has faster current than the surrounding water.

Curler. A wave that curls or falls back on itself (upstream).

Cut-off. *See* **By-pass.**

Deadfalls. Trees that have fallen into the stream totally or partially obstructing it.

Decked boat. A completely enclosed canoe or kayak fitted with a spray skirt. When the boater is properly in place, this forms a nearly waterproof unit.

Downstream ferry. A technique for moving sideways in the current while facing downstream. Can also be done by "surfing" on a wave.

Downward erosion. The wearing away of the bottom of a stream by the current.

Drainage area. Officially defined as an area measured in a horizontal plane, enclosed by a topographic divide, from which direct surface runoff from precipitation normally drains by gravity into a stream above a specified point. In other words, this is an area that has provided the water on which you are paddling at any given time. Accordingly, the drainage area increases as you go downstream. The drainage basin of a river is expressed in square miles. (Also known as a "watershed.")

Drop. Paddler's term for **gradient.**

Eddy. The water behind an obstruction in the current or behind a river bend. The water may be relatively calm or boiling and will flow upstream.

Eddy line. The boundary at the edge of an eddy between two currents of different velocity and direction.

Eddy out. *See* **Eddy turn.**

Eddy turn. Maneuver used to move into an eddy from the downstream current.

Eskimo roll. The technique used to upright an overturned decked canoe or kayak, by the occupant, while remaining in the craft. This is done by coordinated body motion and usually facilitated by the proper use of the paddle.

Expert boater. A person with extensive experience and good judgment who is familiar with up-to-date boating techniques, practical hydrology, and proper safety practices. An expert boater never paddles alone and always uses the proper equipment.

Fall Line. The line between the Piedmont and Coastal Plain where the land slopes sharply.

Falls. A portion of river where the water falls freely over a drop. This designation has nothing to do with hazard rating or difficulty. *See* **Rapids.**

Ferry. Moving sideways to the current facing either up- or downstream.

Flotation. Additional buoyant materials (air bags, styrofoam, inner tubes, etc.) placed in a boat to provide displacement of water and extra buoyancy in case of upset.

Grab loops. Loops (about 6 inches in diameter) of nylon rope or similar material attached to the bow and stern of a boat to facilitate rescue.

Gradient. The geographical drop of the river expressed in feet per mile.

Hair. Turbulent whitewater.

Haystack. A pyramid-shaped standing wave caused by deceleration of current from underwater resistance.

Headward erosion. The wearing away of the rock strata forming the base of ledges or waterfalls by the current.

Heavy water. Fast current and large waves usually associated with holes and boulders.

Hydraulic. General term for souse holes and back-rollers, where there is a hydraulic jump (powerful current differential) and strong reversal current.

K-1. One-person, decked kayak equipped with spray skirt. In this book, this category does not include non-decked kayaks. The kayaker sits in the boat with both feet extended forward. A double-bladed paddle is used.

Keeper. A souse hole or hydraulic with sufficient vacuum in its trough to hold an object (paddler, boat, log, etc.) that floats into it for an undetermined time. Extremely dangerous and to be avoided.

Lateral erosion. The wearing away of the sides or banks of a stream by the current.

Ledge. The exposed edge of a rock stratum that acts as a low, natural dam or as a series of such dams.

Left bank. Left bank of river when facing downstream.

Lining. A compromise between portaging and running a rapids. By the use of a rope (line), a boat can be worked downstream from the shore.

Logjam. A jumbled tangle of fallen trees, branches, and sometimes debris that totally or partially obstructs a stream.

Low-water bridge. A bridge across the river that barely clears the surface of the water or may even be awash; very dangerous for the paddler if in a fast current.

Meander. A large loop in a river's path through a wide floodplain.

PFD. Personal flotation device, e.g., lifejacket.

Painter. A rope attached to the end of a craft.

Pillow. Bulge on surface created by underwater obstruction, usually a rock. Remember: these pillows are stuffed with rocks.

Pool. A section of water that is usually deep and quiet; frequently found below rapids and falls.

Rapids. Portion of a river where there is appreciable turbulence usually accompanied by obstacles. *See* **Falls.**

Riffles. Slight turbulence with or without a few rocks tossed in; usually Class I on the International Scale of River Difficulty.

Right bank. The right bank of the river as you progress downstream.

Rock garden. Rapids that have many exposed or partially submerged rocks necessitating intricate maneuvering or an occasional carry over shallow places.

Roller. *Also* **curler** or **backroller**; a wave that falls back on itself.

Run. *See* **Section** and **Stretch.**

Scout. To look at rapids from the shore to decide whether or not to run them, or to facilitate selection of a suitable route through the rapids.

Section. A portion of river located between two points. *Also* **Stretch** and **Run.**

Shuttle. Movement of at least two vehicles, one to the take-out and one back to the put-in points. Used to avoid having to paddle back upstream at the end of a run.

Slide rapids. An elongated ledge that descends or slopes gently rather than abruptly, and is covered usually with only shallow water.

Souse hole. A wave at the bottom of a ledge that curls back on itself. Water enters the trough of the wave from the upstream and downstream sides with reversal (upstream) current present downstream of the trough.

Spray skirt. A hemmed piece of waterproof material resembling a short skirt, having an elastic hem fitting around the boater's waist and an elastic hem fitting around the cockpit rim of a decked boat.

Standing wave. A regular wave downstream of submerged rocks that does not move in relation to the riverbed (as opposed to a moving wave such as an ocean wave).

Stern. The back end of a boat.

Stopper. Any very heavy wave or turbulence that quickly impedes the downriver progress of a rapidly paddled boat.

Stretch. A portion of river located between two points. *See* **Section** and **Run.**

Surfing. The technique of sitting on the upstream face of a wave or traveling back and forth across the wave when ferrying.

Surfing wave. A very wide wave that is fairly steep. A good paddler can slide into it and either stay balanced on its upstream face or else travel back and forth across it much in the same manner as a surfer in the ocean.

Sweep. The last boat in a group.

TVA. Tennessee Valley Authority.

Technical whitewater. Whitewater where the route is often less than obvious and where maneuvering in the rapids is frequently required.

Thwart. Transverse braces from gunwale to gunwale.

Trim. The balance of a boat in the water. Paddlers and duffel should be positioned so the waterline is even from bow to stern and the boat does not list to either side.

Undercut rock. A potentially dangerous situation where a large boulder has been eroded or undercut by water flow and could trap a paddler accidentally swept under it.

Upstream ferry. Similar to **downstream ferry** except the paddler faces upstream. *See also* **Surfing.**